tENTATIVELY, aN iNTERVIEW

Alan Davies &
tENTATIVELY, a cONVENIENCE

2010-2011(published 2019)

Other Publications

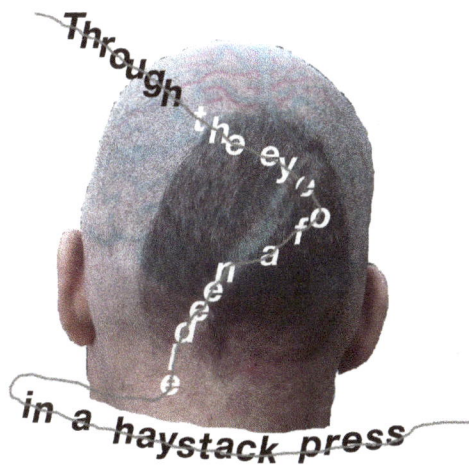

Through the eye of a needle in a haystack press

tENTATIVELY, a cONVENIENCE "Living a Making" - foto: Joe Abeln;
collage: tENTATIVELY, a cONVENIENCE

tENTATIVELY, aN iNTERVIEW

Alan — In one of your missives you made what-I-took-to-be
a-disparaging-remark about rap music / connecting it with
the decline of what we used to call our culture. Would
you care to say more?

tENTATIVELY, a cONVENIENCE [henceforth abbreviated "tENT"]
- Did I? I'd have to reread my remark in order to comment
on it. I don't think of rap music as particularly
representative of the "decline of what we used to call our
culture". I DO usually find it, & almost all other pop
music (& rap/hip-hop is possibly the most popular of pop
musics at the moment) boring b/c of things like its
rhythmic simple-mindedness & its emphasis on lyrics.
People who mostly or only like music w/ lyrics seem to
ultimately be preferring the words 1st, & the music 2nd -
expected mostly to function as a hook/propellant for the
words. Since I'm actually interested in the music, I find
the words to just 'get in the way'. Otherwise, I find the
slam poetry skills of hip-hop vocalists to be phenomenal
at times - but more formally restrictive than other forms
of sound poetry.

Alan — You have made art works [question interrupted by
tENT HERE to make a terminology-specific point]

tENT - As you probably already 'know', I stopped calling
what I produce "art" as of 1978 when I publicly made the
transition from "artist" to "mad scientist". The only
exception to this is when I do something in the name of
Tim Ore. Tim Ore is my "con artist" identity. Therefore,
the vast majority of what you might be referring to as my
"art work" I don't refer to as such. Many people I've
known have been desperate to be thought of & accepted as
"artists". I have the opposite problem: few people, or
perhaps no-one, will accept me as NOT an "artist" unless
their intent is to insult me. In the latter case, they
'think' (if such a word can be used for such minimally
original mental activity) that I'm *trying* to be an

"artist" & that I've failed - even when I tell them that
I'm *not an artist*. This whole notion of calling someone
something that they don't consider themselves to be & then
accusing them of *failing at it* is a peculiar form of
insidiousness.

SO, to reiterate what I've proclaimed many a time before,
I've long since rejected being an "artist" b/c it's my
opinion that art is an uncreative context & I prefer to be
creative. Of course, someone can say: 'But you make films
[eg] & that's an art form!' - to wch I can just as easily
reply that 'Just b/c it's an "art form" to most people
doesn't mean it has to be an "art form" to me. To me,
making movies is just that: making movies - *w/o* the
unnecessary, & downright *boring*, additional baggage of
"art".' - &, of course, it's this position of mine that
makes me anathema to the art world. If I were to go by my
given name & call myself an "artist" I suspect that I'd've
long since become rich & famous - but that wd hardly be
worth doing now wd it?!

AGAIN, of course, I can be criticized for presenting
things in museum & gallery contexts. My response to this,
then, is that I use whatever presentation context can &
will offer me the ways & means that are convenient to what
I'm presenting. THEREFORE, if a museum can: 1. pay me
(although they don't pay me nearly as well as one might
imagine), 2. provide me w/ high quality equipment
(projectors, sound system) - then I'm happy to take
advantage of this. Just as it's boring to be
contextualized (& rendered 'safe') by the art world
context, it's also boring (or annoying or whatever) to
present things under conditions where the projector's so
low quality that my projected text is unreadable, etc..

Alan [continued] - in many of the "available forms" (ie
forms-already-in-use-by-others) / as well as in forms
(using ways-and-means-and-with-results) that are quite

probably unique to yourself. [interrupted]

tENT - I made one feature-length 16mm film entitled "The 'Official' John Lennon's "Erection" is Blocking Our View Homage & Cheese Sandwich". This film is so titled partially b/c it has footage running thru it of a parking garage being built that was blocking the view from my 5th floor warehouse space windows. The view had been panoramic & the parking-lot was doing away w/ that. At one point I thought of not shooting that footage b/c John Lennon (& Yoko Ono) had made a super-8 time-lapse film of a skyscraper being built called "Erection" (& there's a reason why I refer to it as "John Lennon's "Erection"" instead of giving credit to Ono too that's rooted in a prank of sorts of Ono's) & I wanted to be more 'original'. THEN I decided that I shdn't allow *that* to "block my view". I've long since decided to use whatever form I think of that suits my purpose. As such, thru Tim Ore I even leave myself open to the "art world" context - although, humorously perhaps, my Tim Ore work is probably unacceptable to the art world b/c of the way it calculatedly breaks all sorts of subtle unwritten laws. The funny thing is that much of the Tim Ore work is far more conceptual than that by so-called 'conceptual' artists like that idiot Sol LeWitt but isn't likely to ever be acknowledged as such.

Alan [continued] - You have also put a-fair-amount-of-effort into documenting your art actions / in the form of "I did this — I did that — such-and-such-happened — I did the other thing — etc". [question again interrupted by tENT]

tENT - Why not just 'actions'? I document these things largely b/c, yes, I put alotof thought & effort into them & want other people to pay attn to them - but also b/c their partial purpose is to present *examples* of what's POSSIBLE. EG: When my friends Dave Bakker & Randy Hoffman

& I inaugurated the "B.T.O.U.C." (the BalTimOre Underground Club) in the railroad tunnel it was partially to show that *such things cd be done* - that one cd claim a space that other people wdn't expect to be used for such a purpose & have a really good time doing so.

I'm the type of person who likes to do things to show that it's possible - like making 379 movies (the amt I've made as of Jan, 2013; 607 as of October, 2019) for an average of considerably less than $100 a movie - so that other people can become more aware that they're not as trapped by their circumstances as they might feel themselves to be - amongst many, many other reasons. Fortunately, there

are other types of people who then interject longevity
into such possibilities. In other words, while I might
use an illegally-accessed space for a limited-time
purpose, other people make serious squats - & I respect
that - partially b/c *I'm not likely to do it.*

Alan [continued] - Is it possible that if you had refused
to undertake that documenting part of your ongoing-
endeavor / others would have eventually stepped in /
leaving us with something of this sort — "He did this — he
did that — such-and-such-happened — he did the other thing
— etc"? In other words / do you think that if you had not
pursued recognition / it would eventually have pursued you?

tENT - Nah.. One of the other reasons why *I* document (or
as I often prefer: "quasi-document") what I do is b/c so
few other people have ever documented it in any perceptive
way. Unfortunately, I immediately become "Tentatively A.
Convenience, artist" - in other words, **decades** of public
self-contextualizing to the contrary on my part is
immediately usurped into a more 'normal' pattern: 1st
name , middle initial, last name; common 'creative'
'profession'.

Kent Bye started making a documentary about me in 2001.
He & I worked on it for about 7 mnths. He made a pretty
good teaser for it. This teaser wasn't accepted in a
BalTimOre documentary festival. I suspect it might've
been one of the only things rejected. Why? It has a shot
from one of my movies of a girl pissing in my mouth for
one thing. But I'm sure there were many other reasons -
basically it amounted to: 'We will not allow anything
about this guy in our festival. PERIOD.' - This, despite
the theme of the festival being documentaries about
BalTimOreans & my having been a prominent BalTimOre figure
for decades. Just about everything I ever did in

BalTimOre (& after) challenged some 'norm' or another &
somebody somewhere along the line wd try to suppress it -
literally no matter what it was. & I can easily support
this assertion w/ examples - but I'm getting too far
afield for the moment.

Back to the question: "In other words / do you think that
if you had not pursued recognition / it would eventually
have pursued you?" Back to the Kent Bye story: we worked
on the doc for 7 mnths & then he gave up on it saying
something to the effect that he'd wanted to make a simple
one-theme doc about a "political activist" & cdn't
simplify me into that pattern. I proposed that he cd
choose the theme of "free thinker". He didn't go for that
& gave up. For yrs he advertised this doc on his website
& then eventually removed it.

The thing is that I run up against resistance to my very
being that's from angles most people wd never expect. EG:
my bk _footnotes_ - 1st, had its cover picture removed from
Amazon's site [I managed to get it back on again - but the
bk is, as of fall 2012, no longer being printed], 2nd, the
printer has recently refused to print the cover as I
designed it. Why? B/c it's 'upside-down'. Now designing
a cover 'upside-down' certainly wdn't seem like such a big
deal to you or me probably but the printer refuses to do
it - claiming, outrageously, that they technically
"can't". This is such a preposterous lie that it's
amazing. They shd quit the printing business & become
politicians! The basic thing as I see it is that they're
afraid that by printing an 'upside-down' image:

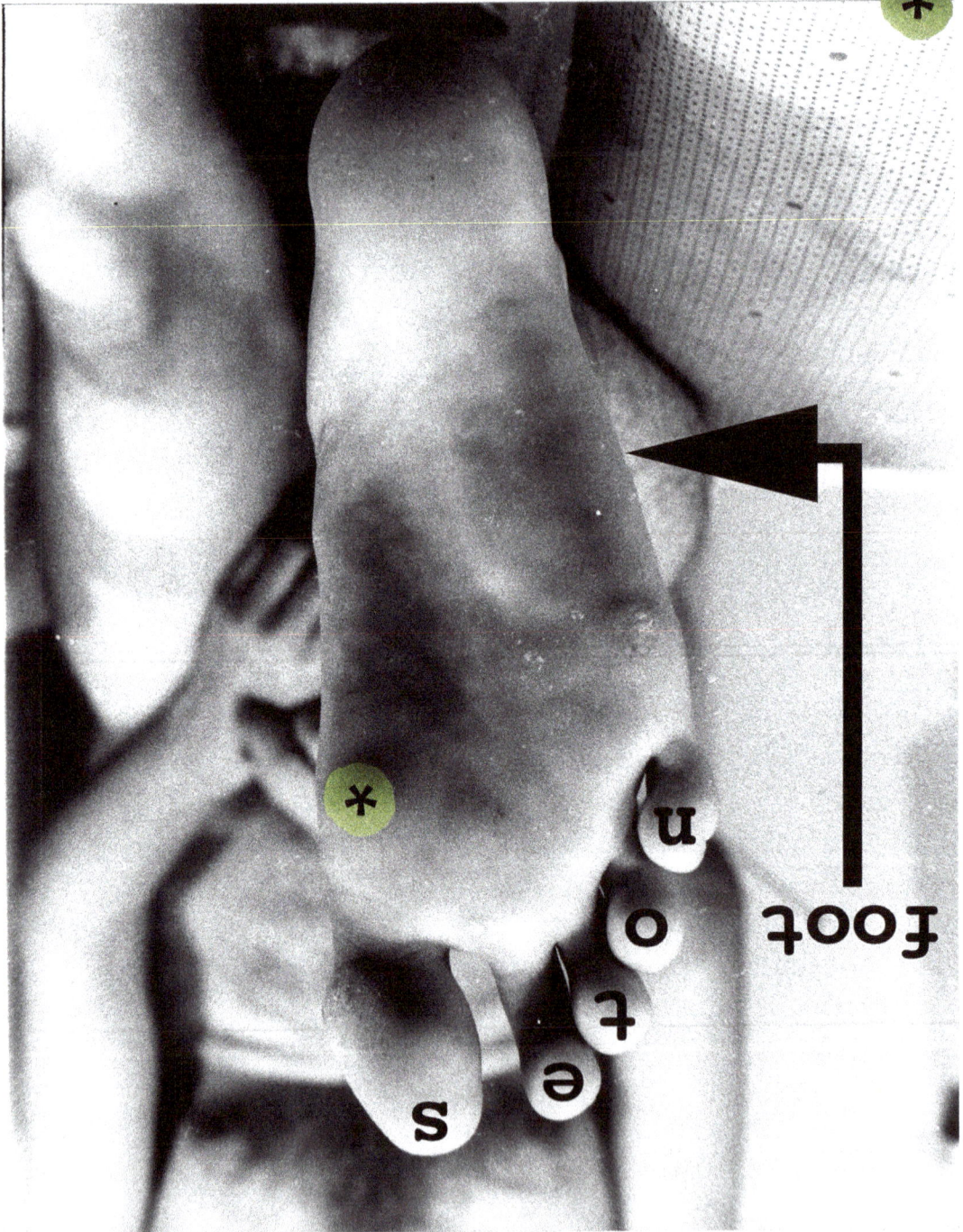

*footnotes

it looks to their potential customers as if they're so bad that they can't even tell that they've printed a cover 'upside-down' (&, actually, they ARE that bad - given that they've sent me at least one copy of the bk w/ something

like 150pp missing - certainly a sign of pathetic quality
control) &/or that they're afraid of being 'satanic' (lest
we forget that we live in a country chock-full of ignorant
religious assholes).

The point here is that in those few instances when
anyone's written about what I do it's been about 99% the
case that the writings have tried to make me into
something that I'm not. If I didn't historicize myself,
I'd be unrecognizable to myself in other people's
historicization.

Alan -- In one of your Bombay Gin reviews [*see footnote
1*] / you note that "I gave this a 5 star rating mainly b/c
there's something by Kenneth Patchen in it that I hadn't
previously read" and in another review you refer to a
collaboration as a "Kenneth Patchen-esque picture poem ".
Until you mentioned Patchen's name / it had been all-but-
lost-to-my-memory / and I don't hear him referred to by
others. Why your strong interest in him/his-work?

tENT - It's been a long time since I've read Patchen,
maybe even decades, & yet a feeling from him sticks w/ me.
I have 6 bks by him in my collection: The Journal of
Albion Moonlight, Sleepers Awake, Aflame and Afun of
Walking Faces, Hallelujah Anyway, But Even So, & The
Argument of Innocence. Sleepers Awake may've been the 1st
one I read. I initially liked him b/c his bks have such
fantastic & playful & visual poetics layouts but have
other things going on too. There's a kind of 'Hallelujah,
I'm a Bum!' joie-de-vivre. Sleepers Awake is great in
these regards & it's from 1946. I don't know what else
there was like it at the time. He seems unique to me.
Your even asking about him makes me want to reread all 6
bks (actually, I've probably only read 2 or 3 of them but
I'm not sure).

Patchen's a droll urban social observer who has fun w/ his

subjects & his techniques. He doesn't seem to feel stuck
w/ having to use 'appropriate' social commentary forms
like a Dos Passos or Steinbeck novel might. (Although, I
like both of them too.) I remember Patchen's playfulness
the most - he seems like a precursor to what I call IMP
ACTIVISM - someone who can address serious socio-political
issues w/ a sense of humor. Such humor is LIBERATING
rather than deadening. But, again, I probably haven't
read him for 25 yrs.

To make things even better, 2 of my favorite composers
have used texts of his. John Cage did a 1942 radio play
in quasi-collaboration w/ Patchen called "The City Wears a
Slouch Hat" that some might consider to be a minor work
(including Cage) but I love it. I don't recall Cage ever
saying anything about Patchen. He always stressed e. e.
cummings, Gertrude Stein, & James Joyce & he dropped
cummings later on in favor of the latter 2 - but I like
Patchen more than cummings (whose work I don't really know
well enuf) or Stein (who, at this point I find somewhat
insufferable - see my review of The Making of Americans:
http://www.goodreads.com/story/show/
42323.As_I_was_Saying_The_Making_of_Americans_y_know_).

The other composer is Franz Kamin. His 3 songs "All the
Roary Night" (1962), "Carnival Late at Night" (1964), &
"May 2nd" (1965) all use Patchen texts - & there are other
pieces too that I haven't heard: "The Sea is Awash with
Roses" (1961), & "The Dark Kingdom (a Patchen
Assemblage)" (1963—65) (wch is actually the 3 songs
mentioned above + "The Lions of Fire", "123rd Street Runs
into Heaven or As We Go Out into the Staring Town…", & 3
others.. - according to a list of Kamin works online.).

[October, 2011 interpolation: I just finished my **100th
feature, Spectral Evidence** (182 features as of October,
2019), & I used "Do The Dead Know What Time It Is?",
"Limericks", & "I Went To The City" from Kenneth Patchen
with the Chamber Jazz Sextet (music composed by Allyn

Ferguson) as part of the soundtrack]

Alan -- Sometimes you (or the-Mad-Scientist / or someone-
else-who-might-be-associated-with-you) makes objects. Do
you think of those objects as residue? / as detritus?
Or / do they in some sense precede you? Or / do they
exist only in the-present-moment (whatever-that-is)? I'm
interested in knowing where your-thinking-about-them
places them / in-time-and/or-otherwise.

tENT - Sometimes I refer to some of my movies as "quasi-
documentary residue" from some action or another. What yr
question mainly makes me think of is my "Frame of
Reference". This is a box that I made in 1975 when I was
21. In my 'resumé' that you published as the last issue
of "A HUNDRED POSTERS" it's listed as item 16 & described
as follows:

"FRAME OF REFERENCE made - originally meant to be my last
commonly understandable (academically?) informational
action/object/reference point for my post FRAME OF
REFERENCE/commonly-understandable schizophrenic existence
to be perceived thru - involving dropping/busting a
"realistic" bust of my head off a 3rd story rooftop into a
box with glue in it's bottom from which an armature was/
is/as erected upon which my representation of my new self
"reality" (including 2 hands with 5 opposable thumbs each)
- disassembleable - multiple layers of subtly different
paint, kinesthetic involvement, ktp, when 21"

This 'description' (or, as I might've written then, 'd
scription') doesn't really tell you very much. This is
THE most elaborately conceived 'sculpture' I ever made.
My bks & movies & (m)usic since then have probably been
more elaborate but this Frame of Reference occupies a
special place. Unlike most 'sculptural' things I've made,
I still have this.

The basic idea of the Frame of Reference was that it be a
medium thru wch I cd communicate after I'd become
completely schizophrenic - or just incomprehensible due to
my having developed a highly complex & personal language.
By the time I made it I'd probably gone to Philadelphia to
see the exhibit of Duchamp works there & had probably read
Arturo Schwarz's The Complete Works of Marcel Duchamp. I
wd've been aware of Alfred Jarry but may not've read his
Caesar Antichrist yet. The extremely esoteric symbolism
of works by Duchamp like "The Bride Stripped Bare by her
Bachelors, Even" was probably important to me at the time,
at least subconsciously, that I was making the Frame of
Reference.

The Frame of Reference has detachable sidewalls & top.
The front is meant to be removed so that a proscenium is
made. What's then seen inside is a 2 floor puppet

theater. The smaller, bottom floor has the fragments of
the bust of my head that I made when I was 17. This bust
was a high school art class assignment. The students were
asked to make a bust of what they'd look like 25 yrs
later. I made a very realistic bust out of clay that I
then painted in primary colors in geometric shapes adapted
to the biomorphism of my face. My primary ways of aging
myself were to add a beard & to have the geometric shapes.
These latter were projections of how willfully perverse I
might become - by changing the appearance of my face to a
quasi-non-biomorphic form. This, perhaps, presaged my
tattoos of later yrs. The larger, top floor has a scroll
backdrop that can be scrolled from side-to-side. This
scroll is made of white paper. The idea was that this is
the moving scenery BUT I don't think I ever intended it to
have any images on it. Instead, it was intended to have
shadows visible on it. As such, the moving white
background wd at most provide a subtle sensation of just
that, movement.

2 circular holes are in the floor separating the bottom &
top floors & thru these holes protrude 2 mannequin hands
w/ 2 thumbs each (contrary to the resumé description
claiming "5"). I molded my own thumbs & cast them to make
these extra thumbs. The hands are hypothetically to be
moved from the bottom floor (but this is frustrated by
limited access). The back wall can be hinged downward to
enable access to the top floor only &/or the back wall can
be removed altogether. The bottom floor has the sidewalls
lined w/ mirrors that have tiny eye-holes in them made by
scraping off the mirror backing. This is to enable
looking into the bottom & seeing 'infinite regress' of
reflections of the bust fragments. On the top floor
there's a central armature made from clothes hanger wire
that's wrapped w/ aluminum foil.

The purpose of the Frame of Reference was to enable my
future self, perhaps a self alienated from most people by

the extremities to wch I'd be willing to go in manifesting my imagination, to communicate w/ an otherwise uncomprehending (v)audience. Ironically, the severity of the symbolic systems used in this object wd probably be even more incomprehensible to the 'average' (v)audience than most things I've made. The Frame of Reference has actually never been used for its intended purpose but Kent Bye & I shot some pretty nice footage of it in 2001 or 2002 for his abandoned "Who is tENTATIVELY, a cONVENIENCE?" documentary. He used this footage in his teaser for the doc & I hope to use it someday in a more elaborate explication of the project. The Frame of Reference has far more significance in my symbolic vocabulary than noted here but that seems like enuf for now.

As for "where your-thinking-about-them places them / in-time-and/or-otherwise"? I don't think I think about them much in the way you seem to be asking about. I make things. These things are an outgrowth of ideas & processes, etc. I make them both to physically manifest the ideas & processes & to make something that people who are interested in things & who enjoy things can experience. They're 'remotes' of me &/or of whatever I 'channel'. I read & witness movies & listen to music every day. I seek out & like the stimulation & the entertainment. What I make is for people who're similarly motivated, for people willing to be challenged by complex signifiers. They're "seeds", as I often call them. I'm hoping that something grows from them that'll create a more intelligent & inspired environment than what I feel I'm generally surrounded by.

Alan -- I see from your Goodreads posts that you read a fair amount of science fiction. Do you find that the genre is capable of predicting the future? Is that why you read it?

tENT - Sometimes people say that such-n-such is *their*
such-n-such - meaning that they feel a close personal bond
to it b/c they grew up w/ it & b/c it addressed issues of
deep personal contemporaneity. In other words, eg, a
person reaching puberty in 1966, as I did, who discovers
music by the Jimi Hendrix Experience, Moby Grape, the
Beatles, the Rolling Stones, the Mothers of Invention,
Captain Beefheart & his Magic Band, Jefferson Airplane,
Bonzo Dog Band, the Soft Machine, etc, as I did, will feel
that this is *their* music b/c it was developing
contemporaneously w/ their own growth & addressing issues
like expanded consciousness, revolt against societal
programming, anti-war, etc..

For me, SF (so abbreviated in order to allow for alternate
readings such as "Speculative Fiction") was developing in
a particular way during the time of my discovery of it
that highly paralleled my own personal development. Of
course, SF can be sd to've originated in the 19th century
& that, therefore, to associate it w/ my discovery of it
in the early-to-mid 1960s is misleading.

& it cd be further claimed that *everything* develops in
sync w/ its time of production. Obviously, the counter-
claim to the latter is that some forms are in use b/c of a
desire to return to the time of the form's origin. Hence
'realistic' social novels cd be taken as expressive of a
desire, of sorts, to return to the time of, say, Jane
Austen. While I don't necessarily claim that, I wd say
that SF, or at least the SF I prefer to read, has more
consistently addressed life as I perceive it, & as I
prefer to be engaged w/ it, than other conventional
narrative genres. Glaring examples of the latter wd be
things like Westerns & Romance novels.

SO, J. G. Ballard's series of contemporary
psychopathological dystopia novels were very easy to
identify w/ even though they're 'exaggerations'. Given

how utterly destructive & obsessive 'car culture' is, is it any wonder that Concrete Island or Crash might result? It's not the 'futuristic' prediction aspect of such bks that I'm necessarily attracted to - it's their re-examination of current existence in analogous fictionalizations.

Like so much SF, Greg Bear's Blood Music & Greg Egan's Permutation City magnify possibilities of technological 'development' that're both exciting & devastating in their broad sweep of paradigm shiftings.

Samuel R. Delaney's Dhalgren depicts a society not so unlike the Baltimore that I spent my early adulthood in & his Triton postulates a world where there's a "u-l", the "unlicensed sector", a lawless zone, from whence come street performers - a lifestyle not so unlike my own at the time I was reading it. Delaney addresses philosophical issues & examines possibilities central to any serious anarchist's concerns: what do you do about sadists in a society w/ or w/o law? What do you do about any non-consensual activities of any sort?

Stanislav Lem explores Probability Theory in The Chain of Chance, Michel Jeury explores multi-national drug companies & the financial politics of entering an alternate universe in Chronolysis. Philip K. Dick explores how 'reality' is structured thru one's often drug-mediated experience of it in just about every bk. Ursula K. LeGuin explores solipsistic possibilities of how 'reality' is determined in The Lathe of Heaven. Much of all the SF I love explores possibilities of what human limits might be superceded by admittedly highly dangerous experiments aimed at transcendence. [yes, yes, I 'know': "superceded" is 'correctly' spelled "superseded" - I prefer the implied relationship to words such as "preceded" - so just think of it as an etymological reference to Middle English & French than as one to Latin]

Vladimir Savchenko's <u>Self-Discovery</u> is another excellent example.

& there's plenty of politics to satisfy me: Arkady & Boris Strugatsky's <u>Prisoners of Power</u> is a remarkably clear-headed piece from 1970s-era USSR. Slightly more recently, there's Joan Slonczewski's 1986 <u>A Door into Ocean</u> - a novel of great interest to anyone who thinks that pacifist resistance to imperialism is possible & preferable to violent revolution.

W/ all that sd, though, for me SF has probably ceased to be the stimulus it once was. Cyberpunk & the 'hard-science' of Egan & Bear bring things up-to-date but it still seems somehow 'antiquated' to me. I 'need' more & I reckon that's what I, personally, am trying to offer. I read an enormous amt of fiction & it serves as stimulus & escape but the type of escape I'm ultimately looking for is *not* the escape from being aware of one's prison by submerging one's mind in an alternate universe - but the escape from one's prison thru actual physical disengagement. Until SF helps accomplish that more directly, it won't really be living up to its potential - less *escapism*, more *actual escape*.

Alan — Even those beginning to become familiar with your work / will note that you work in more genres than do most artists (or (to use your preferred designation) mad scientists) — it is almost a matter of understatement to refer to you as a-Renaissance-man. But / the times in which we live seem to be anything but (but (anything but)) a renaissance. How does this disjunction strike you? and how do you deal with it?

tENT - Ha ha! That's a 'funny' sort of dilemma isn't it?! I'm a very prolific film & vaudeo maker, writer, Low Classical (M)Usician, 'performer', & even (sometimes) a political activist. & I'm a publisher. & I work for a living ("Living a Making" as a movie I'm working on is called). In this latter capacity I've washed dishes, owned & run a bkstore, been a hard-wood floor finisher, installed & deinstalled things in museums, been a projectionist, driven cars, done more general construction work, etc, etc.. I make clothes. Etc, etc..

& how am I generally referred to? 'Oh, he's not really a musician, he's a performance artist; Oh, he's not really a writer, he's a filmmaker.' In other words, I'm so marginalized in any historicization in any of the areas that I'm so prolific in that it's as if I don't exist at all. 358 movies in 35 yrs? [make that 374 movies in 37 yrs as of fall, 2012] Try to find mention of that **anywhere** in any bk or magazine. Therefore, I must not be conceived of by many as a 'Re-naissance-man', but more as an Un-naissance-man, eh!

It seems to be a popular misconception that it's close to impossible for anyone to excel at anything unless they *specialize* in it. To make matters worse, if one exhibits calculatedly *original* facets to what one *does excel in*, esp if one works in what're supposedly separate mediums, then these are commonly considered to be mistakes: 'Obviously the guy can't spell - he writes "alotof" - what kinda word is that?' As such, one can go from being accomplished in many mediums to being perceived as an idiot in all of them.

What doesn't seem to occur to most people is that this separation of activities into categories is *not* some sort of 'law of nature' but is simply something that's done in order to try to have a particular critical language. Hence we have poetry differentiated from fiction *not b/c this is 'absolutely necessary'* but b/c people seem to find it easier to analyze things (or pseudo-analyze them) when they can create boundaries for them.

But boundaries can be fluid or non-existent &, obviously, many people have explored this - often to reluctant critical kudos: 'AN ARTIST WHO EXPLORES TEXT & DANCE ***SIMULTANEOUSLY!***'

What I'm getting at is that for me, it's all under the category of 'What I do' - so is it really so impossible that I might be just 'good' at 'doing what I do'? In other words, all of what I accomplish is somehow part of a whole or interpenetrated or whatever. My movies are often quasi-documentaries of my (m)usic w/ shitloads of text to be read - often w/ a political point somewhere in there. I think this is what partially makes them so insufferable for most people - they seem to require an ability to *pay attn* to too many types of things at once. Big deal, right? Have you ever listened to music w/ headphones on while reading on the subway & still managed to get off at the right stop? Is it that much different from texting while driving? What I'm asking for is just that people text OuLiPian Haikus while driving bumper cars - maybe w/ a little sex thrown in. Is that so much to ask?

As for whether or not we live in a renaissance? Do you know the Mike Judge 2005 movie "Idiocracy"? In my more depressed moments, its look at the future in wch everything dumb about this society (Hooters, eg) becomes the ONLY thing is all too true. I've already commented on this in relation to the way language seems to be continually getting dumbed down: all music is songs, all songs are played by bands, you can buy it all from the iTunes Store, you can listen to it on yr iPod. Who 'needs' anything else? (Unless it's more expensive, of course)

This seems much more where we're headed than any renaissance does. Sometimes I think that the majority of humanity is degenerating into a homogeneous superorganism in wch each 'individual' human is little more than a cell.

This 'superorganism' may be able to 'accomplish' alot more in terms of scale but the types of inspiration that 'individuals' are capable of may be completely lost. Personally, I refuse to be incorporated into the Corpus Reductio Absurdum.

Alan — I would be interested in knowing which books first struck you / as a boy / which authors — and the reading of what things might have pointed (pushed?) you in the direction of writing and the other arts.

tENT - Whew! Considering how much I read & how much I've read, answering that question is a tall order! Some of the bks that still stick w/ me somehow are:

'Victor Appleton' - <u>Tom Swift</u>

J.M. Barrie's <u>Peter Pan and Wendy</u>

Briggs' <u>How to Draw Cartoons</u> - I might not've actually read this one but I remember loving it.

Lewis Carroll's <u>Alice in Wonderland</u> & <u>Through the Looking Glass</u>

'Franklin W. Dixon' <u>The Hardy Boys Mysteries</u>

Madeleine L'Engle's <u>A Wrinkle in Time</u>

A bk on Greek Myths that I no longer have & don't recall much more about - except that it was probably illustrated & aimed at kids.

Norman Juster & Jules Feiffer's <u>The Phantom Tollbooth</u>

Edward Lear's <u>A Book of Nonsense</u>

J.R.R. Tolkien's The Hobbit

Mark Twain's The Adventures of Tom Sawyer & The Adventures of Huckleberry Finn

Evans G. Valens' Me and Frumpet: An Adventure With Size and Science - wch I only learned recently is called that - I always remembered it as just Frumpet.

E.B. White's Stuart Little & Charlotte's Web

That list is a bit misleading since it's in roughly alphabetical order &, therefore, starts w/ Tom Swift followed by Peter Pan and Wendy wch was probably one of the least important of all the bks mentioned.

Of course, the Tom Swift & Hardy Boys bks were series that were written by many authors pseudonymously. Even remembering that these exist at this late date makes me want to reread some of them.

[see footnote 2]

I think I read all of these by the time I was 9. I'm pretty sure that I read The Hobbit when I was 9 & that might be the 'most sophisticated' one of the lot so reading the others by that age isn't too unlikely.

It's not too hard to find things that these bks had in common that're still meaningful to me today. The White bks anthropomorphized a mouse & a spider, etc - wch fed into my natural inclination to identify w/ non-human life. Of course, Carroll & Tolkien did much the same thing. There's science, there's myth, there's fantasy; nonsense, struggle, freedom, hero's journeys. Twain's sense of justice.

Kids bks seem to be generally written by people w/ a sense of ethics, people who want to inspire children to aspire

to leading a life of integrity pushing for just societies.
I often say that I learned my values more from Marvel & DC
comics than I did from church - wch I went to until I
became an atheist at age 15. So the comics were very
important to me too. Wch brings up "Mad" magazine,
"Cracked", "Sick", "Famous Monsters of Filmland"..

Kids who immerse themselves in such things have the
potential to have a superhero fantasy core to their
personality. Probably most of them either 'grow out of
it' or sidetrack it by staying fantasists - most commonly
stoners & gamers these days. Or they get defeated by a
society that's definitely NOT sympathetic: 'Get a job & do
my bidding SLAVE!' may as well be written all over the
'opportunities' for debasement (ie: 'advancement').

Between ages 10 & 13 or so I started reading more authors
like Edgar Rice Burroughs & Robert A. Heinlein. I read
something like 17 Burroughs novels in quick succession -
mostly the "Pellucidar" ones about the Hollow Earth. 17
yrs later, I organized the "Sinnit-Nut Hollow Earth
Symposium" in a cave in WV, recorded the event & published
that as a tape. Heinlein's Have Space Suit Will Travel
was, no doubt, a big stimulus to imagining what just might
be possible someday-in-the-not-necessarily-too-distant-
future. Less than 30 yrs later I was doing things in
conjunction w/ the AAA (Association of Autonomous
Astronauts) - a far cry from what Heinlein imagined but,
still, related (at least in my own personal development).

Heinlein's quite a subject in & of himself. His Farnham's
Freehold is a combination of American cold war bomb
shelter paranoia coupled w/ incest fantasy. It wasn't
until much later that I realized that Heinlein seems to
have had quite a thing for incest. In To Sail Beyond the
Sunset, the last novel published before he died, the SF is
a thin pretext covering up what's basically a full-blown
(pun intended) incest fantasy. I'm happy to say that

Heinlein's incest promotion is *not* one of the things that influenced me. I read his <u>Stranger in a Strange Land</u> when I was 16 & more or less lost interest in him after that. Nonetheless, despite Heinlein's generally imperialist politics, he was a friend to Philip K. Dick & an influence on Samuel Delaney - 2 of my favorite SF writers - & I can certainly understand that. Heinlein inspired me to imagine, as I wrote before, *what might be possible* & I'm forever grateful for that.

Around the same time, I was voraciously reading (I 'know': that's a cliché phrase but nonetheless apt) as many fantasy trilogies as I cd find: Tolkein's <u>Lord of the Rings</u> & Mervyn Peake's <u>Gormenghast Trilogy</u>. William Morris' <u>The Well at the World's End</u> was published in 2 volumes. E.R. Eddison's <u>The Worm Ouroborous</u> deserves to be listed here too even though it was a single volume.

Of course, by the time I was a teenager my literary tastes had considerably expanded to include 'classics' like Dostoyevsky, Tolstoy, Hesse, Dickens, Austen, Gautier, Poe, Maupaussant, Hugo, Swift, Steinbeck.. - so many hundreds of authors that any list here will be misleadingly small.

Richard Brautigan & Kurt Vonnegut, Jr, are 2 examples of more contemporary writers I wd've discovered as a teen.

One of my fondest memories of high school is of when I was in an Honors English class when I was 15: I gave my teacher a list of something like 75 short stories that I'd read in the recent past only to discover that we'd left behind the subject of short stories a wk or so before. I hadn't been paying attn in class at all. The teacher was still impressed anyway.

&, indeed, the small list above is just that: SMALL. I read ALOT - both past & present tense. [October 22, 2011 note: Ever since Alan asked me this question I've been thinking of all the bks I read when I was a child. I must've read 3 or more bks a wk: there may've been THOUSANDS. Another important one that I remembered recently was Rudyard Kipling's <u>The Jungle Book</u>. It's funny thinking about that one in relation to my preference for the 'wild' & 'feral'.]

I started writing 'seriously' when I was 13. I've written about these early days elsewhere (in my bk <u>footnotes</u>). My 1st, & basically ONLY short story was about escaping from a mental institution thru (a) laundry chute(s). Then I kept a dream diary. Alas, neither of those examples of juvenilia escaped my purges of a few yrs later. Perhaps most importantly to me now are my '1st published works': my 3 high school yrbk entries. My 16 yr old self-description:

"Nascent, orthopteran, sabaist, luxated, oleographic, turgid; labiac, excogitate, accentric, hydrophytic, crispy, intarsia, magnetize."

It's practically a miracle that this was allowed into the Woodlawn Senior High School 1970 yrbk. Can you find the hidden message? Alas, my 1971 yrbk entry, wch was far more encoded (& wch I no longer have a copy of) had most of my entry removed altogether & the rest of it butchered. It became this:

""Tinselbrain." 71. Captain Spanzer's Conch Shell, Harmonica, & Kazoo Band. Enjoys box opening, harp destroying, reading. Favorites: Mothers of Invention, Frank Zappa, Captain Beefheart and his Magic Band, Frumpet, "Lord of the Rings," "Stranger in a Strange Land," "Wrinkle in Time," "Gormeing Mast," Trilogy, The Band."

Of course, according to the way the yrbk editors organized things, *Frumpet* shd be "Frumpet" & *"Gormeing Mast," Trilogy* shd be "Gormenghast Trilogy". *"Tinselbrain"* was a nickname that had been preceded by "Tinseltoes" - I don't remember ever having been called *"Tinselbrain"* & it's not in my list of names in my 1st bk (written only a few yrs later) but I suppose it's possible. "Captain Spanzer's Conch Shell, Harmonica, & Kazoo Band" was probably an imaginary group invented by my friend Doug Retzler. "box opening" meant fucking (box = vagina) so I'm glad that made it past the censors. "harp destroying" referenced my rather ferocious harmonica playing.

Writing this reminiscence has been fun - partially b/c it jogged my memory & partially b/c all these stories are what a Jungian might call (but probably wdn't?) my Formative Archetypes.

Alan — What is your take on the spiritual? — how does it figure in your works?

tENT - I remembered the statement "When I hear the word 'culture' I reach for my revolver" as having been attributed to André Breton (the 'Pope' of Surrealism) or some other Surrealist - &, yet, when I look for attribution online I find it credited to Herman Goering (the nazi Commander-in-Chief of the *Luftwaffe*, the German Airforce, & 2nd-in-command under Hitler) & Heinrich Himmler (the nazi Chief of Police, Minister of the Interior, & overseer of the concentration & extermination camps).

SO, in an attempt to clarify this, I searched on Wikiquotes' "List of Misquotations" <http://en.wikiquote.org/wiki/List_of_misquotations> & found this:

"Whenever I hear the word 'culture' I reach for my revolver."
  * The actual quote is "Wenn ich Kultur höre ... entsichere ich meinen Browning!" This translates as: "Whenever I hear [the word] 'culture'... I remove the safety from my

Browning!"

   * This quote is often mistakenly attributed to leading Nazi Hermann Goering, or occasionally to Julius Streicher, a lower-ranking Nazi. This misattribution may date from the famous Frank Capra documentaries (Why We Fight) shown to American troops before shipping out.

   * In fact, it is a line uttered by the character Thiemann in Act 1, Scene 1 of the play Schlageter, written by Hanns Johst. The association with Nazism is appropriate, as the play was first performed in April 1933, in honor of Hitler's birthday.

   * Baldur von Schirach, head of the Hitlerjugend, delivered this sentence in a public speech, circa 1938. A footage of the scene, with von Schirach actually drawing his gun, appears in Frederic Rossif's documentary "from Nurnberg to Nurnberg".

   * Notes: It is possible that this is actually a rather more felicitous phrase in translation than it is in the original. Both the original German and this English translation were juxtaposed by Howard Thomas in his review of an article by Nicholas H Battey in the Journal of Experimental Biology, December 2002, as "the famous words of Hanns Johst: 'Wenn ich Kultur höre ... entsichere ich meinen Browning' - 'Whenever I hear the word culture, I reach for my revolver.'"

   * The phrase itself may be a play on words as the word Browning may refer to both a pistol and the English poet Robert Browning.

   * Additionally it should be noted that a Browning (most likely the M1935 High-Power) is not a revolver, but a magazine-fed semi-automatic pistol. However, at the time the word "Browning" was used to refer to any pistol, much as "Colt" is used for any revolver in westerns.

What I want to 'know' is this: If the play in wch this phrase 1st appeared was in "April 1933", then why is the Browning most likely a "M1935 High-Power" given that the "M1935" was developed in 1935. I mean like, duh, dudes — you're supposed to be *correcting* misinformation not spreading it!

When I hear people speak about their own 'spirituality' I have much the same reaction - I'm immediately suspicious. People often refer to 'spirit' instead of 'god' as a way of expressing their investment in a 'non-material 'higher' 'essence'' 'free' of religious baggage. In other words, 'I believe in the spirit as the pure guiding force of all good impulses'.

What I find that this usually means is something more along the lines of 'I can disguise my own sleazy ulterior motives by camouflaging them w/ references to an

intangible higher authority that I am supposedly deeply in
tune w/.' In other words, bullshit, dogshit, cowshit,
humanshit, eatshit, seenoshit, hearnoshit, speaknoshit.
In OTHER other words, I'm not sure I've ever met a
'spiritual' person who didn't strike me as a fraud.

So what does that say about the concept of the 'spirit' &
the 'spiritual'? At the risk of overquoting Wikiwhatever,
"spirituality" is presented in the opening paragraph of
its Wikipedia definition as:

"Spirituality can refer to an ultimate or immaterial reality; an inner path enabling a
person to discover the essence of their being; or the "deepest values and meanings by
which people live." Spiritual practices, including meditation, prayer and contemplation,
are intended to develop an individual's inner life; such practices often lead to an
experience of connectedness with a larger reality, yielding a more comprehensive self;
with other individuals or the human community; with nature or the cosmos; or with the
divine realm. Spirituality is often experienced as a source of inspiration or orientation
in life. It can encompass belief in immaterial realities or experiences of the immanent
or transcendent nature of the world. "

My questions are:

If spirituality is an "immaterial reality" why is that
"ultimate"? Why is there a hierarchy in wch immateriality
is 'better' than materiality?

I find the immaterial & the material both interesting but
I feel no need to rank them in relation to each other.
Religion & spirituality & the 'divine rights' of kings are
all ways of creating a hierarchy that justifies
domineering & parasitic practices. "Rinpoche"? "Precious
one"? Gimme a break. What makes a Tibetan Buddhist any
more "precious" than anyone or anything else?

"an inner path enabling a person to discover the essence
of their being; or the "deepest values and meanings by
which people live."" An inner path? Fine, I reckon I
have one of those. Does it enable me "to discover the

essence of [my] being"? What makes anyone think there **IS**
an "essence" of being?!   If by "deepest values" is
meant those values that one values most strongly then I'm
all in favor of being conscious of what those are - but it
seems to me that what we're talking about here is simply
SELF-AWARENESS & that references beyond that are more
obfuscating than they are clarifying.

"Spiritual practices, including meditation, prayer and
contemplation, are intended to develop an individual's
inner life": How about *introspection* as a way of
developing one's "inner life"? Why the 'spiritual'
trappings? My 'answer': the 'spiritual' trappings are a
way of *misguiding* a person *away from self-knowledge* by
providing paths w/ externally imposed & prestated limits,
procedures, & outcomes. 'Spiritual leaders' are like
traffic cops in a world where staying on the road serves
no practical purpose. An introspective person may find
things w/in themselves that're *deviant* from established
'spiritual' practices & that's a no-no. As such, I think
that a person's "inner life" is, under spiritualism, more
likely to be a facsimile - a cookie cutter fake, a symbol,
a PR put-on.

"such practices often lead to an experience of
connectedness with a larger reality, yielding a more
comprehensive self; with other individuals or the human
community; with nature or the cosmos; or with the divine
realm": What I often refer to are "entity boundaries":
where does one thing end & another begin? Yes, I define
"me" as a specific physical entity bounded in a particular
way. Nonetheless, I don't need 'spirituality' to realize
that there's an apparently infinite connection between me
& everything else. I'm sitting on a chair breathing in
air - w/o this air I'd be dead. I'll be taking in food,
the food has been made from some other living thing, I
process it, I shit it out. My shit becomes nourishment
for plants to grow. & this is all on an immediate local

obvious level. I AM PART OF A GREATER WHOLE. I don't
need to romanticize this.

A moronicism of Christinanity is: "How can you see such a
beautiful sunset & not believe in God?" What I ask is:
"Why do you need the concept of 'God' to enable you to
appreciate the sunset?" Needing such an extraneous
concept for such appreciation seems disrespectful of the
sunset. I can appreciate the sunset, or whatever else I
witness, for its own intrinsic characteristics. I can
appreciate my own interconnectedness to everything else w/
o adding a superfluous, & interfering, pseudo-philosophy
to it.

SO, "How does [spirituality] figure in [my] works?" It
doesn't. There're ideas/things/whatever that are
important to me. I try to address these, make these more
palpable thru actions/creations. That's good enuf for me.

Alan — Quite a number of the works that you've made have
been driven by concepts (often humorous / pataphysical).
Do you feel an alliance with the conceptual poetry that
has been gaining a slight bit of momentum these past
couple of years? What distinguishes your work (your
works) from theirs?

tENT - I mainly or entirely 'know' about conceptual poetry
thru hearing about it from my girlfriend, the poet/poem
Amy Catanzano, & I can't name a single conceptual poet
other than its most well-known representative, Kenneth
Goldsmith. [actually, I 'know' a little bit about
Christian Bök too - who seems pretty interesting; fall,
2012 insertion: by now I know more] Nonetheless, there're
times when Amy & I think that I've been a 'conceptual
poet' for longer than most, if not *all*, people associated
w/ it - even though I prefer to **NOT** self-define as a poet
(Amy calls me a "poem" - I like that better - but mainly

b/c *she* calls me that). I prefer my own terminology -
such as: homonymphonemiac & practicing promotextual.

Here're quotes from Goldsmith re the subject that I took
offline (http://www.poetryfoundation.org/harriet/2008/06/
conceptual-poetics-kenneth-goldsmith/) as interrupted by
me:

"In brief, Conceptual writing or uncreative writing "

Goldsmith starts off conflating "conceptual writing" w/
"uncreative writing". It seems obvious to me that that's
his personal take & that that has next-to-nothing to do w/
the meanings of the words as they're ordinarily used. In
other words, what's intrinsic to "conceptual" that makes
it "uncreative"? W/ that in mind, why bother to use the
term "conceptual writing" at all? Why not call it "the
motion of the air when a pen is falling on Mars writing"
instead? That has as much to do w/ "uncreative writing"
as "conceptual writing" does. Calling it "uncreative
writing", however, is creative.

"is a poetics of the moment,"

He's defining it w/o seeming to bother much w/ the
etymology & other associations of the words. If
"conceptual writing" were to acknowledge "conceptual
art" (or "concept art") as its precursor, then it wd be
defined very differently. [Amy tells me that Goldsmith
does address conceptual art somewhere but I haven't read
that] I think *not defining it in terms of its obvious
etymological precursors* is *almost* interesting.. but not
really enuf so for me b/c I'm not convinced that doing so
is a highly conscious enuf choice. But, then, Goldsmith
runs UbuWeb so he obviously knows his shit so maybe I'm
underestimating him. I wonder what he thinks about the
texts of Vito Acconci, eg, in wch Acconci used only

clichés - as he did in part of his vaudeo "The Red
Tapes" (1976-77). As w/ my criticism of calling
"conceptual writing" "uncreative writing", I see no
intrinsic reason why it 'shd be' "a poetics of the
moment".

"fusing the avant-garde impulses of the last century with the technologies of the
present, one that proposes an expanded field for 21st century poetry."

That just reads like a grant proposal to me.
Technologies, blah, blah; 21st century, blah, blah.

"Conceptual writing's concerns are generally two-pronged, as manifested in the
tensions between materiality and concept."

Ok.

"Conceptual writing obstinately makes no claims on originality. On the contrary, it
employs intentionally self and ego effacing tactics using uncreativity, unoriginality,
illegibility, appropriation, plagiarism, fraud, theft, and falsification as its precepts;"

This is such a boring subject to me that I can barely
muster the energy to reply to it. The above statement
obviously harkens back to Andy Warhol & I've heard that
Goldsmith's Soliloquy (1997) has been compared to Warhol's
'novel' a (1968). This comparison is based on both being
transcriptions of recordings of speech, etc.. I read a in
the early 1970s & found it interesting b/c it seemed like
such an extreme thing for Warhol to've done at the time -
I admired the efficiency of it as a way of creating a
'novel' w/ very little effort on the part of the 'author'.
Obviously it challenged notions of 'authorship'.

Then there was my own "Compliments to Vesna" (1983) in wch
I carried around a tape recorder & goaded people into
complimenting my girlfriend of the time, video artist
Vesna Miksiç, & recorded the results. Vesna wasn't
necessarily well-liked so the compliments were a bit

forced at times. This was just published in recorded form
since transcription wd've depleted the intonation &
contributed nothing.

However, it's when we come to the Stewart Home notions of
neoism as expressed in his SMILE magazines in the 1980s &
in his novel Pure Mania (1989) that we come
philosophically closest to Goldsmith's above statement.

Emphasis on effacing "the self and the ego" were (& still
are) probably better served thru collective identities
such as Monty Cantsin & Karen Eliot than they were by
attaching Goldsmith's own name to his product. But
Goldsmith's use of his own name (is it his given name?) is
a more conventional artistic career move: 'I'll efface my
self & ego as long as it doesn't interfere w/ my career'.
If he were just another Monty Cantsin it wd be much more
self & ego effacing but it wd be a terrible career move.
Lardy, what a bore.

Goldsmith's statement is close enuf to many of
Homes' (usually made as Monty Cantsin or Karen Eliot) to
be a plagiarism &, of course, Home was also plagiarizing.
As such, there's a tradition in place, a collective
identity. When Cantsin & Eliot were putting forth such
statements in SMILE form in the mid 1980s it was fun for
me. But when it deteriorated into a lazy career-building
technique it wasn't fun for me anymore. Pure Mania was (a
little) fun, the succeeding repetitive novels weren't.
I'll take texts written by 'original' authors anyday. Any
critique of 'originality' made by Goldsmith's manifesto
have already been made better by others & such critiques
serve no purpose for me anymore.

Yes, 'originality' is problematic; there will always be
ways of pointing out that people use language as a system
that *pre-exists* them. I did this in the 1970s by putting

my texts in quotes - to show that I didn't *invent* the
language I was using. But there's still a distinction to
be made between inspired creators & uninspired ones. I'll
take Alfred Jarry over Dean Koontz anyday. Home milked a
lazy technique that grabbed the public's attn for awhile &
that appealed to lazy readers. Of course, Stewart also
had plenty of other things going that were far more
interesting - such as his donor card in wch he leaves his
body to necrophiliacs - or his 'fake' neoist website
designed to irritate other neoists.

In the long run, though, I find both Home's & Goldsmith's
statements re the use of plagiarism & whatnot as not
interesting. Either the products provide me the
stimulation I thirst for or they don't. Mostly they
don't.

"information management, word processing, databasing, and extreme process as its
methodologies; and boredom, valuelessness, and nutritionlessness as its ethos."

Whatever. I don't want to be bored, I don't want my
experience to be valueless & I doubt that Goldsmith does
either. Given that anything that we take into ourself/ves
is a form of food, promoting "nutritionlessness" in
language is ok as a provocation but useless to me
otherwise. I wdn't choose to eat only nutritionless food,
I'd die quicker than I'm already dying; & I'm not going to
do the same w/ language. Goldsmith's strategies wd be
stimulating for me if I hadn't already heard it all before
- but I have.

Obviously, concept(ual) art grew out of Marcel Duchamp's
emphasis on the idea & the ideas were new but Goldsmith's
conceptual writing is a deliberate debasement of that, as
was Home's.

"Language as junk, language as detritus. Nutritionless language, meaningless
language, unloved language, entartete sprache, everyday speech, illegibility,
unreadability, machinistic repetition. Obsessive archiving & cataloging, the debased
language of media & advertising; language more concerned with quantity than

quality."

Right. As my friend Doug Retzler says: "Yadda, yadda." I don't want more "quantity than quality" in my life &, again, I doubt that Goldsmith does either. If he did, UbuWeb wd just have commercials on it - or any kind of filler junk - & he'd invade everyone's computers w/ spam - or publish on billboards or whatever. The problem for me w/ the above statement of his is how he conflates all these things together in one list. But I don't want to fall into the obvious trap of discussing deliberately controversial statements. Some of the above interests me, some of it doesn't. None of it **necessarily** strikes me as conceptual writing - *except as defined by Goldsmith.*

"Conceptual writing is more interested in a thinkership rather than a readership. Readability is the last thing on this poetry's mind."

Alright, I really don't want to spend much more time on responding to Goldsmith's statement so I've deleted a few of the sentences in the interest of jump-cutting ahead. A "thinkership" is fine w/ me. I doubt that conceptual writing promotes that any more than most other theory-based writing. Andy Warhol sd much the same thing about his films. I don't find them very interesting either - & I think most of the 'scholarship' that surrounds them is a waste of energy. I've never read a Goldsmith bk - maybe I will someday but I'm not in any hurry. If he's not interested in "readability" then he shd consider the possibility of not wasting trees for getting them printed. But, of course, that might not explore the "tensions between materiality and concept" that he expresses interest in.

Much of my own writing is certainly 'unreadable' by most people's standards - take things like "rfeEINr Ashaircnm" as published in <u>Vertov from Z to A</u> - so I wdn't claim that "readability", as usually conceived, is exactly my main concern either. As such, much of my writing might be

classified under "conceptual writing" too - but I have no
desire or interest to 'justify' it w/ specious arguments
of the type that Goldsmith provokes w/. Each piece has an
originating concept & the resultant form reinforces this
concept - regardless of whether this makes it
conventionally 'readable' or not.

Brain-Bairn

The biran of hdeas teird & selpt
'til its blarn was in a wreid sacpe.
It cvread the stlay crud on its berad
& in its driay snak in the sitan
of the bran & the bran aklie.

"Conceptual writing is good only when the idea is good; often, the idea is much more
interesting than the resultant texts."

Again, this is just a rehashing of part of Warhol's
philosophy. I want the idea to be interesting & the
result to be interesting - if they aren't **both** interesting
then the originating idea probably won't be interesting to
me either. If both aren't interesting then, to me, making
the result is a waste of time. We already live in an
"Idiocracy" - my intention is to combat this, not to
contribute to it.

As stated earlier, I don't use the term "conceptual
writing" in relation to my own texts - & I'm even less
inclined to do so w/ Goldsmith's dominating the defining
of it. If "the idea is much more interesting than the
resultant texts" then "ineptual writing" is probably a
better term. Unfortunately, Goldsmith's defining is just
what the art market 'needs' - more shallow controversy
that promotes careers. Career artists who rely on
specious theory to place themselves in the public eye are
a waste of intellectual energy. Much of Warhol & Home &
Goldsmith is smack-dab in the middle of that. But putting

their career-building strategies aside there's plenty
there of interest for me. I'm sure Goldsmith's a smart &
funny & stimulating guy. He's probably fun to have a
conversation w/. & if he makes a career out of all this I
don't really resent it.

In the meantime, I, personally, prefer to pursue my Low
Classicism in obscurity rather than adding to the general
dumbing-down w/ theories that encourage any more junk
product than we already have - even if the encouragement
has a contrary subtext. & I'd rather read topology
filtered thru Franz Kamin than Warhol filtered thru
Goldsmith.

Alan — Do you think that art can change political and
social reality? If so / how? and in what ways?

tENT - Perhaps I think that EVERYTHING can change
EVERYTHING. What I might be most interested in is
SOMETHING that changes NOTHING - or, to rephrase,
SOMETHING that cannot change ANYTHING. That wd be quite a
challenge, eh? A rock dropped on the ground blocks out
sunlight for what's underneath it - subsequently plants
needing sunlight won't grow under the rock; a dead body
rots & offgases - this changes the atmosphere.

A question such as yrs is usually loaded w/ implication.
Let's imagine a more specific hypothetical restatement:

A specific socio-political situation exists that a
creative person wants to change. Let's say there's an
oppressive & intolerant government that scapegoats part of
the population by dehumanizing them & persecuting them.
The creative person wants to address this unfairness in a
way that's likely to lead to the government's policy
changing in favor of greater equality & tolerance. Is it
possible for this person to accomplish this? OF COURSE!

But that doesn't mean they will.

In all societies public opinion can shape the overall
socio-political situation - wch is why ruling elites
invest so much time & energy in controlling public opinion
so that it serves the elite interests. Crude
dictatorships enforce their version of consensus 'reality'
thru fear; slick dictatorships enforce it thru mass media
oversimplification.

Creative people find creative ways of putting their own
'realities' out there. They don't even necessarily have
to do so thru mass media means. Ideas can spread & grow
in all sorts of ways. Ask yrself this: where do jokes
originate from? Someone tells you a joke that they heard
from someone else who heard it from someone else, etc..
This joke can spread w/o having to have an identifiable
point of origin &/or dissemination. If people think it's
funny it spreads widely & wildly. Why not the same
process or type of process for socio-political basises?

The thing is that changing conditions thru creative
activity or other means isn't necessarily an obvious
process. [take these examples: "Anti-Neoist Rally" (2000): http://
www/youtube.com/watch?v=QX7963kyl2k & "TV 'News' Commits
Suicide" (2009): http://www.youtube.com/watch?v=hU-_aL7kKBl &
"Vermin Supreme's Real Life Adventures from the Campaign Trail": http://
www.youtube.com/watch?v=n2Eqombld-M - these are on my
"onesownthoughts" YouTube channel] I often suggest
imagining this: if you think that creative activity is
ineffectual, imagine life **w/o** creative activity - for most
of us, including, I suspect, the most hardened proponent
of the ineffectualness of creative activity, life w/o
creative stimulation wd be deathly dull - as such,
creative people have far more influence than might be
ordinarily recognized. Creativity is often influential
just by virtue of being what keeps life interesting!

Alan — You have recently spent a great deal of time and effort memorializing Franz Kamin. Are there other (perhaps under-acknowledged) contemporary creators about whom / about whose work / you feel similarly?

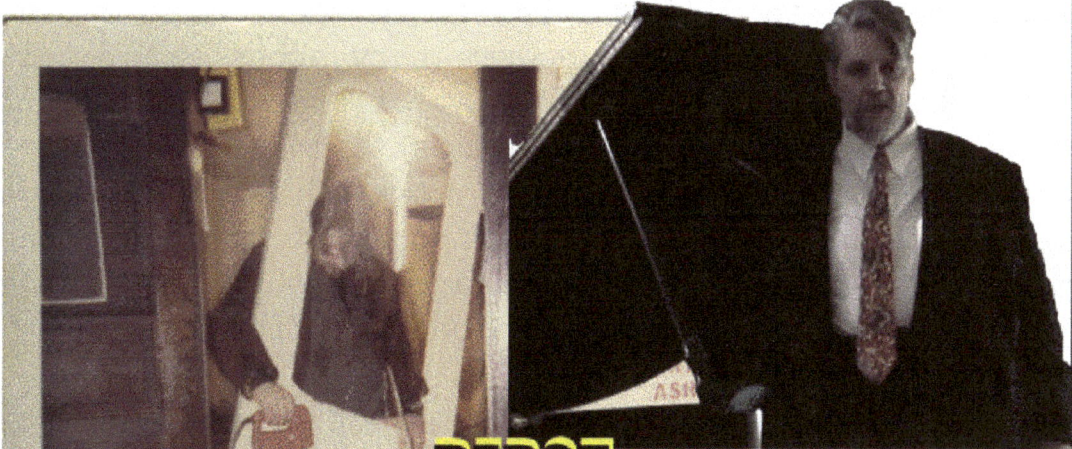

DEPOT
(wherein resides the UNDEAD of Franz Kamin)

- a movie about a very intelligent
& creative man that you may've never heard of
- by tENTATIVELY, a cONVENIENCE

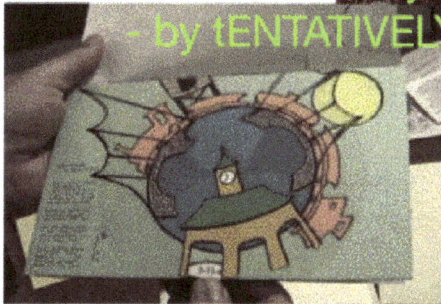

tENT - **OI VEH**! There are so many! Although I might
approach each case differently. I've spent most of the
last 6 mnths making a long documentary about Franz called
"DEPOT (wherein resides the UNDEAD of Franz Kamin)". This
is a major project for me & the most time I've ever
invested in exploring the life & work of another person.
While making it, I've been thinking about how many other
people I'd like to make documentaries about - esp while
they're still alive so they can benefit from it!

For decades I've been fantasizing about writing an entire
"Encyclopedia of Friends" - an encyclopedia in wch I'd
tell stories about all the interesting folks I've known
personally or heard tell of. Of course, an obvious
problem w/ this is that I have a zillion other projects
too.

One of the 1st people I talk about when I mention the
proposed encyclopedia is a former roommate/collaborator of
mine named John Sheehan. I usually explain his "balloon
fishing" & "slow bowling" & I might mention the large
Tesla Coil he built in one of the houses we lived in
together. I might also mention the last phone call I
rc'vd from him - where he'd tapped into someone else's
phone to make the long-distance call to me. While we were
on the phone, the person whose phone it was came on & John
disconnected them. He's since disappeared from my life.
He may be dead or homeless. I doubt that he's prosperous.
I've published a tape by him but I've been unable to find
him to tell him so.

The problem, for me, about telling people about John is
that he was such a pain-in-the-ass when he was in my life
that I hesitate to promote him. It's hard to imagine John
ever doing anything for me. Then again, John DID make the
motorized wings that I used in my "Generic As-Beenism". &
he helped w/ computer use in the late 1980s & early 1990s.
So I'm wrong: he DID do things for me. He had "**DEATH**"

written in big block letters on his forearm.

Another person that I'd promote is etta cetera. She's
consistently been one of my most visionary friends & she
was my main collaborator from 1997 to 2001. In Pittsburgh
I see a guy get an "Artist of the Year" honor & I think:
him instead of etta? What a farce. This "Artist of the
Year" is a completely unoriginal rich drunk who's never
done anything for anyone & who lives totally off the
wealth of his parents. & his work is pathetically
repetitive & based on apparently ill-understood crap he
picked up in college. etta, on the other hand, is
completely original & 100% dedicated to community. So,
yeah, I'd like to see her get more credit - not that she'd
give a shit about "Artist of the Year", mind you - she
wdn't!

But, again, each person's story is different - & as soon
as someone DOES get credit or popularity I usually lose
interest in them.

For the last yr I've been trying to promote my archive so
that at least part of it will be preserved after I die. I
organized a program of movies by friends of mine that're
in my collection that screened as part of Pittsburgh
Filmmakers' annual "Three Rivers Film Festival". Here're
the program notes for that:

Selections from tENTATIVELY, a cONVENIENCE's Movie Archive

"The End" - Jubal **Brown**, Toronto, Canada - 1998? -2:59

Jubal's 1st brush w/ notoriety may've been when he vomited in primary colors on museum
paintings. Since then, he's been associated w/ the video-making group FAME FAME.

"twenty dollar poem" - Brian Douglas **Clemons** + g.g.allin, New Hampshire, us@ - Mar 2, 1987 - 7:10

Brian Clemons was a poet, a junkie, a squatter, & a drifter who once told me that he rode a
passenger train for free from Florida to Chicago - when the conductor asked for his ticket he said:
"What're you gonna do? Beat me? I'd like that." & the conductor left him alone. Here, g.g.allin
reads Brian's poem while he.. beats him.

"Blister Freak Circus' "Cheese Tweezer"" - Skizz P. **Cyzyk**, Baltimore, us@ - 1992 - 2:11

Skizz is a musician, a filmmaker, the former organizer of the H.O.M.E. Group Microcinefest, & a guy w/ a sense of humor.

"Creamy Love" - Dick **Dale**, Adelaide, Australia - 2001 - 6:45

Dick Dale is a drunk punk comedy horror low-budget videomaker extraordinaire. As w/ so many things presented in this program, you're not likely to see his work in the US very often.

Church of the SubGenius ad - **Dobbsfilm**, Cleveland?, us@ - early 2000s? - 1:01

The Church of the SubGenius has been using the subterfuge of bilking the gullible to make them less gullible for 32 yrs. Here we see the Reverend Ivan Stang doing what he does best. I'm a Saint in the church so keep that in mind the next time you think about being anything even slightly less than worshipful to me.

"I Agree with tENTATIVELY, a cONVENIENCE's Position on the Art Strike" - Karen **Eliot** [John Berndt], Baltimore, us@ - 1990 - :36

My position on the Art Strike (1990-1993) was basically that those of us who didn't consider ourselves to be artists in the 1st place couldn't participate in the Strike w/o *reinforcing* art - which we certainly didn't want to do. Here Karen Eliot expresses solidarity by walking naked in the city in daytime. You figure it out.

"Case #4136: 'Hal'" - Jennifer **Fieber**, NYC, us@ - 1997? - 12:30

I've been 'reviving' the use of filmstrips for new purposes since Orgone Cinema got me involved w/ them in 1996. This not-quite-a-filmstrip was contributed to a filmstrip compilation that I was editing & rejected b/c of the "not-quite" aspect.

"The Trinity Session" - Istvan **Kantor** / Monty Cantsin / Amen?!, Hungary / Toronto, Canada - 2001 - 7:30

Kantor is the primary founder of neoism. Here the Machine Sex Action Group shows where neoists get all our energy from for our continual overthrow of easy answers to stupid questions.

"Cellar Sinema" - George **Kuchar** w/ Total Mobile Home Micro Cinema, San Francisco, us@ - 1994 - 12:35

Rebecca Barten & David Sherman may just deserve the credit for coining the term "microcinema" around 1994. Here, the greatest living film & video maker almost completely perverts any serious documentation about what may've been the 1st of these microcinemas.

"Repression" (unfinished) - **L.A. Newsreel**, LA, us@ - 1969? - 12:34

In 1998 or 1999, I curated a 6 part screening series on "The Suppression of Black Radicals in the United States". My seeking rare footage led to my receiving this. I've never screened it before.

Those familiar w/ the history of the Black Panthers in L.A. will realize why this might be a very controversial film. One clue: Kwaanza. 'Nuff said.

"Was it Six" - Vesna **Miksiç**, Yugoslavia / Baltimore, us@ - 1983 - 2:04

Vesna Miksiç came briefly to Baltimore & taught at U.M.B.C. in 1984 back in the day when Yugoslavia still existed. I have no idea what's happened to her since.

"Dances with Mirrors" - Jona **Pelovska**, Bulgaria / Montréal, Canada - 2007 - 6:34

Jona is a Bulgarian expatriate living in Canada. She made this movie partially so she could use Michael Pestel's & my soundtrack & then sent it to me. Boy, was I surprised.

"Superb Lyrebird" - Michael **Pestel** & David Rothenberg, Australia - 2004 - 3:27

David Rothenberg wrote a book called <u>Why Do Birds Sing?</u> that came w/ a CD. Michael Pestel, formerly of Pittsburgh, has done many performances w/ birds & referencing *extinct* birds. David took Michael to Australia just so the 2 could improvise w/ the master imitator, the lyrebird, & included an excerpt on the CD. This includes rare footage of a lyrebird flying.

"Levi's Subvertisement: Button Your Lip" - Jeff **Plansker**, us@ - 1990 - :34

I got this from Jeff's collaborator, my friend Owen O'Toole. I think Jeff & Owen tried to make actual commercials together for money. They might've failed at that. This might've been a precursor to such attempts.

"Breeda to Bag Morph" - **TV Hospital**, Berlin, Germany - 1994 - :35

I lived in Berlin for 3 months in 1994 so that I could help w/ Herr Stilleto Studio's "TV Hospital" installation/cable-tv-show. One of the things that our collaborator, Axel Jagemann, & I did was make morphs of those around us. Axel also made computer graphics. Here's a morph of Breeda from the performance group The Dead Chickens. She made the bag she's morphing into.

"**Vermin Supreme**'s Real Life Adventures from the Campaign Trail" - us@ - 1996 - 9:25

Vermin Supreme is the only candidate for supreme dictator of everything-from-your-teeth-to-your-trust-fund. Here we see him hard at work during his 1996 presidential campaign. Everyone in the know knows that the election was fixed so that he couldn't win. & Sam Donaldson is a prime suspect in the conspiracy.

- superficial notes from tENTATIVELY, a cONVENIENCE

Not all of the people above are totally obscure or unappreciated but most of them are probably somewhat *underappreciated* & I'd like to see some of their work better known - wch isn't to say that I even necessarily currently personally LIKE everyone listed above - but that's somewhat beside the point.

Next friday, April 15, 2011, I've curated another program from my movie archive of the work of friends. It'll be at the Andy Warhol Museum here in Pittsburgh. This program was put together largely to promote the work of Ken Doolittle. [of course, this interview was created over a period of time that's now passed - this particular program has played in 2 different locations & a 3rd program from my archive is 'upcoming' - wch may well *also* be passed/ past by the time YOU read this; fall, 2012 insertion: &, of course, program 3 has also come & gone]

I initially met Ken at my bkstore, "Normal's", in Baltimore in the early 1990s. Then he came to a concert of mine - probably one of the "Official" ones - maybe a trio that Neil Feather, John Berndt, & I did. Ken was living in Baltimore briefly & then returned to Montréal - where I think he might be from. I moved to Canada & Ken & I stayed in touch. He sent me a VHS transfer of his labor-intensive direct-on-film 16mm called "RE:CYCLE" & a few other works. I was impressed. I probably encouraged Orgone Cinema to present him a yr or 2 later in Pittsburgh after I'd moved (t)here.

Then I lost touch w/ Ken. I'd heard something about his having a rare blood disease. I put "RE:CYCLE" on my online list of "Favorite Movies from other People". 13 or 14 yrs later I was contacted by a guy who's making a documentary about Ken. He emailed me b/c he saw my mention of "RE:CYCLE" online. This guy informed me that Ken's blood disease had caused him to go blind. I THEN learned that Ken had just had an operation to restore his eyesight wch had been somewhat successful. *SO*, I've started promoting Ken's work partially b/c I like "RE:CYCLE" so much & partially b/c I like Ken & partially b/c Ken's multi-talented (he's a musician too) & partially b/c the story about his eyes is such an intense human interest story.

Here's the program for the upcoming event:

Indelible Mark, ACE:
Selections from tENTATIVELY, a cONVENIENCE's Movie Archive:
Direct-on-Film / Optical Printing
- notes from tENTATIVELY, a cONVENIENCE (Dec. 17, 2010)

"Pull & Tear the White Air 2 to 9" - Rebecca **Barten** - 1992 - 6:08

Rebecca Barten was the cofounder of "H.O.M.E. Group" (Horse Opera Meanderthal Encounter Group) w/ tENTATIVELY, a cONVENIENCE in Baltimore in 1992. Together they published two 2 hour long compilations of locally produced experimental film work & organized screenings. Skizz Cyzyk went on to run a screening series for many years under the same name. This film uses direct-on-film techniques such as typing on the film & also uses rephotography of her own video.

"Rote Movie" - Dirk **DeBruyn** - 1994 - 11:31

Dirk DeBruyn was part of a Melbourne, Australia direct-on-film group that collaboratively created work under the name of Direct Action. "Rote Movie" was made during a trip to the US. It involves an impressively intricate array of techniques that include shooting using a filmstrip camera & then using the results as 35mm film.

"RE:CYCLE" - Ken **Doolittle** - 1992 - 22:30

Ken Doolittle is a Montréal-based filmmaker whose "RE:CYCLE" is one of the most meticulous & extended direct-on-film films I've ever seen. Largely reworking a found birthing film, the birthing becomes a birthing of filmic possibilities. A few years after Ken made this, he went blind from a rare blood disease. I'm happy to say that he's recently had his sight restored after more than a decade of blindness.

"... For a Moment ... ...Only" - Steve **Estes** - 1997 - 21:42

Steve Estes, like perhaps most of the people whose work is in my archives, is entirely too unknown outside his native city - in this case Baltimore. Starting in the 1970s Steve made minimalist video, with original soundtracks, & laborious rotoscope portraits. Rotoscope is a technique where animated drawings are based around a filmed original. In the 1990s Steve returned to grad school & started incorporating computer animation as well. This film is the resultant hybrid of decades of work.

"Manual Labor" - Mark **Nugent** - 1987 - 16:19

Mark Nugent was another Montréal-based film & video maker. At one time he was also the film & video curator at Hallwalls in Buffalo. After being in Buffalo, he returned to Montréal where he eventually lived a very reclusive life until his death in 2009. "Manual Labor" is a masterpiece of optical printing using both original & found footage. The latter involves some particularly poignant footage of drug experimentation, possibly LSD, using a volunteer laying in bed tripping surrounded by doctors.

"Dark River" - Mark **Nugent** - 1992 - 7:18

Nugent also worked extensively with bands - sometimes touring with them to provide live video projection. In this case, this is another optically printed 16mm film (transferred here to VHS) rather than video but it has a soundtrack made by the post-Psychic TV group Coil. Both of Nugent's works are profoundly evocative of mythic journeys.

So there's another person I'm promoting. The gist of it is that I cd go on & on. It seems that the general public wants & relates to simpletons - the Lowest Common Denominator. & everyone I'm interested in is far more complex. But even that's an oversimplification.

I mentioned etta cetera earlier. etta's much more of a believer in 'the people' than I am. My own personal experience warns me that 'the people' are usually weak & cowardly & will turn on anyone conveniently scapegoated in order to save their ass - even when it's not desperately 'necessary'. As such, I don't believe that people are intrinsically 'good' as many of my fellow anarchists do. My point here is that when I generalize about the general public wanting "simpletons" & about my being interested in people that the general public might reject or have minimal interest in I'm speaking for myself - people like etta wd probably strongly disagree. & I respect her.

Alan -- If things were to have an-ending / what would it look like? / what would you be doing?

tENT - Of course, yr question prompts my asking in turn: "What "things"?" Often, when works address this topic, 'the end' is imagined as the death of most or all people - more rarely it's the death of all living things on this planet, more rare still it's the annihilation of the planet - but how often does it go beyond that? Of my most immediate concern is the death of my closest friends & of myself.

But let's imagine further: you ask about "an-ending" - *not* THE ending, not one-of-many-possible-endings, just *an-ending*. If we were to discuss "an-ending" that's THE ending, "would it look like" anything? Would I be "doing"

anything? It wd be "an-end[ing]" to looking & doing, to
me, to you, to this sentence, to this language, to this
planet, to this solar system, to the possibility of this
solar system, to the galaxy, to the universe, to the
multiverse, to ways of measuring itself, to itself - to
spin off of what my girlfriend Amy Catanzano often
discusses: it'd be not just an end to human scale but to
ALL SCALE. **PERIOD.**

But let's scale it back down again: being a morbid person
from time-to-time & being proactive (to use a word perhaps
overused in contexts I don't necessarily always want to
associate myself w/), I have an ongoing fantasy in wch I
learn that I'm to die soon. *SO*, I get a dr.'s certificate
explaining this (duly notarized, etc) & I take this to
places where I might not ordinarily be able to partake of
what's available there - say an expensive restaurant.

In this example, I go to the restaurant w/ a hidden camera
& mic & I show them the certificate & explain that one of
my dying wishes is to have a free lavish meal there. I
explain this politely but I look as I ordinarily do:
eccentrically dressed, perhaps a little dirty - definitely
not like the rest of the clientele.

If I'm denied a free meal there (perhaps for myself *&* a
friend), then I make the clandestine documentary footage
available to the world as widely as possible - identifying
the restaurant. If they graciously *give me a free meal* I
do the same thing. Thus, I have one of my final roles be
that of a SECRET SHOPPER FOR TRICKSTER CULTURE.

Another human-scale/my-death fantasy is this: I'm on my
death-bed (or death-car-seat or death-sidewalk, etc) & my
last word is:

Methionylthreonylthreonylglutaminylarginyltyrosylglutamylserylleucyl
phenylalanylalanylglutaminylleucyllysylglutamylarginyllysylglutamylg

lycylalanylphenylalanylvalylprolylphenylalanylvalylthreonylleucylglyc
ylaspartylprolylglycylisoleucylglutamylglutaminylserylleucyllysylisole
ucylaspartylthreonylleucylisoleucylglutamylalanylglycylalanylaspartyl
alanylleucylglutamylleucylglycylisoleucylprolylphenylalanylserylaspar
tylprolylleucylalanylaspartylglycylprolylthreonylisoleucylglutaminylas
paraginylalanylthreonylleucylarginylalanylphenylalanylalanylalanylgly
cylvalylthreonylprolylalanylglutaminylcysteinylphenylalanylglutamylm
ethionylleucylalanylleucylisoleucylarginylglutaminyllysylhistidylprolylt
hreonylisoleucylprolylisoleucylglycylleucylleucylmethionyltyrosylalan
ylasparaginylleucylvalylphenylalanylasparaginyllysylglycylisoleucylas
partylglutamylphenylalanyltyrosylalanylglutaminylcysteinylglutamylly
sylvalylglycylvalylaspartylserylvalylleucylvalylalanylaspartylvalylprol
ylvalylglutaminylglutamylserylalanylprolylphenylalanylarginylglutami
nylalanylalanylleucylarginylhistidylasparaginylvalylalanylprolylisoleuc
ylphenylalanylisoleucylcysteinylprolylprolylaspartylalanylaspartylaspa
rtylaspartylleucylleucylarginylglutaminylisoleucylalanylseryltyrosylgly
cylarginylglycyltyrosylthreonyltyrosylleucylleucylserylarginylalanylgly
cylvalylthreonylglycylalanylglutamylasparaginylarginylalanylalanylleu
cylprolylleucylasparaginylhistidylleucylvalylalanyllysylleucyllysylgluta
myltyrosylasparaginylalanylalanylprolylprolylleucylglutaminylglycylph
enylalanylglycylisoleucylserylalanylprolylaspartylglutaminylvalyllysyl
alanylalanylisoleucylaspartylalanylglycylalanylalanylglycylalanylisole
ucylserylglycylserylalanylisoleucylvalyllysylisoleucylisoleucylglutamyl
glutaminylhistidylasparaginylisoleucylglutamylprolylglutamyllysylmet
hionylleucylalanylalanylleucyllysylvalylphenylalanylvalylglutaminylpr
olylmethionyllysylalanylalanylthreonylarginylacetylseryltyrosylserylis
oleucylthreonylserylprolylserylglutaminylphenylalanylvalylphenylalan
ylleucylserylserylvalyltryptophylalanylaspartylprolylisoleucylglutamyl
leucylleucylasparaginylvalylcysteinylthreonylserylserylleucylglycylasp
araginylglutaminylphenylalanylglutaminylthreonylglutaminylglutamin
ylalanylarginylthreonylthreonylglutaminylvalylglutaminylglutaminylph
enylalanylserylglutaminylvalyltryptophyllysylprolylphenylalanylprolyl
glutaminylserylthreonylvalylarginylphenylalanylprolylglycylaspartylva
lyltyrosyllysylvalyltyrosylarginyltyrosylasparaginylalanylvalylleucylas
partylprolylleucylisoleucylthreonylalanylleucylleucylglycylthreonylphe
nylalanylaspartylthreonylarginylasparaginylarginylisoleucylisoleucylgl
utamylvalylglutamylasparaginylglutaminylglutaminylserylprolylthreon
ylthreonylalanylglutamylthreonylleucylaspartylalanylthreonylarginylar
ginylvalylaspartylaspartylalanylthreonylvalylalanylisoleucylarginylser
ylalanylasparaginylisoleucylasparaginylleucylvalylasparaginylglutamy

lleucylvalylarginylglycylthreonylglycylleucyltyrosylasparaginylglutami
nylasparaginylthreonylphenylalanylglutamylserylmethionylserylglycyl
leucylvalyltryptophylthreonylserylalanylprolylalanyltitinmethionylglut
aminylarginyltyrosylglutamylserylleucylphenylalanylalanylisoleucylcy
steinylprolylprolylaspartylalanylaspartylaspartylaspartylleucylleucylar
ginylglutaminylisoleucylalanylseryltyrosylglycylarginylglycyltyrosylthr
eonyltyrosylleucylleucylserylarginylalanylglycylvalylthreonylglycylala
nylglutamylasparaginylarginylalanylalanylleucylprolylleucylasparagin
ylhistidylleucylvalylalanyllysylleucyllysylglutamyltyrosylasparaginylal
anylalanylprolylprolylleucylglutaminylglycylphenylalanylglycylisoleuc
ylserylalanylprolylaspartylglutaminylvalyllysylalanylalanylisoleucylas
partylalanylglycylalanylalanylglycylalanylisoleucylserylglycylserylalan
ylisoleucylvalyllysylisoleucylisoleucylglutamylglutaminylhistidylaspar
aginylisoleucylglutamylprolylglutamyllysylmethionylleucylalanylalanyl
leucyllysylvalylphenylalanylvalylglutaminylprolylmethionyllysylalanyl
alanylthreonylaginylacetylseryltyrosylserylisoleucylthreonylserylproly
lserylglutaminylphenylalanylvalylphenylalanylleucylserylserylvalyltry
ptophylalanylaspartylprolylisoleucylglutamylleucylleucylasparaginylva
lylcysteinylthreonylserylserylleucylglycylasparaginylglutaminylphenyl
alanylglutaminylthreonylglutaminylglutaminylalanylarginylthreonylthr
eonylglutaminylvalylglutaminylglutaminylphenylalanylserylglutaminyl
valyltryptophyllysylprolylphenylalanylprolylglutaminylserylthreonylva
lylarginylphenylalanylprolylglycylaspartylvalyltyrosyllysylvalyltyrosyl
arginyltyrosylasparaginylalanylvalylleucylaspartylprolylleucylisoleucy
lthreonylalanylleucylleucylglycylthreonylphenylalanylaspartylthreonyl
arginylasparaginylarginylisoleucylisoleucylglutamylvalylglutamylaspa
raginylglutaminylglutaminylserylprolylthreonylthreonylalanylglutamyl
threonylleucylaspartylalanylthreonylarginylarginylvalylaspartylaspart
ylalanylthreonylvalylalanylisoleucylarginylserylalanylasparaginylisole
ucylasparaginylleucylvalylasparaginylglutamylleucylvalylarginylglycyl
threonylglycylleucyltyrosylasparaginylglutaminylasparaginylthreonylp
henylalanylglutamylserylmethionylserylglycylleucylvalyltryptophylthr
eonylserylalanylprolylalanyltitinmethionylglutaminylarginyltyrosylglut
amylserylleucylphenylalanylalanylisoleucylcysteinylprolylprolylaspart
ylalanylaspartylaspartylaspartylleucylleucylarginylglutaminylisoleucyl
alanylseryltyrosylglycylarginylglycyltyrosylthreonyltyrosylleucylleucyl
serylarginylalanylglycylvalylthreonylglycylalanylglutamylasparaginyla
rginylalanylalanylleucylprolylleucylasparaginylhistidylleucylvalylalany
llysylleucyllysylglutamyltyrosylasparaginylalanylalanylprolylprolylleu
cylglutaminylglycylphenylalanylglycylisoleucylserylalanylprolylaspart

ylglutaminylvalyllysylalanylalanylisoleucylaspartylalanylglycylalanylal
anylglycylalanylisoleucylserylglycylserylalanylisoleucylvalyllysylisole
ucylisoleucylglutamylglutaminylhistidylasparaginylisoleucylglutamylpr
olylglutamyllysylmethionylleucylalanylalanylleucyllysylvalylphenylala
nylvalylglutaminylprolylmethionyllysylalanylalanylthreonylarginylacet
ylseryltyrosylserylisoleucylthreonylserylprolylserylglutaminylphenylal
anylvalylphenylalanylleucylserylserylvalyltryptophylalanylaspartylpro
lylisoleucylglutamylleucylleucylasparaginylvalylcysteinylthreonylseryl
serylleucylglycylasparaginylglutaminylphenylalanylglutaminylthreonyl
glutaminylglutaminylalanylarginylthreonylthreonylglutaminylvalylglut
aminylglutaminylphenylalanylserylglutaminylvalyltryptophyllysylproly
lphenylalanylprolylglutaminylserylthreonylvalylarginylphenylalanylpro
lylglycylaspartylvalyltyrosyllysylvalyltyrosylarginyltyrosylasparaginyl
alanylvalylleucylaspartylprolylleucylisoleucylthreonylalanylleucylleuc
ylglycylthreonylphenylalanylaspartylthreonylarginylasparaginylarginyl
isoleucylisoleucylglutamylvalylglutamylasparaginylglutaminylglutami
nylserylprolylthreonylthreonylalanylglutamylthreonylleucylaspartylala
nylthreonylarginylarginylvalylaspartylaspartylalanylthreonylvalylalan
ylisoleucylarginylserylalanylasparaginylisoleucylasparaginylleucylvaly
lasparaginylglutamylleucylvalylarginylglycylthreonylglycylleucyltyros
ylasparaginylglutaminylasparaginylthreonylphenylalanylglutamylseryl
methionylserylglycylleucylvalyltryptophylthreonylserylalanylprolylala
nyltitinmethionylglutaminylarginyltyrosylglutamylserylleucylphenylala
nylalanylisoleucylcysteinylprolylprolylaspartylalanylaspartylaspartyla
spartylleucylleucylarginylglutaminylisoleucylalanylseryltyrosylglycyla
rginylglycyltyrosylthreonyltyrosylleucylleucylserylarginylalanylglycylv
alylthreonylglycylalanylglutamylasparaginylarginylalanylalanylleucylp
rolylleucylasparaginylhistidylleucylvalylalanyllysylleucyllysylglutamyl
tyrosylasparaginylalanylalanylprolylprolylleucylglutaminylglycylpheny
lalanylglycylisoleucylserylalanylprolylaspartylglutaminylvalyllysylalan
ylalanylisoleucylaspartylalanylglycylalanylalanylglycylalanylisoleucyls
erylglycylserylalanylisoleucylvalyllysylisoleucylisoleucylglutamylgluta
minylhistidylasparaginylisoleucylglutamylprolylglutamyllysylmethiony
lleucylalanylalanylleucyllysylvalylphenylalanylvalylglutaminylprolylm
ethionyllysylalanylalanylthreonylarginylacetylseryltyrosylserylisoleuc
ylthreonylserylprolylserylglutaminylphenylalanylvalylphenylalanylleuc
ylserylserylvalyltryptophylalanylaspartylprolylisoleucylglutamylleucyl
leucylasparaginylvalylcysteinylthreonylserylserylleucylglycylasparagi
nylglutaminylphenylalanylglutaminylthreonylglutaminylglutaminylalan
ylarginylthreonylthreonylglutaminylvalylglutaminylglutaminylphenylal

anylserylglutaminylvalyltryptophyllysylprolylphenylalanylprolylglutam
inylserylthreonylvalylarginylphenylalanylprolylglycylaspartylvalyltyro
syllysylvalyltyrosylarginyltyrosylasparaginylalanylvalylleucylaspartyl
prolylleucylisoleucylthreonylalanylleucylleucylglycylthreonylphenylala
nylaspartylthreonylarginylasparaginylarginylisoleucylisoleucylglutamy
lvalylglutamylasparaginylglutaminylglutaminylserylprolylthreonylthre
onylalanylglutamylthreonylleucylaspartylalanylthreonylarginylarginyl
valylaspartylaspartylalanylthreonylvalylalanylisoleucylarginylserylala
nylasparaginylisoleucylasparaginylleucylvalylasparaginylglutamylleuc
ylvalylarginylglycylthreonylglycylleucyltyrosylasparaginylglutaminyla
sparaginylthreonylphenylalanylglutamylserylmethionylserylglycylleuc
ylvalyltryptophylthreonylserylalanylprolylalanyltitinmethionylglutamin
ylarginyltyrosylglutamylserylleucylphenylalanylalanylmethionylthreon
ylthreonylglutaminylarginyltyrosylglutamylserylleucylphenylalanylala
nylglutaminylleucyllysylglutamylarginyllysylglutamylglycylalanylphen
ylalanylvalylprolylphenylalanylvalylthreonylleucylglycylaspartylprolyl
glycylisoleucylglutamylglutaminylserylleucyllysylisoleucylaspartylthre
onylleucylisoleucylglutamylalanylglycylalanylaspartylalanylleucylgluta
mylleucylglycylisoleucylprolylphenylalanylserylaspartylprolylleucylala
nylaspartylglycylprolylthreonylisoleucylglutaminylasparaginylalanylth
reonylleucylarginylalanylphenylalanylalanylalanylglycylvalylthreonylp
rolylalanylglutaminylcysteinylphenylalanylglutamylmethionylleucylala
nylleucylisoleucylarginylglutaminyllysylhistidylprolylthreonylisoleucyl
prolylisoleucylglycylleucylleucylmethionyltyrosylalanylasparaginylleu
cylvalylphenylalanylasparaginyllysylglycylisoleucylaspartylglutamylph
enylalanyltyrosylalanylglutaminylcysteinylglutamyllysylvalylglycylval
ylaspartylserylvalylleucylvalylalanylaspartylvalylprolylvalylglutaminyl
glutamylserylalanylprolylphenylalanylarginylglutaminylalanylalanylle
ucylarginylhistidylasparaginylvalylalanylprolylisoleucylphenylalanylis
oleucylcysteinylprolylprolylaspartylalanylaspartylaspartylaspartylleuc
ylleucylarginylglutaminylisoleucylalanylseryltyrosylglycylarginylglycyl
tyrosylthreonyltyrosylleucylleucylserylarginylalanylglycylvalylthreony
lglycylalanylglutamylasparaginylarginylalanylalanylleucylprolylleucyla
sparaginylhistidylleucylvalylalanyllysylleucyllysylglutamyltyrosylaspa
raginylalanylalanylprolylprolylleucylglutaminylglycylphenylalanylglyc
ylisoleucylserylalanylprolylaspartylglutaminylvalyllysylalanylalanyliso
leucylaspartylalanylglycylalanylalanylglycylalanylisoleucylserylglycyls
erylalanylisoleucylvalyllysylisoleucylisoleucylglutamylglutaminylhistid
ylasparaginylisoleucylglutamylprolylglutamyllysylmethionylleucylalan
ylalanylleucyllysylvalylphenylalanylvalylglutaminylprolylmethionyllys

ylalanylalanylthreonylarginylacetylserylthreonylserylisoleucylthreonyls
erylprolylserylglutaminylphenylalanylvalylphenylalanylleucylserylsery
lvalyltryptophylalanylaspartylprolylisoleucylglutamylleucylleucylaspar
aginylvalylcysteinylthreonylserylserylleucylglycylasparaginylglutamin
ylphenylalanylglutaminylthreonylglutaminylglutaminylalanylarginylthr
eonylthreonylglutaminylvalylglutaminylglutaminylphenylalanylserylgl
utaminylvalyltryptophyllysylprolylphenylalanylprolylglutaminylserylth
reonylvalylarginylphenylalanylprolylglycylaspartylvalyltyrosyllysylval
yltyrosylarginyltyrosylasparaginylalanylvalylleucylaspartylprolylleucy
lisoleucylthreonylalanylleucylleucylglycylthreonylphenylalanylaspartyl
threonylarginylasparaginylarginylisoleucylisoleucylglutamylvalylgluta
mylasparaginylglutaminylglutaminylserylprolylthreonylthreonylalanyl
glutamylthreonylleucylaspartylalanylthreonylarginylarginylvalylaspart
ylaspartylalanylthreonylvalylalanylisoleucylarginylserylalanylasparagi
nylisoleucylasparaginylleucylvalylasparaginylglutamylleucylvalylargin
ylglycylthreonylglycylleucyltyrosylasparaginylglutaminylasparaginylth
reonylphenylalanylglutamylserylmethionylserylglycylleucylvalyltrypto
phylthreonylserylalanylprolylalanyltitinmethionylglutaminylarginyltyr
osylglutamylserylleucylphenylalanylalanylisoleucylcysteinylprolylprol
ylaspartylalanylaspartylaspartylaspartylleucylleucylarginylglutaminyli
soleucylalanylseryltyrosylglycylarginylglycyltyrosylthreonyltyrosylleu
cylleucylserylarginylalanylglycylvalylthreonylglycylalanylglutamylasp
araginylarginylalanylalanylleucylprolylleucylasparaginylhistidylleucylv
alylalanyllysylleucyllysylglutamyltyrosylasparaginylalanylalanylprolyl
prolylleucylglutaminylglycylphenylalanylglycylisoleucylserylalanylprol
ylaspartylglutaminylvalyllysylalanylalanylisoleucylaspartylalanylglycy
lalanylalanylglycylalanylisoleucylserylglycylserylalanylisoleucylvalylly
sylisoleucylisoleucylglutamylglutaminylhistidylasparaginylisoleucylglu
tamylprolylglutamyllysylmethionylleucylalanylalanylleucyllysylvalylph
enylalanylvalylglutaminylprolylmethionyllysylalanylalanylthreonylargi
nylacetylseryltyrosylserylisoleucylthreonylserylprolylserylglutaminylp
henylalanylvalylphenylalanylleucylserylserylvalyltryptophylalanylaspa
rtylprolylisoleucylglutamylleucylleucylasparaginylvalylcysteinylthreon
ylserylserylleucylglycylasparaginylglutaminylphenylalanylglutaminylt
hreonylglutaminylglutaminylalanylarginylthreonylthreonylglutaminylv
alylglutaminylglutaminylphenylalanylserylglutaminylvalyltryptophylly
sylprolylphenylalanylprolylglutaminylserylthreonylvalylarginylphenyla
lanylprolylglycylaspartylvalyltyrosyllysylvalyltyrosylarginyltyrosylasp
araginylalanylvalylleucylaspartylprolylleucylisoleucylthreonylalanylle
ucylleucylglycylthreonylphenylalanylaspartylthreonylarginylasparagin

ylarginylisoleucylisoleucylglutamylvalylglutamylasparaginylglutaminy
lglutaminylserylprolylthreonylthreonylalanylglutamylthreonylleucylas
partylalanylthreonylarginylarginylvalylaspartylaspartylalanylthreonyl
valylalanylisoleucylarginylserylalanylasparaginylisoleucylasparaginyll
eucylvalylasparaginylglutamylleucylvalylarginylglycylthreonylglycylle
ucyltyrosylasparaginylglutaminylasparaginylthreonylphenylalanylglut
amylserylmethionylserylglycylleucylvalyltryptophylthreonylserylalany
lprolylalanyltitinmethionylglutaminylarginyltyrosylglutamylserylleucyl
phenylalanylalanylisoleucylcysteinylprolylprolylaspartylalanylaspartyl
aspartylaspartylleucylleucylarginylglutaminylisoleucylalanylseryltyros
ylglycylarginylglycyltyrosylthreonyltyrosylleucylleucylserylarginylalan
ylglycylvalylthreonylglycylalanylglutamylasparaginylarginylalanylalan
ylleucylprolylleucylasparaginylhistidylleucylvalylalanyllysylleucyllysyl
glutamyltyrosylasparaginylalanylalanylprolylprolylleucylglutaminylgly
cylphenylalanylglycylisoleucylserylalanylprolylaspartylglutaminylvalyl
lysylalanylalanylisoleucylaspartylalanylglycylalanylalanylglycylalanyli
soleucylserylglycylserylalanylisoleucylvalyllysylisoleucylisoleucylglut
amylglutaminylhistidylasparaginylisoleucylglutamylprolylglutamyllysy
lmethionylleucylalanylalanylleucyllysylvalylphenylalanylvalylglutamin
ylprolylmethionyllysylalanylalanylthreonylarginylacetylseryltyrosylser
ylisoleucylthreonylserylprolylserylglutaminylphenylalanylvalylphenyla
lanylleucylserylserylvalyltryptophylalanylaspartylprolylisoleucylgluta
mylleucylleucylasparaginylvalylcysteinylthreonylserylserylleucylglycy
lasparaginylglutaminylphenylalanylglutaminylthreonylglutaminylgluta
minylalanylarginylthreonylthreonylglutaminylvalylglutaminylglutamin
ylphenylalanylserylglutaminylvalyltryptophyllysylprolylphenylalanylpr
olylglutaminylserylthreonylvalylarginylphenylalanylprolylglycylaspart
ylvalyltyrosyllysylvalyltyrosylarginyltyrosylasparaginylalanylvalylleuc
ylaspartylprolylleucylisoleucylthreonylalanylleucylleucylglycylthreonyl
phenylalanylaspartylthreonylarginylasparaginylarginylisoleucylisoleuc
ylglutamylvalylglutamylasparaginylglutaminylglutaminylserylprolylthr
eonylthreonylalanylglutamylthreonylleucylaspartylalanylthreonylargin
ylarginylvalylaspartylaspartylalanylthreonylvalylalanylisoleucylarginy
lserylalanylasparaginylisoleucylasparaginylleucylvalylasparaginylglut
amylleucylvalylarginylglycylthreonylglycylleucyltyrosylasparaginylglu
taminylasparaginylthreonylphenylalanylglutamylserylmethionylserylgl
ycylleucylvalyltryptophylthreonylserylalanylprolylalanyltitinmethionyl
glutaminylarginyltyrosylglutamylserylleucylphenylalanylalanylisoleuc
ylcysteinylprolylprolylaspartylalanylaspartylaspartylaspartylleucylleu
cylarginylglutaminylisoleucylalanylseryltyrosylglycylarginylglycyltyro

sylthreonyltyrosylleucylleucylserylarginylalanylglycylvalylthreonylgly
cylalanylglutamylasparaginylarginylalanylalanylleucylprolylleucylaspa
raginylhistidylleucylvalylalanyllysylleucyllysylglutamyltyrosylasparagi
nylalanylalanylprolylprolylleucylglutaminylglycylphenylalanylglycyliso
leucylserylalanylprolylaspartylglutaminylvalyllysylalanylalanylisoleuc
ylaspartylalanylglycylalanylalanylglycylalanylisoleucylserylglycylseryl
alanylisoleucylvalyllysylisoleucylisoleucylglutamylglutaminylhistidylas
paraginylisoleucylglutamylprolylglutamyllysylmethionylleucylalanylal
anylleucyllysylvalylphenylalanylvalylglutaminylprolylmethionyllysylal
anylalanylthreonylarginylacetylseryltyrosylserylisoleucylthreonylseryl
prolylserylglutaminylphenylalanylvalylphenylalanylleucylserylserylval
yltryptophylalanylaspartylprolylisoleucylglutamylleucylleucylasparagi
nylvalylcysteinylthreonylserylserylleucylglycylasparaginylglutaminylp
henylalanylglutaminylthreonylglutaminylglutaminylalanylarginylthreo
nylthreonylglutaminylvalylglutaminylglutaminylphenylalanylserylgluta
minylvalyltryptophyllysylprolylphenylalanylprolylglutaminylserylthreo
nylvalylarginylphenylalanylprolylglycylaspartylvalyltyrosyllysylvalylty
rosylarginyltyrosylasparaginylalanylvalylleucylaspartyprolylleucylisol
eucylthreonylalanylleucylleucylglycylthreonylphenylalanylaspartylthre
onylarginylasparaginylarginylisoleucylisoleucylglutamylvalylglutamyl
asparaginylglutaminylglutaminylserylprolylthreonylthreonylalanylglut
amylthreonylleucylaspartylalanylthreonylarginylarginylvalylaspartyla
spartylalanylthreonylvalylalanylisoleucylarginylserylalanylasparaginyl
isoleucylasparaginylleucylvalylasparaginylglutamylleucylvalylarginylg
lycylthreonylglycylleucyltyrosylasparaginylglutaminylasparaginylthre
onylphenylalanylglutamylserylmethionylserylglycylleucylvalyltryptoph
ylthreonylserylalanylprolylalanylTitinmethionylglutaminylarginyltyros
ylglutamylserylleucylphenylalanylalanylmethionylthreonylthreonylglut
aminylarginyltyrosylglutamylserylleucylphenylalanylalanylglutaminyll
eucyllysylglutamylarginyllysylglutamylglycylalanylphenylalanylvalylpr
olylphenylalanylvalylthreonylleucylglycylaspartylprolylglycylisoleucyl
glutamylglutaminylserylleucyllysylisoleucylaspartylthreonylleucylisole
ucylglutamylalanylglycylalanylaspartylalanylleucylglutamylleucylglycy
lisoleucylprolylphenylalanylserylaspartylprolylleucylalanylaspartylgly
cylprolylhreonylisoleucylglutaminylasparaginylalanylthreonylleucylarg
inylalanylphenylalanylalanylalanylglycylalylthreonylprolylalanylgluta
minylcysteinylphenylalanylglutamylmethionylleucylalanylleucylisoleuc
ylarginylglutaminyllysylhistidylprolylthreonylisoleucylprolylisoleucylgl
ycylleucylleucylmethionyltyrosylalanylasparaginylleucylvalylphenylal
anylasparaginyllysylglycylisoleucylaspartylglutamylphenylalanyltyros

ylalanylglutaminylcysteinylglutamyllysylvalylglycylvalylaspartylserylv
alylleucylvalylalanylaspartylvalylprolylvalylglutaminylglutamylserylal
anylprolylphenylalanylarginylglutaminylalanylalanylleucylarginylhistid
ylasparaginylvalylalanylprolylisoleucylphenylalanylisoleucylcysteinylp
rolylprolylaspartylalanylaspartylaspartylaspartylleucylleucylarginylglu
taminylisoleucylalanylseryltyrosylglycylarginylglycyltyrosylthreonylty
rosylleucylleucylserylarginylalanylglycylvalylthreonylglycylalanylgluta
mylasparaginylarginylalanylalanylleucylprolylleucylasparaginylhistidy
lleucylvalylalanyllysylleucyllysylglutamyltyrosylasparaginylalanylalan
ylprolylprolylleucylglutaminylglycylphenylalanylglycylisoleucylserylal
anylprolylaspartylglutaminylvalyllysylalanylalanylisoleucylaspartylala
nylglycylalanylalanylglycylalanylisoleucylserylglycylserylalanylisoleuc
ylvalyllysylisoleucylisoleucylglutamylglutaminylhistidylasparaginylisol
eucylglutamylprolylglutamyllysylmethionylleucylalanylalanylleucyllys
ylvalylphenylalanylvalylglutaminylprolylmethionyllysylalanylalanylthr
eonylarginylacetylseryltyrosylserylisoleucylthreonylserylprolylserylgl
utaminylphenylalanylvalylphenylalanylleucylserylserylvalyltryptophyl
alanylaspartylprolylisoleucylglutamylleucylleucylasparaginylvalylcyst
einylthreonylserylserylleucylglycylasparaginylglutaminylphenylalanyl
glutaminylthreonylglutaminylglutaminylalanylarginylthreonylthreonyl
glutaminylvalylglutaminylglutaminylphenylalanylserylglutaminylvalylt
ryptophyllysylprolylphenylalanylprolylglutaminylserylthreonylvalylarg
inylphenylalanylprolylglycylaspartylvalyltyrosyllysylvalyltyrosylarginy
ltyrosylasparaginylalanylvalylleucylaspartylprolylleucylisoleucylthreo
nylalanylleucylleucylglycylthreonylphenylalanylaspartylthreonylarginy
lasparaginylarginylisoleucylisoleucylglutamylvalylglutamylasparaginyl
glutaminylglutaminylserylprolylthreonylthreonylalanylglutamylthreon
ylleucylaspartylalanylthreonylarginylarginylvalylaspartylaspartylalany
lthreonylvalylalanylisoleucylarginylserylalanylasparaginylisoleucylasp
araginylleucylvalylasparaginylglutamylleucylvalylarginylglycylthreony
lglycylleucyltyrosylasparaginylglutaminylasparaginylthreonylphenylal
anylglutamylserylmethionylserylglycylleucylvalyltryptophylthreonylse
rylalanylprolylalanyltitinmethionylglutaminylarginyltyrosylglutamylse
rylleucylphenylalanylalanylisoleucylcysteinylprolylprolylaspartylalanyl
aspartylaspartylaspartylleucylleucylarginylglutaminylisoleucylalanyls
eryltyrosylglycylarginylglycyltyrosylthreonyltyrosylleucylleucylserylar
ginylalanylglycylvalylthreonylglycylalanylglutamylasparaginylarginyla
lanylalanylleucylprolylleucylasparaginylhistidylleucylvalylalanyllysylle
ucyllysylglutamyltyrosylasparaginylalanylalanylprolylprolylleucylgluta
minylglycylphenylalanylglycylisoleucylserylalanylprolylaspartylglutam

inylvalylllysylalanylalanylisoleucylaspartylalanylglycylalanylalanylglyc
ylalanylisoleucylserylglycylserylalanylisoleucylvalylllysylisoleucylisole
ucylglutamylglutaminylhistidylasparaginylisoleucylglutamylprolylgluta
myllysylmethionylleucylalanylalanylleucylllysylvalylphenylalanylvalylg
lutaminylprolylmethionylllysylalanylalanylthreonylarginylacetylserylty
rosylserylisoleucylthreonylserylprolylserylglutaminylphenylalanylvaly
lphenylalanylleucylserylserylvalyltryptophylalanylaspartylprolylisoleu
cylglutamylleucylleucylasparaginylvalylcysteinylthreonylserylserylleu
cylglycylasparaginylglutaminylphenylalanylglutaminylthreonylglutami
nylglutaminylalanylarginylthreonylthreonylglutaminylvalylglutaminylg
lutaminylphenylalanylserylglutaminylvalyltryptophyllysylprolylphenyl
alanylprolylglutaminylserylthreonylvalylarginylphenylalanylprolylglyc
ylaspartylvalyltyrosylllysylvalyltyrosylarginyltyrosylasparaginylalanyl
valylleucylaspartylprolylleucylisoleucylthreonylalanylleucylleucylglycy
lthreonylphenylalanylaspartylthreonylarginylasparaginylarginylisoleuc
ylisoleucylglutamylvalylglutamylasparaginylglutaminylglutaminylseryl
prolylthreonylthreonylalanylglutamylthreonylleucylaspartylalanylthre
onylarginylarginylvalylaspartylaspartylalanylthreonylvalylalanylisoleu
cylarginylserylalanylasparaginylisoleucylasparaginylleucylvalylaspara
ginylglutamylleucylvalylarginylglycylthreonylglycylleucyltyrosylaspar
aginylglutaminylasparaginylthreonylphenylalanylglutamylserylmethio
nylserylglycylleucylvalyltryptophylthreonylserylalanylprolylalanyltitin
methionylglutaminylarginyltyrosylglutamylserylleucylphenylalanylala
nylisoleucylcysteinylprolylprolylaspartylalanylaspartylaspartylasparty
lleucylleucylarginylglutaminylisoleucylalanylseryltyrosylglycylarginylg
lycyltyrosylthreonyltyrosylleucylleucylserylarginylalanylglycylvalylthr
eonylglycylalanylglutamylasparaginylarginylalanylalanylleucylprolylle
ucylasparaginylhistidylleucylvalylalanylllysylleucylllysylglutamyltyrosyl
asparaginylalanylalanylprolylprolylleucylglutaminylglycylphenylalanyl
glycylisoleucylserylalanylprolylaspartylglutaminylvalylllysylalanylalan
ylisoleucylaspartylalanylglycylalanylalanylglycylalanylisoleucylserylgl
ycylserylalanylisoleucylvalylllysylisoleucylisoleucylglutamylglutaminyl
histidylasparaginylisoleucylglutamylprolylglutamyllysylmethionylleuc
ylalanylalanylleucylllysylvalylphenylalanylvalylglutaminylprolylmethio
nyllysylalanylalanylthreonylarginylacetylseryltyrosylserylisoleucylthr
eonylserylprolylserylglutaminylphenylalanylvalylphenylalanylleucylse
rylserylvalyltryptophylalanylaspartylprolylisoleucylglutamylleucylleuc
ylasparaginylvalylcysteinylthreonylserylserylleucylglycylasparaginylgl
utaminylphenylalanylglutaminylthreonylglutaminylglutaminylalanylar
ginylthreonylthreonylglutaminylvalylglutaminylglutaminylphenylalanyl

serylglutaminylvalyltryptophyllysylprolylphenylalanylprolylglutaminyl
serylthreonylvalylarginylphenylalanylprolylglycylaspartylvalyltyrosyll
ysylvalyltyrosylarginyltyrosylasparaginylalanylvalylleucylaspartylprol
ylleucylisoleucylthreonylalanylleucylleucylglycylthreonylphenylalanyla
spartylthreonylarginylasparaginylarginylisoleucylisoleucylglutamylval
ylglutamylasparaginylglutaminylglutaminylserylprolylthreonylthreonyl
alanylglutamylthreonylleucylaspartylalanylthreonylarginylarginylvalyl
aspartylaspartylalanylthreonylvalylalanylisoleucylarginylserylalanylas
paraginylisoleucylasparaginylleucylvalylasparaginylglutamylleucylval
ylarginylglycylthreonylglycylleucyltyrosylasparaginylglutaminylaspara
ginylthreonylphenylalanylglutamylserylmethionylserylglycylleucylvaly
ltryptophylthreonylserylalanylprolylalanyltitinmethionylglutaminylargi
nyltyrosylglutamylserylleucylphenylalanylalanylisoleucylcysteinylprol
ylprolylaspartylalanylaspartylaspartylaspartylleucylleucylarginylgluta
minylisoleucylalanylseryltyrosylglycylarginylglycyltyrosylthreonyltyro
sylleucylleucylserylarginylalanylglycylvalylthreonylglycylalanylglutam
ylasparaginylarginylalanylalanylleucylprolylleucylasparaginylhistidylle
ucylvalylalanyllysylleucyllysylglutamyltyrosylasparaginylalanylalanyl
prolylprolylleucylglutaminylglycylphenylalanylglycylisoleucylserylalan
ylprolylaspartylglutaminylvalyllysylalanylalanylisoleucylaspartylalany
lglycylalanylalanylglycylalanylisoleucylserylglycylserylalanylisoleucyl
valyllysylisoleucylisoleucylglutamylglutaminylhistidylasparaginylisole
ucylglutamylprolylglutamyllysylmethionylleucylalanylalanylleucyllysyl
valylphenylalanylvalylglutaminylprolylmethionyllysylalanylalanylthreo
nylarginylacetylseryltyrosylserylisoleucylthreonylserylprolylserylgluta
minylphenylalanylvalylphenylalanylleucylserylserylvalyltryptophylala
nylaspartylprolylisoleucylglutamylleucylleucylasparaginylvalylcystein
ylthreonylserylserylleucylglycylasparaginylglutaminylphenylalanylglut
aminylthreonylglutaminylglutaminylalanylarginylthreonylthreonylglut
aminylvalylglutaminylglutaminylphenylalanylserylglutaminylvalyltrypt
ophyllysylprolylphenylalanylprolylglutaminylserylthreonylvalylarginyl
phenylalanylprolylglycylaspartylvalyltyrosyllysylvalyltyrosylarginyltyr
osylasparaginylalanylvalylleucylaspartylprolylleucylisoleucylthreonyla
lanylleucylleucylglycylthreonylphenylalanylaspartylthreonylarginylasp
araginylarginylisoleucylisoleucylglutamylvalylglutamylasparaginylglut
aminylglutaminylserylprolylthreonylthreonylalanylglutamylthreonylle
ucylaspartylalanylthreonylarginylarginylvalylaspartylaspartylalanylthr
eonylvalylalanylisoleucylarginylserylalanylasparaginylisoleucylaspara
ginylleucylvalylasparaginylglutamylleucylvalylarginylglycylthreonylgl
ycylleucyltyrosylasparaginylglutaminylasparaginylthreonylphenylalan

ylglutamylserylmethionylserylglycylleucylvalyltryptophylthreonylseryl
alanylprolylalanyltitinmethionylglutaminylarginyltyrosylglutamylseryll
eucylphenylalanylalanylmethionylthreonylthreonylglutaminylarginylty
rosylglutamylserylleucylphenylalanylalanylglutaminylleucyllysylgluta
mylarginyllysylglutamylglycylalanylphenylalanylvalylprolylphenylalan
ylvalylthreonylleucylglycylaspartylprolylglycylisoleucylglutamylgluta
minylserylleucyllysylisoleucylaspartylthreonylleucylisoleucylglutamyl
alanylglycylalanylaspartylalanylleucylglutamylleucylglycylisoleucylpro
lylphenylalanylserylaspartylprolylleucylalanylaspartylglycylprolylthre
onylisoleucylglutaminylasparaginylalanylthreonylleucylarginylalanylp
henylalanylalanylalanylglycylvalylthreonylprolylalanylglutaminylcyste
inylphenylalanylglutamylmethionylleucylalanylleucylisoleucylarginylgl
utaminyllysylhistidylprolylthreonylisoleucylprolylisoleucylglycylleucyll
eucylmethionyltyrosylalanylasparaginylleucylvalylphenylalanylaspara
ginyllysylglycylisoleucylaspartylglutamylphenylalanyltyrosylalanylglut
aminylcysteinylglutamyllysylvalylglycylvalylaspartylserylvalylleucylv
alylalanylaspartylvalylprolylvalylglutaminylglutamylserylalanylprolylp
henylalanylarginylglutaminylalanylalanylleucylarginylhistidylasparagi
nylvalylalanylprolylisoleucylphenylalanylisoleucylcysteinylprolylprolyl
aspartylalanylaspartylaspartylaspartylleucylleucylarginylglutaminylis
oleucylalanylseryltyrosylglycylarginylglycyltyrosylthreonyltyrosylleuc
ylleucylserylarginylalanylglycylvalylthreonylglycylalanylglutamylaspa
raginylarginylalanylalanylleucylprolylleucylasparaginylhistidylleucylva
lylalanyllysylleucyllysylglutamyltyrosylasparaginylalanylalanylprolylp
rolylleucylglutaminylglycylphenylalanylglycylisoleucylserylalanylproly
laspartylglutaminylvalyllysylalanylalanylisoleucylaspartylalanylglycyl
alanylalanylglycylalanylisoleucylserylglycylserylalanylisoleucylvalylly
sylisoleucylisoleucylglutamylglutaminylhistidylasparaginylisoleucylglu
tamylprolylglutamyllysylmethionylleucylalanylalanylleucyllysylvalylph
enylalanylvalylglutaminylprolylmethionyllysylalanylalanylthreonylargi
nylacetylseryltyrosylserylisoleucylthreonylserylprolylserylglutaminylp
henylalanylvalylphenylalanylleucylserylserylvalyltryptophylalanylaspa
rtylprolylisoleucylglutamylleucylleucylasparaginylvalylcysteinylthreon
ylserylserylleucylglycylasparaginylglutaminylphenylalanylglutaminylt
hreonylglutaminylglutaminylalanylarginylthreonylthreonylglutaminylv
alylglutaminylglutaminylphenylalanylserylglutaminylvalyltryptophylly
sylprolylphenylalanylprolylglutaminylserylthreonylvalylarginylphenyla
lanylprolylglycylaspartylvalyltyrosyllysylvalyltyrosylarginyltyrosylasp
araginylalanylvalylleucylaspartylprolylleucylisoleucylthreonylalanylle
ucylleucylglycylthreonylphenylalanylaspartylthreonylarginylasparagin

ylarginylisoleucylisoleucylglutamylvalylglutamylasparaginylglutaminy
lglutaminylserylprolylthreonylthreonylalanylglutamylthreonylleucylas
partylalanylthreonylarginylarginylvalylaspartylaspartylalanylthreonyl
valylalanylisoleucylarginylserylalanylasparaginylisoleucylasparaginyll
eucylvalylasparaginylglutamylleucylvalylarginylglycylthreonylglycylle
ucyltyrosylasparaginylglutaminylasparaginylthreonylphenylalanylglut
amylserylmethionylserylglycylleucylvalyltryptophylthreonylserylalany
lprolylalanyltitinmethionylglutaminylarginyltyrosylglutamylserylleucyl
phenylalanylalanylisoleucylcysteinylprolylprolylaspartylalanylaspartyl
aspartylaspartylleucylleucylarginylglutaminylisoleucylalanylseryltyros
ylglycylarginylglycyltyrosylthreonyltyrosylleucylleucylserylarginylalan
ylglycylvalylthreonylglycylalanylglutamylasparaginylarginylalanylalan
ylleucylprolylleucylasparaginylhistidylleucylvalylalanyllysylleucyllysyl
glutamyltyrosylasparaginylalanylalanylprolylprolylleucylglutaminylgly
cylphenylalanylglycylisoleucylserylalanylprolylaspartylglutaminylvalyl
lysylalanylalanylisoleucylaspartylalanylglycylalanylalanylglycylalanyli
soleucylserylglycylserylalanylisoleucylvalyllysylisoleucylisoleucylglut
amylglutaminylhistidylasparaginylisoleucylglutamylprolylglutamyllysy
lmethionylleucylalanylalanylleucyllysylvalylphenylalanylvalylglutamin
ylprolylmethionyllysylalanylalanylthreonylarginylacetylseryltyrosylser
ylisoleucylthreonylserylprolylserylglutaminylphenylalanylvalylphenyla
lanylleucylserylserylvalyltryptophylalanylaspartylprolylisoleucylgluta
mylleucylleucylasparaginylvalylcysteinylthreonylserylserylleucylglycy
lasparaginylglutaminylphenylalanylglutaminylthreonylglutaminylgluta
minylalanylarginylthreonylthreonylglutaminylvalylglutaminylglutamin
ylphenylalanylserylglutaminylvalyltryptophyllysylprolylphenylalanylpr
olylglutaminylserylthreonylvalylarginylphenylalanylprolylglycylaspart
ylvalyltyrosyllysylvalyltyrosylarginyltyrosylasparaginylalanylvalylleuc
ylaspartylprolylleucylisoleucylthreonylalanylleucylleucylglycylthreonyl
phenylalanylaspartylthreonylarginylasparaginylarginylisoleucylisoleuc
ylglutamylvalylglutamylasparaginylglutaminylglutaminylserylprolylthr
eonylthreonylalanylglutamylthreonylleucylaspartylalanylthreonylargin
ylarginylvalylaspartylaspartylalanylthreonylvalylalanylisoleucylarginy
lserylalanylasparaginylisoleucylasparaginylleucylvalylasparaginylglut
amylleucylvalylarginylglycylthreonylglycylleucyltyrosylasparaginylglu
taminylasparaginylthreonylphenylalanylglutamylserylmethionylserylgl
ycylleucylvalyltryptophylthreonylserylalanylprolylalanyltitinmethionyl
glutaminylarginyltyrosylglutamylserylleucylphenylalanylalanylisoleuc
ylcysteinylprolylprolylaspartylalanylaspartylaspartylaspartylleucylleu
cylarginylglutaminylisoleucylalanylseryltyrosylglycylarginylglycyltyro

sylthreonyltyrosylleucylleucylserylarginylalanylglycylvalylthreonylgly
cylalanylglutamylasparaginylarginylalanylalanylleucylprolylleucylaspa
raginylhistidylleucylvalylalanyllysylleucyllysylglutamyltyrosylasparagi
nylalanylalanylprolylprolylleucylglutaminylglycylphenylalanylglycyliso
leucylserylalanylprolylaspartylglutaminylvalyllysylalanylalanylisoleuc
ylaspartylalanylglycylalanylalanylglycylalanylisoleucylserylglycylseryl
alanylisoleucylvalyllysylisoleucylisoleucylglutamylglutaminylhistidylas
paraginylisoleucylglutamylprolylglutamyllysylmethionylleucylalanylal
anylleucyllysylvalylphenylalanylvalylglutaminylprolylmethionyllysylal
anylalanylthreonylarginylacetylseryltyrosylserylisoleucylthreonylseryl
prolylserylglutaminylphenylalanylvalylphenylalanylleucylserylserylval
yltryptophylalanylaspartylprolylisoleucylglutamylleucylleucylasparagi
nylvalylcysteinylthreonylserylserylleucylglycylasparaginylglutaminylp
henylalanylglutaminylthreonylglutaminylglutaminylalanylarginylthreo
nylthreonylglutaminylvalylglutaminylglutaminylphenylalanylserylgluta
minylvalyltryptophyllysylprolylphenylalanylprolylglutaminylserylthreo
nylvalylarginylphenylalanylprolylglycylaspartylvalyltyrosyllysylvalylty
rosylarginyltyrosylasparaginylalanylvalylleucylaspartylprolylleucylisol
eucylthreonylalanylleucylleucylglycylthreonylphenylalanylaspartylthre
onylarginylasparaginylarginylisoleucylisoleucylglutamylvalylglutamyl
asparaginylglutaminylglutaminylserylprolylthreonylthreonylalanylglut
amylthreonylleucylaspartylalanylthreonylarginylarginylvalylaspartyla
spartylalanylthreonylvalylalanylisoleucylarginylserylalanylasparaginyl
isoleucylasparaginylleucylvalylasparaginylglutamylleucylvalylarginylg
lycylthreonylglycylleucyltyrosylasparaginylglutaminylasparaginylthre
onylphenylalanylglutamylserylmethionylserylglycylleucylvalyltryptoph
ylthreonylserylalanylprolylalanyltitinmethionylglutaminylarginyltyrosy
lglutamylserylleucylphenylalanylalanylisoleucylcysteinylprolylprolylas
partylalanylaspartylaspartylaspartylleucylleucylarginylglutaminylisole
ucylalanylseryltyrosylglycylarginylglycyltyrosylthreonyltyrosylleucylle
ucylserylarginylalanylglycylvalylthreonylglycylalanylglutamylasparagi
nylarginylalanylalanylleucylprolylleucylasparaginylhistidylleucylvalyla
lanyllysylleucyllysylglutamyltyrosylasparaginylalanylalanylprolylproly
lleucylglutaminylglycylphenylalanylglycylisoleucylserylalanylprolylasp
artylglutaminylvalyllysylalanylalanylisoleucylaspartylalanylglycylalan
ylalanylglycylalanylisoleucylserylglycylserylalanylisoleucylvalyllysylis
oleucylisoleucylglutamylglutaminylhistidylasparaginylisoleucylglutam
ylprolylglutamyllysylmethionylleucylalanylalanylleucyllysylvalylpheny
lalanylvalylglutaminylprolylmethionyllysylalanylalanylthreonylarginyl
acetylseryltyrosylserylisoleucylthreonylserylprolylserylglutaminylphe

nylalanylvalylphenylalanylleucylserylserylvalyltryptophylalanylaspart
ylprolylisoleucylglutamylleucylleucylasparaginylvalylcysteinylthreonyl
serylserylleucylglycylasparaginylglutaminylphenylalanylglutaminylthr
eonylglutaminylglutaminylalanylarginylthreonylthreonylglutaminylval
ylglutaminylglutaminylphenylalanylserylglutaminylvalyltryptophyllysy
lprolylphenylalanylprolylglutaminylserylthreonylvalylarginylphenylala
nylprolylglycylaspartylvalyltyrosyllysylvalyltyrosylarginyltyrosylaspar
aginylalanylvalylleucylaspartylprolylleucylisoleucylthreonylalanylleuc
ylleucylglycylthreonylphenylalanylaspartylthreonylarginylasparaginyl
arginylisoleucylisoleucylglutamylvalylglutamylasparaginylglutaminylg
lutaminylserylprolylthreonylthreonylalanylglutamylthreonylleucylaspa
rtylalanylthreonylarginylarginylvalylaspartylaspartylalanylthreonylval
ylalanylisoleucylarginylserylalanylasparaginylisoleucylasparaginylleuc
ylvalylasparaginylglutamylleucylvalylarginylglycylthreonylglycylleucyl
tyrosylasparaginylglutaminylasparaginylthreonylphenylalanylglutamyl
serylmethionylserylglycylleucylvalyltryptophylthreonylserylalanylprol
ylalanyltitinmethionylglutaminylarginyltyrosylglutamylserylleucylphen
ylalanylalanylmethionylthreonylthreonylglutaminylarginyltyrosylgluta
mylserylleucylphenylalanylalanylglutaminylleucyllysylglutamylarginyl
lysylglutamylglycylalanylphenylalanylvalylprolylphenylalanylvalylthre
onylleucylglycylaspartylprolylglycylisoleucylglutamylglutaminylserylle
ucyllysylisoleucylaspartylthreonylleucylisoleucylglutamylalanylglycyla
lanylaspartylalanylleucylglutamylleucylglycylisoleucylprolylphenylala
nylserylaspartylprolylleucylalanylaspartylglycylprolylthreonylisoleucyl
glutaminylasparaginylalanylthreonylleucylarginylalanylphenylalanylal
anylalanylglycylvalylthreonylprolylalanylglutaminylcysteinylphenylala
nylglutamylmethionylleucylalanylleucylisoleucylarginylglutaminyllysyl
histidylprolylthreonylisoleucylprolylisoleucylglycylleucylleucylmethion
yltyrosylalanylasparaginylleucylvalylphenylalanylasparaginyllysylglyc
ylisoleucylaspartylglutamylphenylalanyltyrosylalanylglutaminylcystei
nylglutamyllysylvalylglycylvalylaspartylserylvalylleucylvalylalanylasp
artylvalylprolylvalylglutaminylglutamylserylalanylprolylphenylalanyla
rginylglutaminylalanylalanylleucylarginylhistidylasparaginylvalylalany
lprolylisoleucylphenylalanylisoleucylcysteinylprolylprolylaspartylalany
laspartylaspartylaspartylleucylleucylarginylglutaminylisoleucylalanyls
eryltyrosylglycylarginylglycyltyrosylthreonyltyrosylleucylleucylserylar
ginylalanylglycylvalylthreonylglycylalanylglutamylasparaginylarginyla
lanylalanylleucylprolylleucylasparaginylhistidylleucylvalylalanyllysylle
ucyllysylglutamyltyrosylasparaginylalanylalanylprolylprolylleucylgluta
minylglycylphenylalanylglycylisoleucylserylalanylprolylaspartylglutam

inylvalylllysylalanylalanylisoleucylaspartylalanylglycylalanylalanylglyc
ylalanylisoleucylserylglycylserylalanylisoleucylvalylllysylisoleucylisole
ucylglutamylglutaminylhistidylasparaginylisoleucylglutamylprolylgluta
myllysylmethionylleucylalanylalanylleucylllysylvalylphenylalanylvalylg
lutaminylprolylmethionylllysylalanylalanylthreonylarginylacetylserylty
rosylserylisoleucylthreonylserylprolylserylglutaminylphenylalanylvaly
lphenylalanylleucylserylserylvalyltryptophylalanylaspartylprolylisoleu
cylglutamylleucylleucylasparaginylvalylcysteinylthreonylserylserylleu
cylglycylasparaginylglutaminylphenylalanylglutaminylthreonylglutami
nylglutaminylalanylarginylthreonylthreonylglutaminylvalylglutaminylg
lutaminylphenylalanylserylglutaminylvalyltryptophyllysylprolylphenyl
alanylprolylglutaminylserylthreonylvalylarginylphenylalanylprolylglyc
ylaspartylvalyltyrosylllysylvalyltyrosylarginyltyrosylasparaginylalanyl
valylleucylaspartylprolylleucylisoleucylthreonylalanylleucylleucylglycy
lthreonylphenylalanylaspartylthreonylarginylasparaginylarginylisoleuc
ylisoleucylglutamylvalylglutamylasparaginylglutaminylglutaminylseryl
prolylthreonylthreonylalanylglutamylthreonylleucylaspartylalanylthre
onylarginylarginylvalylaspartylaspartylalanylthreonylvalylalanylisoleu
cylarginylserylalanylasparaginylisoleucylasparaginylleucylvalylaspara
ginylglutamylleucylvalylarginylglycylthreonylglycylleucyltyrosylaspar
aginylglutaminylasparaginylthreonylphenylalanylglutamylserylmethio
nylserylglycylleucylvalyltryptophylthreonylserylalanylprolylalanyltitin
methionylglutaminylarginyltyrosylglutamylserylleucylphenylalanylala
nylisoleucylcysteinylprolylprolylaspartylalanylaspartylaspartylasparty
lleucylleucylarginylglutaminylisoleucylalanylseryltyrosylglycylarginylg
lycyltyrosylthreonyltyrosylleucylleucylserylarginylalanylglycylvalylthr
eonylglycylalanylglutamylasparaginylarginylalanylalanylleucylprolylle
ucylasparaginylhistidylleucylvalylalanylllysylleucylllysylglutamyltyrosyl
asparaginylalanylalanylprolylprolylleucylglutaminylglycylphenylalanyl
glycylisoleucylserylalanylprolylaspartylglutaminylvalylllysylalanylalan
ylisoleucylaspartylalanylglycylalanylalanylglycylalanylisoleucylserylgl
ycylserylalanylisoleucylvalylllysylisoleucylisoleucylglutamylglutaminyl
histidylasparaginylisoleucylglutamylprolylglutamylllysylmethionylleuc
ylalanylalanylleucylllysylvalylphenylalanylvalylglutaminylprolylmethio
nylllysylalanylalanylthreonylarginylacetylseryltyrosylserylisoleucylthr
eonylserylprolylserylglutaminylphenylalanylvalylphenylalanylleucylse
rylserylvalyltryptophylalanylaspartylprolylisoleucylglutamylleucylleuc
ylasparaginylvalylcysteinylthreonylserylserylleucylglycylasparaginylgl
utaminylphenylalanylglutaminylthreonylglutaminylglutaminylalanylar
ginylthreonylthreonylglutaminylvalylglutaminylglutaminylphenylalanyl

serylglutaminylvalyltryptophyllysylprolylphenylalanylprolylglutaminyl
serylthreonylvalylarginylphenylalanylprolylglycylaspartylvalyltyrosyll
ysylvalyltyrosylarginyltyrosylasparaginylalanylvalylleucylaspartylprol
ylleucylisoleucylthreonylalanylleucylleucylglycylthreonylphenylalanyla
spartylthreonylarginylasparaginylarginylisoleucylisoleucylglutamylval
ylglutamylasparaginylglutaminylglutaminylserylprolylthreonylthreonyl
alanylglutamylthreonylleucylaspartylalanylthreonylarginylarginylvalyl
aspartylaspartylalanylthreonylvalylalanylisoleucylarginylserylalanylas
paraginylisoleucylasparaginylleucylvalylasparaginylglutamylleucylval
ylarginylglycylthreonylglycylleucyltyrosylasparaginylglutaminylaspara
ginylthreonylphenylalanylglutamylserylmethionylserylglycylleucylvaly
ltryptophylthreonylserylalanylprolylalanyltitinmethionylglutaminylargi
nyltyrosylglutamylserylleucylphenylalanylalanylisoleucylcysteinylprol
ylprolylaspartylalanylaspartylaspartylaspartylleucylleucylarginylgluta
minylisoleucylalanylseryltyrosylglycylarginylglycyltyrosylthreonyltyro
sylleucylleucylserylarginylalanylglycylvalylthreonylglycylalanylglutam
ylasparaginylarginylalanylalanylleucylprolylleucylasparaginylhistidylle
ucylvalylalanyllysylleucyllysylglutamyltyrosylasparaginylalanylalanyl
prolylprolylleucylglutaminylglycylphenylalanylglycylisoleucylserylalan
ylprolylaspartylglutaminylvalyllysylalanylalanylisoleucylaspartylalany
lglycylalanylalanylglycylalanylisoleucylserylglycylserylalanylisoleucyl
valyllysylisoleucylisoleucylglutamylglutaminylhistidylasparaginylisole
ucylglutamylprolylglutamyllysylmethionylleucylalanylalanylleucyllysyl
valylphenylalanylvalylglutaminylprolylmethionyllysylalanylalanylthreo
nylarginylacetylseryltyrosylserylisoleucylthreonylserylprolylserylgluta
minylphenylalanylvalylphenylalanylleucylserylserylvalyltryptophylala
nylaspartylprolylisoleucylglutamylleucylleucylasparaginylvalylcystein
ylthreonylserylserylleucylglycylasparaginylglutaminylphenylalanylglut
aminylthreonylglutaminylglutaminylalanylarginylthreonylthreonylglut
aminylvalylglutaminylglutaminylphenylalanylserylglutaminylvalyltrypt
ophyllysylprolylphenylalanylprolylglutaminylserylthreonylvalylarginyl
phenylalanylprolylglycylaspartylvalyltyrosyllysylvalyltyrosylarginyltyr
osylasparaginylalanylvalylleucylaspartylprolylleucylisoleucylthreonyla
lanylleucylleucylglycylthreonylphenylalanylaspartylthreonylarginylasp
araginylarginylisoleucylisoleucylglutamylvalylglutamylasparaginylglut
aminylglutaminylserylprolylthreonylthreonylalanylglutamylthreonylle
ucylaspartylalanylthreonylarginylarginylvalylaspartylaspartylalanylthr
eonylvalylalanylisoleucylarginylserylalanylasparaginylisoleucylaspara
ginylleucylvalylasparaginylglutamylleucylvalylarginylglycylthreonylgl
ycylleucyltyrosylasparaginylglutaminylasparaginylthreonylphenylalan

ylglutamylserylmethionylserylglycylleucylvalyltryptophylthreonylseryl
alanylprolylalanyltitinmethionylglutaminylarginyltyrosylglutamylseryll
eucylphenylalanylalanylisoleucylcysteinylprolylprolylaspartylalanylas
partylaspartylaspartylleucylleucylarginylglutaminylisoleucylalanylsery
ltyrosylglycylarginylglycyltyrosylthreonyltyrosylleucylleucylserylargin
ylalanylglycylvalylthreonylglycylalanylglutamylasparaginylarginylalan
ylalanylleucylprolylleucylasparaginylhistidylleucylvalylalanyllysylleuc
yllysylglutamyltyrosylasparaginylalanylalanylprolylprolylleucylglutam
inylglycylphenylalanylglycylisoleucylserylalanylprolylaspartylglutamin
ylvalyllysylalanylalanylisoleucylaspartylalanylglycylalanylalanylglycyl
alanylisoleucylserylglycylserylalanylisoleucylvalyllysylisoleucylisoleuc
ylglutamylglutaminylhistidylasparaginylisoleucylglutamylprolylglutam
yllysylmethionylleucylalanylalanylleucyllysylvalylphenylalanylvalylglu
taminylprolylmethionyllysylalanylalanylthreonylarginylacetylseryltyro
sylserylisoleucylthreonylserylprolylserylglutaminylphenylalanylvalylp
henylalanylleucylserylserylvalyltryptophylalanylaspartylprolylisoleucy
lglutamylleucylleucylasparaginylvalylcysteinylthreonylserylserylleucyl
glycylasparaginylglutaminylphenylalanylglutaminylthreonylglutaminyl
glutaminylalanylarginylthreonylthreonylglutaminylvalylglutaminylglut
aminylphenylalanylserylglutaminylvalyltryptophyllysylprolylphenylala
nylprolylglutaminylserylthreonylvalylarginylphenylalanylprolylglycyla
spartylvalyltyrosyllysylvalyltyrosylarginyltyrosylasparaginylalanylval
ylleucylaspartylprolylleucylisoleucylthreonylalanylleucylleucylglycylth
reonylphenylalanylaspartylthreonylarginylasparaginylarginylisoleucyli
soleucylglutamylvalylglutamylasparaginylglutaminylglutaminylserylpr
olylthreonylthreonylalanylglutamylthreonylleucylaspartylalanylthreon
ylarginylarginylvalylaspartylaspartylalanylthreonylvalylalanylisoleucy
larginylserylalanylasparaginylisoleucylasparaginylleucylvalylasparagi
nylglutamylleucylvalylarginylglycylthreonylglycylleucyltyrosylasparag
inylglutaminylasparaginylthreonylphenylalanylglutamylserylmethionyl
serylglycylleucylvalyltryptophylthreonylserylalanylprolylalanyltitinme
thionylglutaminylarginyltyrosylglutamylserylleucylphenylalanylalanyl
methionylthreonylthreonylglutaminylarginyltyrosylglutamylserylleucyl
phenylalanylalanylglutaminylleucyllysylglutamylarginyllysylglutamylg
lycylalanylphenylalanylvalylprolylphenylalanylvalylthreonylleucylglyc
ylaspartylprolylglycylisoleucylglutamylglutaminylserylleucyllysylisole
ucylaspartylthreonylleucylisoleucylglutamylalanylglycylalanylaspartyl
alanylleucylglutamylleucylglycylisoleucylprolylphenylalanylserylaspar
tylprolylleucylalanylaspartylglycylprolylthreonylisoleucylglutaminylas
paraginylalanylthreonylleucylarginylalanylphenylalanylalanylalanylgly

cylvalylthreonylprolylalanylglutaminylcysteinylphenylalanylglutamylm
ethionylleucylalanylleucylisoleucylarginylglutaminyllysylhistidylprolylt
hreonylisoleucylprolylisoleucylglycylleucylleucylmethionyltyrosylalan
ylasparaginylleucylvalylphenylalanylasparaginyllysylglycylisoleucylas
partylglutamylphenylalanyltyrosylalanylglutaminylcysteinylglutamylly
sylvalylglycylvalylaspartylserylvalylleucylvalylalanylaspartylvalylprol
ylvalylglutaminylglutamylserylalanylprolylphenylalanylarginylglutami
nylalanylalanylleucylarginylhistidylasparaginylvalylalanylprolylisoleuc
ylphenylalanylisoleucylcysteinylprolylprolylaspartylalanylaspartylaspa
rtylaspartylleucylleucylarginylglutaminylisoleucylalanylseryltyrosylgly
cylarginylglycyltyrosylthreonyltyrosylleucylleucylserylarginylalanylgly
cylvalylthreonylglycylalanylglutamylasparaginylarginylalanylalanylleu
cylprolylleucylasparaginylhistidylleucylvalylalanyllysylleucyllysylgluta
myltyrosylasparaginylalanylalanylprolylprolylleucylglutaminylglycylph
enylalanylglycylisoleucylserylalanylprolylaspartylglutaminylvalyllysyl
alanylalanylisoleucylaspartylalanylglycylalanylalanylglycylalanylisole
ucylserylglycylserylalanylisoleucylvalyllysylisoleucylisoleucylglutamyl
glutaminylhistidylasparaginylisoleucylglutamylprolylglutamyllysylmet
hionylleucylalanylalanylleucyllysylvalylphenylalanylvalylglutaminylpr
olylmethionyllysylalanylalanylthreonylarginylacetylseryltyrosylserylis
oleucylthreonylserylprolylserylglutaminylphenylalanylvalylphenylalan
ylleucylserylserylvalyltryptophylalanylaspartylprolylisoleucylglutamyl
leucylleucylasparaginylvalylcysteinylthreonylserylserylleucylglycylasp
araginylglutaminylphenylalanylglutaminylthreonylglutaminylglutamin
ylalanylarginylthreonylthreonylglutaminylvalylglutaminylglutaminylph
enylalanylserylglutaminylvalyltryptophyllysylprolylphenylalanylprolyl
glutaminylserylthreonylvalylarginylphenylalanylprolylglycylaspartylva
lyltyrosyllysylvalyltyrosylarginyltyrosylasparaginylalanylvalylleucylas
partylprolylleucylisoleucylthreonylalanylleucylleucylglycylthreonylphe
nylalanylaspartylthreonylarginylasparaginylarginylisoleucylisoleucylgl
utamylvalylglutamylasparaginylglutaminylglutaminylserylprolylthreon
ylthreonylalanylglutamylthreonylleucylaspartylalanylthreonylarginylar
ginylvalylaspartylaspartylalanylthreonylvalylalanylisoleucylarginylser
ylalanylasparaginylisoleucylasparaginylleucylvalylasparaginylglutamy
lleucylvalylarginylglycylthreonylglycylleucyltyrosylasparaginylglutami
nylasparaginylthreonylphenylalanylglutamylserylmethionylserylglycyl
leucylvalyltryptophylthreonylserylalanylprolylalanyltitinmethionylglut
aminylarginyltyrosylglutamylserylleucylphenylalanylalanylisoleucylcy
steinylprolylprolylaspartylalanylaspartylaspartylaspartylleucylleucylar
ginylglutaminylisoleucylalanylseryltyrosylglycylarginylglycyltyrosylthr

eonyltyrosylleucylleucylserylarginylalanylglycylvalylthreonylglycylala
nylglutamylasparaginylarginylalanylalanylleucylprolylleucylasparagin
ylhistidylleucylvalylalanyllysylleucyllysylglutamyltyrosylasparaginylal
anylalanylprolylprolylleucylglutaminylglycylphenylalanylglycylisoleuc
ylserylalanylprolylaspartylglutaminylvalyllysylalanylalanylisoleucylas
partylalanylglycylalanylalanylglycylalanylisoleucylserylglycylserylalan
ylisoleucylvalyllysylisoleucylisoleucylglutamylglutaminylhistidylaspar
aginylisoleucylglutamylprolylglutamyllysylmethionylleucylalanylalanyl
leucyllysylvalylphenylalanylvalylglutaminylprolylmethionyllysylalanyl
alanylthreonylarginylacetylseryltyrosylserylisoleucylthreonylserylprol
ylserylglutaminylphenylalanylvalylphenylalanylleucylserylserylvalyltr
yptophylalanylaspartylprolylisoleucylglutamylleucylleucylasparaginylv
alylcysteinylthreonylserylserylleucylglycylasparaginylglutaminylphen
ylalanylglutaminylthreonylglutaminylglutaminylalanylarginylthreonylt
hreonylglutaminylvalylglutaminylglutaminylphenylalanylserylglutamin
ylvalyltryptophyllysylprolylphenylalanylprolylglutaminylserylthreonyl
valylarginylphenylalanylprolylglycylaspartylvalyltyrosyllysylvalyltyros
ylarginyltyrosylasparaginylalanylvalylleucylaspartylprolylleucylisoleu
cylthreonylalanylleucylleucylglycylthreonylphenylalanylaspartylthreon
ylarginylasparaginylarginylisoleucylisoleucylglutamylvalylglutamylasp
araginylglutaminylglutaminylserylprolylthreonylthreonylalanylglutam
ylthreonylleucylaspartylalanylthreonylarginylarginylvalylaspartylaspa
rtylalanylthreonylvalylalanylisoleucylarginylserylalanylasparaginylisol
eucylasparaginylleucylvalylasparaginylglutamylleucylvalylarginylglyc
ylthreonylglycylleucyltyrosylasparaginylglutaminylasparaginylthreony
lphenylalanylglutamylserylmethionylserylglycylleucylvalyltryptophylt
hreonylserylalanylprolylalanyltitinmethionylglutaminylarginyltyrosylgl
utamylserylleucylphenylalanylalanylisoleucylcysteinylprolylprolylaspa
rtylalanylaspartylaspartylaspartylleucylleucylarginylglutaminylisoleuc
ylalanylseryltyrosylglycylarginylglycyltyrosylthreonyltyrosylleucylleuc
ylserylarginylalanylglycylvalylthreonylglycylalanylglutamylasparaginy
larginylalanylalanylleucylprolylleucylasparaginylhistidylleucylvalylala
nyllysylleucyllysylglutamyltyrosylasparaginylalanylalanylprolylprolyll
eucylglutaminylglycylphenylalanylglycylisoleucylserylalanylprolylaspa
rtylglutaminylvalyllysylalanylalanylisoleucylaspartylalanylglycylalanyl
alanylglycylalanylisoleucylserylglycylserylalanylisoleucylvalyllysylisol
eucylisoleucylglutamylglutaminylhistidylasparaginylisoleucylglutamyl
prolylglutamyllysylmethionylleucylalanylalanylleucyllysylvalylphenyla
lanylvalylglutaminylprolylmethionyllysylalanylalanylthreonylarginylac
etylseryltyrosylserylisoleucylthreonylserylprolylserylglutaminylphenyl

alanylvalylphenylalanylleucylserylserylvalyltryptophylalanylaspartylp
rolylisoleucylglutamylleucylleucylasparaginylvalylcysteinylthreonylser
ylserylleucylglycylasparaginylglutaminylphenylalanylglutaminylthreon
ylglutaminylglutaminylalanylarginylthreonylthreonylglutaminylvalylgl
utaminylglutaminylphenylalanylserylglutaminylvalyltryptophyllysylpro
lylphenylalanylprolylglutaminylserylthreonylvalylarginylphenylalanylp
rolylglycylaspartylvalyltyrosyllysylvalyltyrosylarginyltyrosylasparagin
ylalanylvalylleucylaspartylprolylleucylisoleucylthreonylalanylleucylleu
cylglycylthreonylphenylalanylaspartylthreonylarginylasparaginylargin
ylisoleucylisoleucylglutamylvalylglutamylasparaginylglutaminylgluta
minylserylprolylthreonylthreonylalanylglutamylthreonylleucylaspartyl
alanylthreonylarginylarginylvalylaspartylaspartylalanylthreonylvalylal
anylisoleucylarginylserylalanylasparaginylisoleucylasparaginylleucylv
alylasparaginylglutamylleucylvalylarginylglycylthreonylglycylleucyltyr
osylasparaginylglutaminylasparaginylthreonylphenylalanylglutamylse
rylmethionylserylglycylleucylvalyltryptophylthreonylserylalanylprolyl
alanyltitinmethionylglutaminylarginyltyrosylglutamylserylleucylphenyl
alanylalanylisoleucylcysteinylprolylprolylaspartylalanylaspartylaspart
ylaspartylleucylleucylarginylglutaminylisoleucylalanylseryltyrosylglyc
ylarginylglycyltyrosylthreonyltyrosylleucylleucylserylarginylalanylglyc
ylvalylthreonylglycylalanylglutamylasparaginylarginylalanylalanylleuc
ylprolylleucylasparaginylhistidylleucylvalylalanyllysylleucyllysylgluta
myltyrosylasparaginylalanylalanylprolylprolylleucylglutaminylglycylph
enylalanylglycylisoleucylserylalanylprolylaspartylglutaminylvalyllysyl
alanylalanylisoleucylaspartylalanylglycylalanylalanylglycylalanylisole
ucylserylglycylserylalanylisoleucylvalyllysylisoleucylisoleucylglutamyl
glutaminylhistidylasparaginylisoleucylglutamylprolylglutamyllysylmet
hionylleucylalanylalanylleucyllysylvalylphenylalanylvalylglutaminylpr
olylmethionyllysylalanylalanylthreonylarginylacetylseryltyrosylserylis
oleucylthreonylserylprolylserylglutaminylphenylalanylvalylphenylalan
ylleucylserylserylvalyltryptophylalanylaspartylprolylisoleucylglutamyl
leucylleucylasparaginylvalylcysteinylthreonylserylserylleucylglycylasp
araginylglutaminylphenylalanylglutaminylthreonylglutaminylglutamin
ylalanylarginylthreonylthreonylglutaminylvalylglutaminylglutaminylph
enylalanylserylglutaminylvalyltryptophyllysylprolylphenylalanylprolyl
glutaminylserylthreonylvalylarginylphenylalanylprolylglycylaspartylva
lyltyrosyllysylvalyltyrosylarginyltyrosylasparaginylalanylvalylleucylas
partylprolylleucylisoleucylthreonylalanylleucylleucylglycylthreonylphe
nylalanylaspartylthreonylarginylasparaginylarginylisoleucylisoleucylgl
utamylvalylglutamylasparaginylglutaminylglutaminylserylprolylthreon

ylthreonylalanylglutamylthreonylleucylaspartylalanylthreonylarginylar
ginylvalylaspartylaspartylalanylthreonylvalylalanylisoleucylarginylser
ylalanylasparaginylisoleucylasparaginylleucylvalylasparaginylglutamy
lleucylvalylarginylglycylthreonylglycylleucyltyrosylasparaginylglutami
nylasparaginylthreonylphenylalanylglutamylserylmethionylserylglycyl
leucylvalyltryptophylthreonylserylalanylprolylalanyltitinmethionylglut
aminylarginyltyrosylglutamylserylleucylphenylalanylalanylmethionylt
hreonylthreonylglutaminylarginyltyrosylglutamylserylleucylphenylala
nylalanylglutaminylleucyllysylglutamylarginyllysylglutamylglycylalany
lphenylalanylvalylprolylphenylalanylvalylthreonylleucylglycylaspartyl
prolylglycylisoleucylglutamylglutaminylserylleucyllysylisoleucylaspart
ylthreonylleucylisoleucylglutamylalanylglycylalanylaspartylalanylleuc
ylglutamylleucylglycylisoleucylprolylphenylalanylserylaspartylprolylle
ucylalanylaspartylglycylprolylthreonylisoleucylglutaminylasparaginyla
lanylthreonylleucylarginylalanylphenylalanylalanylalanylglycylvalylthr
eonylprolylalanylglutaminylcysteinylphenylalanylglutamylmethionylle
ucylalanylleucylisoleucylarginylglutaminyllysylhistidylprolylthreonylis
oleucylprolylisoleucylglycylleucylleucylmethionyltyrosylalanylasparag
inylleucylvalylphenylalanylasparaginyllysylglycylisoleucylaspartylglut
amylphenylalanyltyrosylalanylglutaminylcysteinylglutamyllysylvalylgl
ycylvalylaspartylserylvalylleucylvalylalanylaspartylvalylprolylvalylglu
taminylglutamylserylalanylprolylphenylalanylarginylglutaminylalanyla
lanylleucylarginylhistidylasparaginylvalylalanylprolylisoleucylphenylal
anylisoleucylcysteinylprolylprolylaspartylalanylaspartylaspartylaspart
ylleucylleucylarginylglutaminylisoleucylalanylseryltyrosylglycylarginyl
glycyltyrosylthreonyltyrosylleucylleucylserylarginylalanylglycylvalylth
reonylglycylalanylglutamylasparaginylarginylalanylalanylleucylprolyll
eucylasparaginylhistidylleucylvalylalanyllysylleucyllysylglutamyltyros
ylasparaginylalanylalanylprolylprolylleucylglutaminylglycylphenylalan
ylglycylisoleucylserylalanylprolylaspartylglutaminylvalyllysylalanylala
nylisoleucylaspartylalanylglycylalanylalanylglycylalanylisoleucylseryl
glycylserylalanylisoleucylvalyllysylisoleucylisoleucylglutamylglutamin
ylhistidylasparaginylisoleucylglutamylprolylglutamyllysylmethionylleu
cylalanylalanylleucyllysylvalylphenylalanylvalylglutaminylprolylmethi
onyllysylalanylalanylthreonylarginylacetylseryltyrosylserylisoleucylth
reonylserylprolylserylglutaminylphenylalanylvalylphenylalanylleucyls
erylserylvalyltryptophylalanylaspartylprolylisoleucylglutamylleucylleu
cylasparaginylvalylcysteinylthreonylserylserylleucylglycylasparaginyl
glutaminylphenylalanylglutaminylthreonylglutaminylglutaminylalanyla
rginylthreonylthreonylglutaminylvalylglutaminylglutaminylphenylalan

ylserylglutaminylvalyltryptophyllysylprolylphenylalanylprolylglutamin
ylserylthreonylvalylarginylphenylalanylprolylglycylaspartylvalyltyrosy
llysylvalyltyrosylarginyltyrosylasparaginylalanylvalylleucylaspartylpr
olylleucylisoleucylthreonylalanylleucylleucylglycylthreonylphenylalany
laspartylthreonylarginylasparaginylarginylisoleucylisoleucylglutamylv
alylglutamylasparaginylglutaminylglutaminylserylprolylthreonylthreon
ylalanylglutamylthreonylleucylaspartylalanylthreonylarginylarginylval
ylaspartylaspartylalanylthreonylvalylalanylisoleucylarginylserylalanyl
asparaginylisoleucylasparaginylleucylvalylasparaginylglutamylleucylv
alylarginylglycylthreonylglycylleucyltyrosylasparaginylglutaminylaspa
raginylthreonylphenylalanylglutamylserylmethionylserylglycylleucylv
alyltryptophylthreonylserylalanylprolylalanyltitinmethionylglutaminyla
rginyltyrosylglutamylserylleucylphenylalanylalanylisoleucylcysteinylp
rolylprolylaspartylalanylaspartylaspartylaspartylleucylleucylarginylglu
taminylisoleucylalanylseryltyrosylglycylarginylglycyltyrosylthreonylty
rosylleucylleucylserylarginylalanylglycylvalylthreonylglycylalanylgluta
mylasparaginylarginylalanylalanylleucylprolylleucylasparaginylhistidy
lleucylvalylalanyllysylleucyllysylglutamyltyrosylasparaginylalanylalan
ylprolylprolylleucylglutaminylglycylphenylalanylglycylisoleucylserylal
anylprolylaspartylglutaminylvalyllysylalanylalanylisoleucylaspartylala
nylglycylalanylalanylglycylalanylisoleucylserylglycylserylalanylisoleuc
ylvalyllysylisoleucylisoleucylglutamylglutaminylhistidylasparaginylisol
eucylglutamylprolylglutamyllysylmethionylleucylalanylalanylleucyllys
ylvalylphenylalanylvalylglutaminylprolylmethionyllysylalanylalanylthr
eonylarginylacetylseryltyrosylserylisoleucylthreonylserylprolylserylgl
utaminylphenylalanylvalylphenylalanylleucylserylserylvalyltryptophyl
alanylaspartylprolylisoleucylglutamylleucylleucylasparaginylvalylcyst
einylthreonylserylserylleucylglycylasparaginylglutaminylphenylalanyl
glutaminylthreonylglutaminylglutaminylalanylarginylthreonylthreonyl
glutaminylvalylglutaminylglutaminylphenylalanylserylglutaminylvalylt
ryptophyllysylprolylphenylalanylprolylglutaminylserylthreonylvalylarg
inylphenylalanylprolylglycylaspartylvalyltyrosyllysylvalyltyrosylarginy
ltyrosylasparaginylalanylvalylleucylaspartylprolylleucylisoleucylthreo
nylalanylleucylleucylglycylthreonylphenylalanylaspartylthreonylarginy
lasparaginylarginylisoleucylisoleucylglutamylvalylglutamylasparaginyl
glutaminylglutaminylserylprolylthreonylthreonylalanylglutamylthreon
ylleucylaspartylalanylthreonylarginylarginylvalylaspartylaspartylalany
lthreonylvalylalanylisoleucylarginylserylalanylasparaginylisoleucylasp
araginylleucylvalylasparaginylglutamylleucylvalylarginylglycylthreony
lglycylleucyltyrosylasparaginylglutaminylasparaginylthreonylphenylal

anylglutamylserylmethionylserylglycylleucylvalyltryptophylthreonylse
rylalanylprolylalanyltitinmethionylglutaminylarginyltyrosylglutamylse
rylleucylphenylalanylalanylisoleucylcysteinylprolylprolylaspartylalanyl
aspartylaspartylaspartylleucylleucylarginylglutaminylisoleucylalanyls
eryltyrosylglycylarginylglycyltyrosylthreonyltyrosylleucylleucylserylar
ginylalanylglycylvalylthreonylglycylalanylglutamylasparaginylarginyla
lanylalanylleucylprolylleucylasparaginylhistidylleucylvalylalanyllysylle
ucyllysylglutamyltyrosylasparaginylalanylalanylprolylprolylleucylgluta
minylglycylphenylalanylglycylisoleucylserylalanylprolylaspartylglutam
inylvalyllysylalanylalanylisoleucylaspartylalanylglycylalanylalanylglyc
ylalanylisoleucylserylglycylserylalanylisoleucylvalyllysylisoleucylisole
ucylglutamylglutaminylhistidylasparaginylisoleucylglutamylprolylgluta
myllysylmethionylleucylalanylalanylleucyllysylvalylphenylalanylvalylg
lutaminylprolylmethionyllysylalanylalanylthreonylarginylacetylserylty
rosylserylisoleucylthreonylserylprolylserylglutaminylphenylalanylvaly
lphenylalanylleucylserylserylvalyltryptophylalanylaspartylprolylisoleu
cylglutamylleucylleucylasparaginylvalylcysteinylthreonylserylserylleu
cylglycylasparaginylglutaminylphenylalanylglutaminylthreonylglutami
nylglutaminylalanylarginylthreonylthreonylglutaminylvalylglutaminylg
lutaminylphenylalanylserylglutaminylvalyltryptophyllysylprolylphenyl
alanylprolylglutaminylserylthreonylvalylarginylphenylalanylprolylglyc
ylaspartylvalyltyrosyllysylvalyltyrosylarginyltyrosylasparaginylalanyl
valylleucylaspartylprolylleucylisoleucylthreonylalanylleucylleucylglycy
lthreonylphenylalanylaspartylthreonylarginylasparaginylarginylisoleuc
ylisoleucylglutamylvalylglutamylasparaginylglutaminylglutaminylseryl
prolylthreonylthreonylalanylglutamylthreonylleucylaspartylalanylthre
onylarginylarginylvalylaspartylaspartylalanylthreonylvalylalanylisoleu
cylarginylserylalanylasparaginylisoleucylasparaginylleucylvalylaspara
ginylglutamylleucylvalylarginylglycylthreonylglycylleucyltyrosylaspar
aginylglutaminylasparaginylthreonylphenylalanylglutamylserylmethio
nylserylglycylleucylvalyltryptophylthreonylserylalanylprolylalanyltitin
methionylglutaminylarginyltyrosylglutamylserylleucylphenylalanylala
nylisoleucylcysteinylprolylprolylaspartylalanylaspartylaspartylasparty
lleucylleucylarginylglutaminylisoleucylalanylseryltyrosylglycylarginylg
lycyltyrosylthreonyltyrosylleucylleucylserylarginylalanylglycylvalylthr
eonylglycylalanylglutamylasparaginylarginylalanylalanylleucylprolylle
ucylasparaginylhistidylleucylvalylalanyllysylleucyllysylglutamyltyrosyl
asparaginylalanylalanylprolylprolylleucylglutaminylglycylphenylalanyl
glycylisoleucylserylalanylprolylaspartylglutaminylvalyllysylalanylalan
ylisoleucylaspartylalanylglycylalanylalanylglycylalanylisoleucylserylgl

ycylserylalanylisoleucylvalyllysylisoleucylisoleucylglutamylglutaminyl
histidylasparaginylisoleucylglutamylprolylglutamyllysylmethionylleuc
ylalanylalanylleucyllysylvalylphenylalanylvalylglutaminylprolylmethio
nyllysylalanylalanylthreonylarginylacetylseryltyrosylserylisoleucylthr
eonylserylprolylserylglutaminylphenylalanylvalylphenylalanylleucylse
rylserylvalyltryptophylalanylaspartylprolylisoleucylglutamylleucylleuc
ylasparaginylvalylcysteinylthreonylserylserylleucylglycylasparaginylgl
utaminylphenylalanylglutaminylthreonylglutaminylglutaminylalanylar
ginylthreonylthreonylglutaminylvalylglutaminylglutaminylphenylalanyl
serylglutaminylvalyltryptophyllysylprolylphenylalanylprolylglutaminyl
serylthreonylvalylarginylphenylalanylprolylglycylaspartylvalyltyrosyll
ysylvalyltyrosylarginyltyrosylasparaginylalanylvalylleucylaspartylprol
ylleucylisoleucylthreonylalanylleucylleucylglycylthreonylphenylalanyla
spartylthreonylarginylasparaginylarginylisoleucylisoleucylglutamylval
ylglutamylasparaginylglutaminylglutaminylserylprolylthreonylthreonyl
alanylglutamylthreonylleucylaspartylalanylthreonylarginylarginylvalyl
aspartylaspartylalanylthreonylvalylalanylisoleucylarginylserylalanylas
paraginylisoleucylasparaginylleucylvalylasparaginylglutamylleucylval
ylarginylglycylthreonylglycylleucyltyrosylasparaginylglutaminylaspara
ginylthreonylphenylalanylglutamylserylmethionylserylglycylleucylvaly
ltryptophylthreonylserylalanylprolylalanyltitinmethionylglutaminylargi
nyltyrosylglutamylserylleucylphenylalanylalanylmethionylthreonylthre
onylglutaminylarginyltyrosylglutamylserylleucylphenylalanylalanylglu
taminylleucyllysylglutamylarginyllysylglutamylglycylalanylphenylalan
ylvalylprolylphenylalanylvalylthreonylleucylglycylaspartylprolylglycyli
soleucylglutamylglutaminylserylleucyllysylisoleucylaspartylthreonylle
ucylisoleucylglutamylalanylglycylalanylaspartylalanylleucylglutamylle
ucylglycylisoleucylprolylphenylalanylserylaspartylprolylleucylalanylas
partylglycylprolylthreonylisoleucylglutaminylasparaginylalanylthreony
lleucylarginylalanylphenylalanylalanylalanylglycylvalylthreonylprolyla
lanylglutaminylcysteinylphenylalanylglutamylmethionylleucylalanylleu
cylisoleucylarginylglutaminyllysylhistidylprolylthreonylisoleucylprolyli
soleucylglycylleucylleucylmethionyltyrosylalanylasparaginylleucylvaly
lphenylalanylasparaginyllysylglycylisoleucylaspartylglutamylphenylal
anyltyrosylalanylglutaminylcysteinylglutamyllysylvalylglycylvalylaspa
rtylserylvalylleucylvalylalanylaspartylvalylprolylvalylglutaminylgluta
mylserylalanylprolylphenylalanylarginylglutaminylalanylalanylleucyla
rginylhistidylasparaginylvalylalanylprolylisoleucylphenylalanylisoleuc
ylcysteinylprolylprolylaspartylalanylaspartylaspartylaspartylleucylleu
cylarginylglutaminylisoleucylalanylseryltyrosylglycylarginylglycyltyro

sylthreonyltyrosyllleucyllleucylserylarginylalanylglycylvalylthreonylgly
cylalanylglutamylasparaginylarginylalanylalanyllleucylprolyllleucylaspa
raginylhistidyllleucylvalylalanyllysyllleucyllysylglutamyltyrosylasparagi
nylalanylalanylprolylprolyllleucylglutaminylglycylphenylalanylglycyliso
leucylserylalanylprolylaspartylglutaminylvalyllysylalanylalanylisoleuc
ylaspartylalanylglycylalanylalanylglycylalanylisoleucylserylglycylseryl
alanylisoleucylvalyllysylisoleucylisoleucylglutamylglutaminylhistidylas
paraginylisoleucylglutamylprolylglutamyllysylmethionyllleucylalanylal
anyllleucyllysylvalylphenylalanylvalylglutaminylprolylmethionyllysylal
anylalanylthreonylarginylacetylseryltyrosylserylisoleucylthreonylseryl
prolylserylglutaminylphenylalanylvalylphenylalanyllleucylserylserylval
yltryptophylalanylaspartylprolylisoleucylglutamyllleucyllleucylasparagi
nylvalylcysteinylthreonylserylseryllleucylglycylasparaginylglutaminylp
henylalanylglutaminylthreonylglutaminylglutaminylalanylarginylthreo
nylthreonylglutaminylvalylglutaminylglutaminylphenylalanylserylgluta
minylvalyltryptophyllysylprolylphenylalanylprolylglutaminylserylthreo
nylvalylarginylphenylalanylprolylglycylaspartylvalyltyrosyllysylvalylty
rosylarginyltyrosylasparaginylalanylvalyllleucylaspartylprolyllleucylisol
eucylthreonylalanyllleucyllleucylglycylthreonylphenylalanylaspartylthre
onylarginylasparaginylarginylisoleucylisoleucylglutamylvalylglutamyl
asparaginylglutaminylglutaminylserylprolylthreonylthreonylalanylglut
amylthreonyllleucylaspartylalanylthreonylarginylarginylvalylaspartyla
spartylalanylthreonylvalylalanylisoleucylarginylserylalanylasparaginyl
isoleucylasparaginyllleucylvalylasparaginylglutamyllleucylvalylarginylg
lycylthreonylglycyllleucyltyrosylasparaginylglutaminylasparaginylthre
onylphenylalanylglutamylserylmethionylserylglycyllleucylvalyltryptoph
ylthreonylserylalanylprolylalanyltitinmethionylglutaminylarginyltyrosy
lglutamylseryllleucylphenylalanylalanylisoleucylcysteinylprolylprolylas
partylalanylaspartylaspartylaspartyllleucyllleucylarginylglutaminylisole
ucylalanylseryltyrosylglycylarginylglycyltyrosylthreonyltyrosyllleucylle
ucylserylarginylalanylglycylvalylthreonylglycylalanylglutamylasparagi
nylarginylalanylalanyllleucylprolyllleucylasparaginylhistidyllleucylvalyla
lanyllysyllleucyllysylglutamyltyrosylasparaginylalanylalanylprolylproly
lleucylglutaminylglycylphenylalanylglycylisoleucylserylalanylprolylasp
artylglutaminylvalyllysylalanylalanylisoleucylaspartylalanylglycylalan
ylalanylglycylalanylisoleucylserylglycylserylalanylisoleucylvalyllysylis
oleucylisoleucylglutamylglutaminylhistidylasparaginylisoleucylglutam
ylprolylglutamyllysylmethionyllleucylalanylalanyllleucyllysylvalylpheny
lalanylvalylglutaminylprolylmethionyllysylalanylalanylthreonylarginyl
acetylseryltyrosylserylisoleucylthreonylserylprolylserylglutaminylphe

nylalanylvalylphenylalanylleucylserylserylvalyltryptophylalanylaspart
ylprolylisoleucylglutamylleucylleucylasparaginylvalylcysteinylthreonyl
serylserylleucylglycylasparaginylglutaminylphenylalanylglutaminylthr
eonylglutaminylglutaminylalanylarginylthreonylthreonylglutaminylval
ylglutaminylglutaminylphenylalanylserylglutaminylvalyltryptophyllysy
lprolylphenylalanylprolylglutaminylserylthreonylvalylarginylphenylala
nylprolylglycylaspartylvalyltyrosyllysylvalyltyrosylarginyltyrosylaspar
aginylalanylvalylleucylaspartylprolylleucylisoleucylthreonylalanylleuc
ylleucylglycylthreonylphenylalanylaspartylthreonylarginylasparaginyl
arginylisoleucylisoleucylglutamylvalylglutamylasparaginylglutaminylg
lutaminylserylprolylthreonylthreonylalanylglutamylthreonylleucylaspa
rtylalanylthreonylarginylarginylvalylaspartylaspartylalanylthreonylval
ylalanylisoleucylarginylserylalanylasparaginylisoleucylasparaginylleuc
ylvalylasparaginylglutamylleucylvalylarginylglycylthreonylglycylleucyl
tyrosylasparaginylglutaminylasparaginylthreonylphenylalanylglutamyl
serylmethionylserylglycylleucylvalyltryptophylthreonylserylalanylprol
ylalanyltitinmethionylglutaminylarginyltyrosylglutamylserylleucylphen
ylalanylalanylisoleucylcysteinylprolylprolylaspartylalanylaspartylaspa
rtylaspartylleucylleucylarginylglutaminylisoleucylalanylseryltyrosylgly
cylarginylglycyltyrosylthreonyltyrosylleucylleucylserylarginylalanylgly
cylvalylthreonylglycylalanylglutamylasparaginylarginylalanylalanylleu
cylprolylleucylasparaginylhistidylleucylvalylalanyllysylleucyllysylgluta
myltyrosylasparaginylalanylalanylprolylprolylleucylglutaminylglycylph
enylalanylglycylisoleucylserylalanylprolylaspartylglutaminylvalyllysyl
alanylalanylisoleucylaspartylalanylglycylalanylalanylglycylalanylisole
ucylserylglycylserylalanylisoleucylvalyllysylisoleucylisoleucylglutamyl
glutaminylhistidylasparaginylisoleucylglutamylprolylglutamyllysylmet
hionylleucylalanylalanylleucyllysylvalylphenylalanylvalylglutaminylpr
olylmethionyllysylalanylalanylthreonylarginylacetylseryltyrosylserylis
oleucylthreonylserylprolylserylglutaminylphenylalanylvalylphenylalan
ylleucylserylserylvalyltryptophylalanylaspartylprolylisoleucylglutamyl
leucylleucylasparaginylvalylcysteinylthreonylserylserylleucylglycylasp
araginylglutaminylphenylalanylglutaminylthreonylglutaminylglutamin
ylalanylarginylthreonylthreonylglutaminylvalylglutaminylglutaminylph
enylalanylserylglutaminylvalyltryptophyllysylprolylphenylalanylprolyl
glutaminylserylthreonylvalylarginylphenylalanylprolylglycylaspartylva
lyltyrosyllysylvalyltyrosylarginyltyrosylasparaginylalanylvalylleucylas
partylprolylleucylisoleucylthreonylalanylleucylleucylglycylthreonylphe
nylalanylaspartylthreonylarginylasparaginylarginylisoleucylisoleucylgl
utamylvalylglutamylasparaginylglutaminylglutaminylserylprolylthreon

ylthreonylalanylglutamylthreonylleucylaspartylalanylthreonylarginylar
ginylvalylaspartylaspartylalanylthreonylvalylalanylisoleucylarginylser
ylalanylasparaginylisoleucylasparaginylleucylvalylasparaginylglutamy
lleucylvalylarginylglycylthreonylglycylleucyltyrosylasparaginylglutami
nylasparaginylthreonylphenylalanylglutamylserylmethionylserylglycyl
leucylvalyltryptophylthreonylserylalanylprolylalanyltitinmethionylglut
aminylarginyltyrosylglutamylserylleucylphenylalanylalanylisoleucylcy
steinylprolylprolylaspartylalanylaspartylaspartylaspartylleucylleucylar
ginylglutaminylisoleucylalanylseryltyrosylglycylarginylglycyltyrosylthr
eonyltyrosylleucylleucylserylarginylalanylglycylvalylthreonylglycylala
nylglutamylasparaginylarginylalanylalanylleucylprolylleucylasparagin
ylhistidylleucylvalylalanyllysylleucyllysylglutamyltyrosylasparaginylal
anylalanylprolylprolylleucylglutaminylglycylphenylalanylglycylisoleuc
ylserylalanylprolylaspartylglutaminylvalyllysylalanylalanylisoleucylas
partylalanylglycylalanylalanylglycylalanylisoleucylserylglycylserylalan
ylisoleucylvalyllysylisoleucylisoleucylglutamylglutaminylhistidylaspar
aginylisoleucylglutamylprolylglutamyllysylmethionylleucylalanylalanyl
leucyllysylvalylphenylalanylvalylglutaminylprolylmethionyllysylalanyl
alanylthreonylarginylacetylseryltyrosylserylisoleucylthreonylserylprol
ylserylglutaminylphenylalanylvalylphenylalanylleucylserylserylvalyltr
yptophylalanylaspartylprolylisoleucylglutamylleucylleucylasparaginylv
alylcysteinylthreonylserylserylleucylglycylasparaginylglutaminylphen
ylalanylglutaminylthreonylglutaminylglutaminylalanylarginylthreonylt
hreonylglutaminylvalylglutaminylglutaminylphenylalanylserylglutamin
ylvalyltryptophyllysylprolylphenylalanylprolylglutaminylserylthreonyl
valylarginylphenylalanylprolylglycylaspartylvalyltyrosyllysylvalyltyros
ylarginyltyrosylasparaginylalanylvalylleucylaspartylprolylleucylisoleu
cylthreonylalanylleucylleucylglycylthreonylphenylalanylaspartylthreon
ylarginylasparaginylarginylisoleucylisoleucylglutamylvalylglutamylasp
araginylglutaminylglutaminylserylprolylthreonylthreonylalanylglutam
ylthreonylleucylaspartylalanylthreonylarginylarginylvalylaspartylaspa
rtylalanylthreonylvalylalanylisoleucylarginylserylalanylasparaginylisol
eucylasparaginylleucylvalylasparaginylglutamylleucylvalylarginylglyc
ylthreonylglycylleucyltyrosylasparaginylglutaminylasparaginylthreony
lphenylalanylglutamylserylmethionylserylglycylleucylvalyltryptophylt
hreonylserylalanylprolylalanyltitinmethionylglutaminylarginyltyrosylgl
utamylserylleucylphenylalanylalanylmethionylthreonylthreonylglutami
nylarginyltyrosylglutamylserylleucylphenylalanylalanylglutaminylleuc
yllysylglutamylarginyllysylglutamylglycylalanylphenylalanylvalylproly
lphenylalanylvalylthreonylleucylglycylaspartylprolylglycylisoleucylglut

amylglutaminylserylleucyllysylisoleucylaspartylthreonylleucylisoleucy
lglutamylalanylglycylalanylaspartylalanylleucylglutamylleucylglycylis
oleucylprolylphenylalanylserylaspartylprolylleucylalanylaspartylglycyl
prolylthreonylisoleucylglutaminylasparaginylalanylthreonylleucylargin
ylalanylphenylalanylalanylalanylglycylvalylthreonylprolylalanylglutam
inylcysteinylphenylalanylglutamylmethionylleucylalanylleucylisoleucyl
arginylglutaminyllysylhistidylprolylthreonylisoleucylprolylisoleucylgly
cylleucylleucylmethionyltyrosylalanylasparaginylleucylvalylphenylala
nylasparaginyllysylglycylisoleucylaspartylglutamylphenylalanyltyrosyl
alanylglutaminylcysteinylglutamyllysylvalylglycylvalylaspartylserylval
ylleucylvalylalanylaspartylvalylprolylvalylglutaminylglutamylserylalan
ylprolylphenylalanylarginylglutaminylalanylalanylleucylarginylhistidyl
asparaginylvalylalanylprolylisoleucylphenylalanylisoleucylcysteinylpro
lylprolylaspartylalanylaspartylaspartylaspartylleucylleucylarginylgluta
minylisoleucylalanylseryltyrosylglycylarginylglycyltyrosylthreonyltyro
sylleucylleucylserylarginylalanylglycylvalylthreonylglycylalanylglutam
ylasparaginylarginylalanylalanylleucylprolylleucylasparaginylhistidylle
ucylvalylalanyllysylleucyllysylglutamyltyrosylasparaginylalanylalanyl
prolylprolylleucylglutaminylglycylphenylalanylglycylisoleucylserylalan
ylprolylaspartylglutaminylvalyllysylalanylalanylisoleucylaspartylalany
lglycylalanylalanylglycylalanylisoleucylserylglycylserylalanylisoleucyl
valyllysylisoleucylisoleucylglutamylglutaminylhistidylasparaginylisole
ucylglutamylprolylglutamyllysylmethionylleucylalanylalanylleucyllysyl
valylphenylalanylvalylglutaminylprolylmethionyllysylalanylalanylthreo
nylarginylacetylseryltyrosylserylisoleucylthreonylserylprolylserylgluta
minylphenylalanylvalylphenylalanylleucylserylserylvalyltryptophylala
nylaspartylprolylisoleucylglutamylleucylleucylasparaginylvalylcystein
ylthreonylserylserylleucylglycylasparaginylglutaminylphenylalanylglut
aminylthreonylglutaminylglutaminylalanylarginylthreonylthreonylglut
aminylvalylglutaminylglutaminylphenylalanylserylglutaminylvalyltrypt
ophyllysylprolylphenylalanylprolylglutaminylserylthreonylvalylarginyl
phenylalanylprolylglycylaspartylvalyltyrosyllysylvalyltyrosylarginyltyr
osylasparaginylalanylvalylleucylaspartylprolylleucylisoleucylthreonyla
lanylleucylleucylglycylthreonylphenylalanylaspartylthreonylarginylasp
araginylarginylisoleucylisoleucylglutamylvalylglutamylasparaginylglut
aminylglutaminylserylprolylthreonylthreonylalanylglutamylthreonylle
ucylaspartylalanylthreonylarginylarginylvalylaspartylaspartylalanylthr
eonylvalylalanylisoleucylarginylserylalanylasparaginylisoleucylaspara
ginylleucylvalylasparaginylglutamylleucylvalylarginylglycylthreonylgl
ycylleucyltyrosylasparaginylglutaminylasparaginylthreonylphenylalan

ylglutamylserylmethionylserylglycylleucylvalyltryptophylthreonylseryl
alanylprolylalanyltitinmethionylglutaminylarginyltyrosylglutamylseryll
eucylphenylalanylalanylisoleucylcysteinylprolylprolylaspartylalanylas
partylaspartylaspartylleucylleucylarginylglutaminylisoleucylalanylsery
ltyrosylglycylarginylglycyltyrosylthreonyltyrosylleucylleucylserylargin
ylalanylglycylvalylthreonylglycylalanylglutamylasparaginylarginylalan
ylalanylleucylprolylleucylasparaginylhistidylleucylvalylalanyllysylleuc
yllysylglutamyltyrosylasparaginylalanylalanylprolylprolylleucylglutam
inylglycylphenylalanylglycylisoleucylserylalanylprolylaspartylglutamin
ylvalyllysylalanylalanylisoleucylaspartylalanylglycylalanylalanylglycyl
alanylisoleucylserylglycylserylalanylisoleucylvalyllysylisoleucylisoleuc
ylglutamylglutaminylhistidylasparaginylisoleucylglutamylprolylglutam
yllysylmethionylleucylalanylalanylleucyllysylvalylphenylalanylvalylglu
taminylprolylmethionyllysylalanylalanylthreonylarginylacetylseryltyro
sylserylisoleucylthreonylserylprolylserylglutaminylphenylalanylvalylp
henylalanylleucylserylserylvalyltryptophylalanylaspartylprolylisoleucy
lglutamylleucylleucylasparaginylvalylcysteinylthreonylserylserylleucyl
glycylasparaginylglutaminylphenylalanylglutaminylthreonylglutaminyl
glutaminylalanylarginylthreonylthreonylglutaminylvalylglutaminylglut
aminylphenylalanylserylglutaminylvalyltryptophyllysylprolylphenylala
nylprolylglutaminylserylthreonylvalylarginylphenylalanylprolylglycyla
spartylvalyltyrosyllysylvalyltyrosylarginyltyrosylasparaginylalanylval
ylleucylaspartylprolylleucylisoleucylthreonylalanylleucylleucylglycylth
reonylphenylalanylaspartylthreonylarginylasparaginylarginylisoleucyli
soleucylglutamylvalylglutamylasparaginylglutaminylglutaminylserylpr
olylthreonylthreonylalanylglutamylthreonylleucylaspartylalanylthreon
ylarginylarginylvalylaspartylaspartylalanylthreonylvalylalanylisoleucy
larginylserylalanylasparaginylisoleucylasparaginylleucylvalylasparagi
nylglutamylleucylvalylarginylglycylthreonylglycylleucyltyrosylasparag
inylglutaminylasparaginylthreonylphenylalanylglutamylserylmethionyl
serylglycylleucylvalyltryptophylthreonylserylalanylprolylalanyltitinme
thionylglutaminylarginyltyrosylglutamylserylleucylphenylalanylalanyli
soleucylcysteinylprolylprolylaspartylalanylaspartylaspartylaspartylleu
cylleucylarginylglutaminylisoleucylalanylseryltyrosylglycylarginylglyc
yltyrosylthreonyltyrosylleucylleucylserylarginylalanylglycylvalylthreo
nylglycylalanylglutamylasparaginylarginylalanylalanylleucylprolylleuc
ylasparaginylhistidylleucylvalylalanyllysylleucyllysylglutamyltyrosylas
paraginylalanylalanylprolylprolylleucylglutaminylglycylphenylalanylgl
ycylisoleucylserylalanylprolylaspartylglutaminylvalyllysylalanylalanyli
soleucylaspartylalanylglycylalanylalanylglycylalanylisoleucylserylglyc

ylserylalanylisoleucylvalyllysylisoleucylisoleucylglutamylglutaminylhi
stidylasparaginylisoleucylglutamylprolylglutamyllysylmethionylleucyl
alanylalanylleucyllysylvalylphenylalanylvalylglutaminylprolylmethiony
llysylalanylalanylthreonylarginylacetylseryltyrosylserylisoleucylthreo
nylserylprolylserylglutaminylphenylalanylvalylphenylalanylleucylseryl
serylvalyltryptophylalanylaspartylprolylisoleucylglutamylleucylleucyla
sparaginylvalylcysteinylthreonylserylserylleucylglycylasparaginylglut
aminylphenylalanylglutaminylthreonylglutaminylglutaminylalanylargin
ylthreonylthreonylglutaminylvalylglutaminylglutaminylphenylalanylse
rylglutaminylvalyltryptophyllysylprolylphenylalanylprolylglutaminylse
rylthreonylvalylarginylphenylalanylprolylglycylaspartylvalyltyrosyllys
ylvalyltyrosylarginyltyrosylasparaginylalanylvalylleucylaspartylprolyll
eucylisoleucylthreonylalanylleucylleucylglycylthreonylphenylalanylasp
artylthreonylarginylasparaginylarginylisoleucylisoleucylglutamylvalyl
glutamylasparaginylglutaminylglutaminylserylprolylthreonylthreonylal
anylglutamylthreonylleucylaspartylalanylthreonylarginylarginylvalylas
partylaspartylalanylthreonylvalylalanylisoleucylarginylserylalanylaspa
raginylisoleucylasparaginylleucylvalylasparaginylglutamylleucylvalyla
rginylglycylthreonylglycylleucyltyrosylasparaginylglutaminylasparagin
ylthreonylphenylalanylglutamylserylmethionylserylglycylleucylvalyltr
yptophylthreonylserylalanylprolylalanyltitinmethionylglutaminylarginy
ltyrosylglutamylserylleucylphenylalanylalanylisoleucylcysteinylprolylp
rolylaspartylalanylaspartylaspartylaspartylleucylleucylarginylglutamin
ylisoleucylalanylseryltyrosylglycylarginylglycyltyrosylthreonyltyrosyll
eucylleucylserylarginylalanylglycylvalylthreonylglycylalanylglutamyla
sparaginylarginylalanylalanylleucylprolylleucylasparaginylhistidylleuc
ylvalylalanyllysylleucyllysylglutamyltyrosylasparaginylalanylalanylpro
lylprolylleucylglutaminylglycylphenylalanylglycylisoleucylserylalanylp
rolylaspartylglutaminylvalyllysylalanylalanylisoleucylaspartylalanylgl
ycylalanylalanylglycylalanylisoleucylserylglycylserylalanylisoleucylval
yllysylisoleucylisoleucylglutamylglutaminylhistidylasparaginylisoleucy
lglutamylprolylglutamyllysylmethionylleucylalanylalanylleucyllysylval
ylphenylalanylvalylglutaminylprolylmethionyllysylalanylalanylthreonyl
arginylacetylseryltyrosylserylisoleucylthreonylserylprolylserylglutami
nylphenylalanylvalylphenylalanylleucylserylserylvalyltryptophylalanyl
aspartylprolylisoleucylglutamylleucylleucylasparaginylvalylcysteinylth
reonylserylserylleucylglycylasparaginylglutaminylphenylalanylglutami
nylthreonylglutaminylglutaminylalanylarginylthreonylthreonylglutami
nylvalylglutaminylglutaminylphenylalanylserylglutaminylvalyltryptoph
yllysylprolylphenylalanylprolylglutaminylserylthreonylvalylarginylphe

nylalanylpolylglycylaspartylvalyltyrosyllysylvalyltyrosylarginyltyrosyl
asparaginylalanylvalylleucylaspartylprolylleucylisoleucylthreonylalany
lleucylleucylglycylthreonylphenylalanylaspartylthreonylarginylasparag
inylarginylisoleucylisoleucylglutamylvalylglutamylasparaginylglutami
nylglutaminylserylprolylthreonylthreonylalanylglutamylthreonylleucyl
aspartylalanylthreonylarginylarginylvalylaspartylaspartylalanylthreon
ylvalylalanylisoleucylarginylserylalanylasparaginylisoleucylasparagin
ylleucylvalylasparaginylglutamylleucylvalylarginylglycylthreonylglycyl
leucyltyrosylasparaginylglutaminylasparaginylthreonylphenylalanylglu
tamylserylmethionylserylglycylleucylvalyltryptophylthreonylserylalan
ylprolylalanyltitinmethionylglutaminylarginyltyrosylglutamylserylleuc
ylphenylalanylalanylmethionylthreonylthreonylglutaminylarginyltyros
ylglutamylserylleucylphenylalanylalanylglutaminylleucyllysylglutamyl
arginyllysylglutamylglycylalanylphenylalanylvalylprolylphenylalanylva
lylthreonylleucylglycylaspartylprolylglycylisoleucylglutamylglutaminyl
serylleucyllysylisoleucylaspartylthreonylleucylisoleucylglutamylalanyl
glycylalanylaspartylalanylleucylglutamylleucylglycylisoleucylprolylphe
nylalanylserylaspartylprolylleucylalanylaspartylglycylprolylthreonylis
oleucylglutaminylasparaginylalanylthreonylleucylarginylalanylphenyla
lanylalanylalanylglycylvalylthreonylprolylalanylglutaminylcysteinylph
enylalanylglutamylmethionylleucylalanylleucylisoleucylarginylglutami
nyllysylhistidylprolylthreonylisoleucylprolylisoleucylglycylleucylleucyl
methionyltyrosylalanylasparaginylleucylvalylphenylalanylasparaginyll
ysylglycylisoleucylaspartylglutamylphenylalanyltyrosylalanylglutamin
ylcysteinylglutamyllysylvalylglycylvalylaspartylserylvalylleucylvalylal
anylaspartylvalylprolylvalylglutaminylglutamylserylalanylprolylphenyl
alanylarginylglutaminylalanylalanylleucylarginylhistidylasparaginylval
ylalanylprolylisoleucylphenylalanylisoleucylcysteinylprolylprolylaspart
ylalanylaspartylaspartylaspartylleucylleucylarginylglutaminylisoleucyl
alanylseryltyrosylglycylarginylglycyltyrosylthreonyltyrosylleucylleucyl
serylarginylalanylglycylvalylthreonylglycylalanylglutamylasparaginyla
rginylalanylalanylleucylprolylleucylasparaginylhistidylleucylvalylalany
llysylleucyllysylglutamyltyrosylasparaginylalanylalanylprolylprolylleu
cylglutaminylglycylphenylalanylglycylisoleucylserylalanylprolylaspart
ylglutaminylvalyllysylalanylalanylisoleucylaspartylalanylglycylalanylal
anylglycylalanylisoleucylserylglycylserylalanylisoleucylvalyllysylisole
ucylisoleucylglutamylglutaminylhistidylasparaginylisoleucylglutamylpr
olylglutamyllysylmethionylleucylalanylalanylleucyllysylvalylphenylala
nylvalylglutaminylprolylmethionyllysylalanylalanylthreonylarginylacet
ylseryltyrosylserylisoleucylthreonylserylprolylserylglutaminylphenylal

anylvalylphenylalanylleucylserylserylvalyltryptophylalanylaspartylpro
lylisoleucylglutamylleucylleucylasparaginylvalylcysteinylthreonylseryl
serylleucylglycylasparaginylglutaminylphenylalanylglutaminylthreonyl
glutaminylglutaminylalanylarginylthreonylthreonylglutaminylvalylglut
aminylglutaminylphenylalanylserylglutaminylvalyltryptophyllysylproly
lphenylalanylprolylglutaminylserylthreonylvalylarginylphenylalanylpro
lylglycylaspartylvalyltyrosyllysylvalyltyrosylarginyltyrosylasparaginyl
alanylvalylleucylaspartylprolylleucylisoleucylthreonylalanylleucylleuc
ylglycylthreonylphenylalanylaspartylthreonylarginylasparaginylarginyl
isoleucylisoleucylglutamylvalylglutamylasparaginylglutaminylglutami
nylserylprolylthreonylthreonylalanylglutamylthreonylleucylaspartylala
nylthreonylarginylarginylvalylaspartylaspartylalanylthreonylvalylalan
ylisoleucylarginylserylalanylasparaginylisoleucylasparaginylleucylvaly
lasparaginylglutamylleucylvalylarginylglycylthreonylglycylleucyltyros
ylasparaginylglutaminylasparaginylthreonylphenylalanylglutamylseryl
methionylserylglycylleucylvalyltryptophylthreonylserylalanylprolylala
nyltitinmethionylglutaminylarginyltyrosylglutamylserylleucylphenylala
nylalanylisoleucylcysteinylprolylprolylaspartylalanylaspartylaspartyla
spartylleucylleucylarginylglutaminylisoleucylalanylseryltyrosylglycyla
rginylglycyltyrosylthreonyltyrosylleucylleucylserylarginylalanylglycylv
alylthreonylglycylalanylglutamylasparaginylarginylalanylalanylleucylp
rolylleucylasparaginylhistidylleucylvalylalanyllysylleucyllysylglutamyl
tyrosylasparaginylalanylalanylprolylprolylleucylglutaminylglycylpheny
lalanylglycylisoleucylserylalanylprolylaspartylglutaminylvalyllysylalan
ylalanylisoleucylaspartylalanylglycylalanylalanylglycylalanylisoleucyls
erylglycylserylalanylisoleucylvalyllysylisoleucylisoleucylglutamylgluta
minylhistidylasparaginylisoleucylglutamylprolylglutamyllysylmethiony
lleucylalanylalanylleucyllysylvalylphenylalanylvalylglutaminylprolylm
ethionyllysylalanylalanylthreonylarginylacetylseryltyrosylserylisoleuc
ylthreonylserylprolylserylglutaminylphenylalanylvalylphenylalanylleuc
ylserylserylvalyltryptophylalanylaspartylprolylisoleucylglutamylleucyl
leucylasparaginylvalylcysteinylthreonylserylserylleucylglycylasparagi
nylglutaminylphenylalanylglutaminylthreonylglutaminylglutaminylalan
ylarginylthreonylthreonylglutaminylvalylglutaminylglutaminylphenylal
anylserylglutaminylvalyltryptophyllysylprolylphenylalanylprolylglutam
inylserylthreonylvalylarginylphenylalanylprolylglycylaspartylvalyltyro
syllysylvalyltyrosylarginyltyrosylasparaginylalanylvalylleucylaspartyl
prolylleucylisoleucylthreonylalanylleucylleucylglycylthreonylphenylala
nylaspartylthreonylarginylasparaginylarginylisoleucylisoleucylglutamy
lvalylglutamylasparaginylglutaminylglutaminylserylprolylthreonylthre

onylalanylglutamylthreonylleucylaspartylalanylthreonylarginylarginyl
valylaspartylaspartylalanylthreonylvalylalanylisoleucylarginylserylala
nylasparaginylisoleucylasparaginylleucylvalylasparaginylglutamylleuc
ylvalylarginylglycylthreonylglycylleucyltyrosylasparaginylglutaminyla
sparaginylthreonylphenylalanylglutamylserylmethionylserylglycylleuc
ylvalyltryptophylthreonylserylalanylprolylalanyltitinmethionylglutamin
ylarginyltyrosylglutamylserylleucylphenylalanylalanylisoleucylcystein
ylprolylprolylaspartylalanylaspartylaspartylaspartylleucylleucylarginyl
glutaminylisoleucylalanylseryltyrosylglycylarginylglycyltyrosylthreony
ltyrosylleucylleucylserylarginylalanylglycylvalylthreonylglycylalanylgl
utamylasparaginylarginylalanylalanylleucylprolylleucylasparaginylhist
idylleucylvalylalanyllysylleucyllysylglutamyltyrosylasparaginylalanyla
lanylprolylprolylleucylglutaminylglycylphenylalanylglycylisoleucylsery
lalanylprolylaspartylglutaminylvalyllysylalanylalanylisoleucylaspartyl
alanylglycylalanylalanylglycylalanylisoleucylserylglycylserylalanylisol
eucylvalyllysylisoleucylisoleucylglutamylglutaminylhistidylasparaginyl
isoleucylglutamylprolylglutamyllysylmethionylleucylalanylalanylleucyl
lysylvalylphenylalanylvalylglutaminylprolylmethionyllysylalanylalanyl
threonylarginylacetylseryltyrosylserylisoleucylthreonylserylprolylsery
lglutaminylphenylalanylvalylphenylalanylleucylserylserylvalyltryptoph
ylalanylaspartylprolylisoleucylglutamylleucylleucylasparaginylvalylcy
steinylthreonylserylserylleucylglycylasparaginylglutaminylphenylalan
ylglutaminylthreonylglutaminylglutaminylalanylarginylthreonylthreon
ylglutaminylvalylglutaminylglutaminylphenylalanylserylglutaminylval
yltryptophyllysylprolylphenylalanylprolylglutaminylserylthreonylvalyl
arginylphenylalanylprolylglycylaspartylvalyltyrosyllysylvalyltyrosylar
ginyltyrosylasparaginylalanylvalylleucylaspartylprolylleucylisoleucylth
reonylalanylleucylleucylglycylthreonylphenylalanylaspartylthreonylar
ginylasparaginylarginylisoleucylisoleucylglutamylvalylglutamylaspara
ginylglutaminylglutaminylserylprolylthreonylthreonylalanylglutamylth
reonylleucylaspartylalanylthreonylarginylarginylvalylaspartylaspartyl
alanylthreonylvalylalanylisoleucylarginylserylalanylasparaginylisoleuc
ylasparaginylleucylvalylasparaginylglutamylleucylvalylarginylglycylth
reonylglycylleucyltyrosylasparaginylglutaminylasparaginylthreonylph
enylalanylglutamylserylmethionylserylglycylleucylvalyltryptophylthre
onylserylalanylprolylalanyltitinmethionylglutaminylarginyltyrosylgluta
mylserylleucylphenylalanylalanylisoleucylcysteinylprolylprolylaspartyl
alanylaspartylaspartylaspartylleucylleucylarginylglutaminylisoleucylal
anylseryltyrosylglycylarginylglycyltyrosylthreonyltyrosylleucylleucyls
erylarginylalanylglycylvalylthreonylglycylalanylglutamylasparaginylar

ginylalanylalanylleucylprolylleucylasparaginylhistidylleucylvalylalanyll
ysylleucyllysylglutamyltyrosylasparaginylalanylalanylprolylprolylleuc
ylglutaminylglycylphenylalanylglycylisoleucylserylalanylprolylaspartyl
glutaminylvalyllysylalanylalanylisoleucylaspartylalanylglycylalanylala
nylglycylalanylisoleucylserylglycylserylalanylisoleucylvalyllysylisoleu
cylisoleucylglutamylglutaminylhistidylasparaginylisoleucylglutamylpro
lylglutamyllysylmethionylleucylalanylalanylleucyllysylvalylphenylalan
ylvalylglutaminylprolylmethionyllysylalanylalanylthreonylarginylacety
lseryltyrosylserylisoleucylthreonylserylprolylserylglutaminylphenylala
nylvalylphenylalanylleucylserylserylvalyltryptophylalanylaspartylprol
ylisoleucylglutamylleucylleucylasparaginylvalylcysteinylthreonylseryl
serylleucylglycylasparaginylglutaminylphenylalanylglutaminylthreonyl
glutaminylglutaminylalanylarginylthreonylthreonylglutaminylvalylglut
aminylglutaminylphenylalanylserylglutaminylvalyltryptophyllysylproly
lphenylalanylprolylglutaminylserylthreonylvalylarginylphenylalanylpro
lylglycylaspartylvalyltyrosyllysylvalyltyrosylarginyltyrosylasparaginyl
alanylvalylleucylaspartylprolylleucylisoleucylthreonylalanylleucylleuc
ylglycylthreonylphenylalanylaspartylthreonylarginylasparaginylarginyl
isoleucylisoleucylglutamylvalylglutamylasparaginylglutaminylglutami
nylserylprolylthreonylthreonylalanylglutamylthreonylleucylaspartylala
nylthreonylarginylarginylvalylaspartylaspartylalanylthreonylvalylalan
ylisoleucylarginylserylalanylasparaginylisoleucylasparaginylleucylvaly
lasparaginylglutamylleucylvalylarginylglycylthreonylglycylleucyltyros
ylasparaginylglutaminylasparaginylthreonylphenylalanylglutamylseryl
methionylserylglycylleucylvalyltryptophylthreonylserylalanylprolylala
nyltitinmethionylglutaminylarginyltyrosylglutamylserylleucylphenylala
nylalanylethionylthreonylthreonylglutaminylarginyltyrosylglutamylser
ylleucylphenylalanylalanylglutaminylleucyllysylglutamylarginyllysylgl
utamylglycylalanylphenylalanylvalylprolylphenylalanylvalylthreonylle
ucylglycylaspartylprolylglycylisoleucylglutamylglutaminylserylleucylly
sylisoleucylaspartylthreonylleucylisoleucylglutamylalanylglycylalanyla
spartylalanylleucylglutamylleucylglycylisoleucylprolylphenylalanylser
ylaspartylprolylleucylalanylaspartylglycylprolylthreonylisoleucylgluta
minylasparaginylalanylthreonylleucylarginylalanylphenylalanylalanyla
lanylglycylvalylthreonylprolylalanylglutaminylcysteinylphenylalanylgl
utamylmethionylleucylalanylleucylisoleucylarginylglutaminyllysylhisti
dylprolylthreonylisoleucylprolylisoleucylglycylleucylleucylmethionylty
rosylalanylasparaginylleucylvalylphenylalanylasparaginyllysylglycylis
oleucylaspartylglutamylphenylalanyltyrosylalanylglutaminylcysteinylg
lutamyllysylvalylglycylvalylaspartylserylvalylleucylvalylalanylaspartyl

valylprolylvalylglutaminylglutamylserylalanylprolylphenylalanylarginy
lglutaminylalanylalanylleucylarginylhistidylasparaginylvalylalanylprol
ylisoleucylphenylalanylisoleucylcysteinylprolylprolylaspartylalanylasp
artylaspartylaspartylleucylleucylarginylglutaminylisoleucylalanylseryl
tyrosylglycylarginylglycyltyrosylthreonyltyrosylleucylleucylserylargin
ylalanylglycylvalylthreonylglycylalanylglutamylasparaginylarginylalan
ylalanylleucylprolylleucylasparaginylhistidylleucylvalylalanyllysylleuc
yllysylglutamyltyrosylasparaginylalanylalanylprolylprolylleucylglutam
inylglycylphenylalanylglycylisoleucylserylalanylprolylaspartylglutamin
ylvalyllysylalanylalanylisoleucylaspartylalanylglycylalanylalanylglycyl
alanylisoleucylserylglycylserylalanylisoleucylvalyllysylisoleucylisoleuc
ylglutamylglutaminylhistidylasparaginylisoleucylglutamylprolylglutam
yllysylmethionylleucylalanylalanylleucyllysylvalylphenylalanylvalylglu
taminylprolylmethionyllysylalanylalanylthreonylarginylacetylserylltyro
sylserylisoleucylthreonylserylprolylserylglutaminylphenylalanylvalylp
henylalanylleucylserylserylvalyltryptophylalanylaspartylprolylisoleucy
lglutamylleucylleucylasparaginylvalylcysteinylthreonylserylserylleucyl
glycylasparaginylglutaminylphenylalanylglutaminylthreonylglutaminyl
glutaminylalanylarginylthreonylthreonylglutaminylvalylglutaminylglut
aminylphenylalanylserylglutaminylvalyltryptophyllysylprolylphenylala
nylprolylglutaminylserylthreonylvalylarginylphenylalanylprolylglycyla
spartylvalyltyrosyllysylvalyltyrosylarginyltyrosylasparaginylalanylval
ylleucylaspartylprolylleucylisoleucylthreonylalanylleucylleucylglycylth
reonylphenylalanylaspartylthreonylarginylasparaginylarginylisoleucyli
soleucylglutamylvalylglutamylasparaginylglutaminylglutaminylserylpr
olylthreonylthreonylalanylglutamylthreonylleucylaspartylalanylthreon
ylarginylarginylvalylaspartylaspartylalanylthreonylvalylalanylisoleucy
larginylserylalanylasparaginylisoleucylasparaginylleucylvalylasparagi
nylglutamylleucylvalylarginylglycylthreonylglycylleucyltyrosylasparag
inylglutaminylasparaginylthreonylphenylalanylglutamylserylmethionyl
serylglycylleucylvalyltryptophylthreonylserylalanylprolylalanyltitinme
thionylglutaminylarginyltyrosylglutamylserylleucylphenylalanylalanyli
soleucylcysteinylprolylprolylaspartylalanylaspartylaspartylaspartylleu
cylleucylarginylglutaminylisoleucylalanylseryltyrosylglycylarginylglyc
yltyrosylthreonyltyrosylleucylleucylserylarginylalanylglycylvalylthreo
nylglycylalanylglutamylasparaginylarginylalanylalanylleucylprolylleuc
ylasparaginylhistidylleucylvalylalanyllysylleucyllysylglutamyltyrosylas
paraginylalanylalanylprolylprolylleucylglutaminylglycylphenylalanylgl
ycylisoleucylserylalanylprolylaspartylglutaminylvalyllysylalanylalanyli
soleucylaspartylalanylglycylalanylalanylglycylalanylisoleucylserylglyc

ylserylalanylisoleucylvalyllysylisoleucylisoleucylglutamylglutaminylhi
stidylasparaginylisoleucylglutamylprolylglutamyllysylmethionylleucyl
alanylalanylleucyllysylvalylphenylalanylvalylglutaminylprolylmethiony
llysylalanylalanylthreonylarginylacetylseryltyrosylserylisoleucylthreo
nylserylprolylserylglutaminylphenylalanylvalylphenylalanylleucylseryl
serylvalyltryptophylalanylaspartylprolylisoleucylglutamylleucylleucyla
sparaginylvalylcysteinylthreonylserylserylleucylglycylasparaginylglut
aminylphenylalanylglutaminylthreonylglutaminylglutaminylalanylargin
ylthreonylthreonylglutaminylvalylglutaminylglutaminylphenylalanylse
rylglutaminylvalyltryptophyllysylprolylphenylalanylprolylglutaminylse
rylthreonylvalylarginylphenylalanylprolylglycylaspartylvalyltyrosyllys
ylvalyltyrosylarginyltyrosylasparaginylalanylvalylleucylaspartylprolyll
eucylisoleucylthreonylalanylleucylleucylglycylthreonylphenylalanylasp
artylthreonylarginylasparaginylarginylisoleucylisoleucylglutamylvalyl
glutamylasparaginylglutaminylglutaminylserylprolylthreonylthreonylal
anylglutamylthreonylleucylaspartylalanylthreonylarginylarginylvalylas
partylaspartylalanylthreonylvalylalanylisoleucylarginylserylalanylaspa
raginylisoleucylasparaginylleucylvalylasparaginylglutamylleucylvalyla
rginylglycylthreonylglycylleucyltyrosylasparaginylglutaminylAsparagi
nylthreonylphenylalanylglutamylserylmethionylserylglycylleucylvalylt
ryptophylthreonylserylalanylprolylalanyltitinmethionylglutaminylargin
yltyrosylglutamylserylleucylphenylalanylalanylisoleucylcysteinylprolyl
prolylaspartylalanylaspartylaspartylaspartylleucylleucylarginylglutami
nylisoleucylalanylseryltyrosylglycylarginylglycyltyrosylthreonyltyrosyl
leucylleucylserylarginylalanylglycylvalylthreonylglycylalanylglutamyla
sparaginylarginylalanylalanylleucylprolylleucylasparaginylhistidylleuc
ylvalylalanyllysylleucyllysylglutamyltyrosylasparaginylalanylalanylpro
lylprolylleucylglutaminylglycylphenylalanylglycylisoleucylserylalanylp
rolylaspartylglutaminylvalyllysylalanylalanylisoleucylaspartylalanylgl
ycylalanylalanylglycylalanylisoleucylserylglycylserylalanylisoleucylval
yllysylisoleucylisoleucylglutamylglutaminylhistidylasparaginylisoleucy
lglutamylprolylglutamyllysylmethionylleucylalanylalanylleucyllysylval
ylphenylalanylvalylglutaminylprolylmethionyllysylalanylalanylthreonyl
arginylacetylseryltyrosylserylisoleucylthreonylserylprolylserylglutami
nylphenylalanylvalylphenylalanylleucylserylserylvalyltryptophylalanyl
aspartylprolylisoleucylglutamylleucylleucylasparaginylvalylcysteinylth
reonylserylserylleucylglycylasparaginylglutaminylphenylalanylglutami
nylthreonylglutaminylglutaminylalanylarginylthreonylthreonylglutami
nylvalylglutaminylglutaminylphenylalanylserylglutaminylvalyltryptoph
yllysylprolylphenylalanylprolylglutaminylserylthreonylvalylarginylphe

nylalanylprolylglycylaspartylvalyltyrosyllysylvalyltyrosylarginyltyrosy
lasparaginylalanylvalylleucylaspartylprolylleucylisoleucylthreonylalan
ylleucylleucylglycylthreonylphenylalanylaspartylthreonylarginylaspara
ginylarginylisoleucylisoleucylglutamylvalylglutamylasparaginylglutam
inylglutaminylserylprolylthreonylthreonylalanylglutamylthreonylleucyl
aspartylalanylthreonylarginylarginylvalylaspartylaspartylalanylthreon
ylvalylalanylisoleucylarginylserylalanylasparaginylisoleucylasparagin
ylleucylvalylasparaginylglutamylleucylvalylarginylglycylthreonylglycyl
leucyltyrosylasparaginylglutaminylasparaginylthreonylphenylalanylglu
tamylserylmethionylserylglycylleucylvalyltryptophylthreonylserylalan
ylprolylalanyltitinmethionylglutaminylarginyltyrosylglutamylserylleuc
ylphenylalanylalanylisoleucylcysteinylprolylprolylaspartylalanylaspart
ylaspartylaspartylleucylleucylarginylglutaminylisoleucylalanylseryltyr
osylglycylarginylglycyltyrosylthreonyltyrosylleucylleucylserylarginylal
anylglycylvalylthreonylglycylalanylglutamylasparaginylarginylalanylal
anylleucylprolylleucylasparaginylhistidylleucylvalylalanyllysylleucylly
sylglutamyltyrosylasparaginylalanylalanylprolylprolylleucylglutaminyl
glycylphenylalanylglycylisoleucylserylalanylprolylaspartylglutaminylv
alyllysylalanylalanylisoleucylaspartylalanylglycylalanylalanylglycylala
nylisoleucylserylglycylserylalanylisoleucylvalyllysylisoleucylisoleucylg
lutamylglutaminylhistidylasparaginylisoleucylglutamylprolylglutamyll
ysylmethionylleucylalanylalanylleucyllysylvalylphenylalanylvalylgluta
minylprolylmethionyllysylalanylalanylthreonylarginylacetylseryltyrosy
lserylisoleucylthreonylserylprolylserylglutaminylphenylalanylvalylphe
nylalanylleucylserylserylvalyltryptophylalanylaspartylprolylisoleucylgl
utamylleucylleucylasparaginylvalylcysteinylthreonylserylserylleucylgl
ycylasparaginylglutaminylphenylalanylglutaminylthreonylglutaminylgl
utaminylalanylarginylthreonylthreonylglutaminylvalylglutaminylgluta
minylphenylalanylserylglutaminylvalyltryptophyllysylprolylphenylalan
ylprolylglutaminylserylthreonylvalylarginylphenylalanylprolylglycylas
partylvalyltyrosyllysylvalyltyrosylarginyltyrosylasparaginylalanylvalyl
leucylaspartylprolylleucylisoleucylthreonylalanylleucylleucylglycylthre
onylphenylalanylaspartylthreonylarginylasparaginylarginylisoleucyliso
leucylglutamylvalylglutamylasparaginylglutaminylglutaminylserylprol
ylthreonylthreonylalanylglutamylthreonylleucylaspartylalanylthreonyl
arginylarginylvalylaspartylaspartylalanylthreonylvalylalanylisoleucyla
rginylserylalanylasparaginylisoleucylasparaginylleucylvalylasparaginy
lglutamylleucylvalylarginylglycylthreonylglycylleucyltyrosylasparagin
ylglutaminylasparaginylthreonylphenylalanylglutamylserylmethionyls
erylglycylleucylvalyltryptophylthreonylserylalanylprolylalanyltitinmet

hionylglutaminylarginyltyrosylglutamylserylleucylphenylalanylalanyl
methionylthreonylthreonylglutaminylarginyltyrosylglutamylserylleucyl
phenylalanylalanylglutaminylleucyllysylglutamylarginyllysylglutamylg
lycylalanylphenylalanylvalylprolylphenylalanylvalylthreonylleucylglyc
ylaspartylprolylglycylisoleucylglutamylglutaminylserylleucyllysylisole
ucylaspartylthreonylleucylisoleucylglutamylalanylglycylalanylaspartyl
alanylleucylglutamylleucylglycylisoleucylprolylphenylalanylserylaspar
tylprolylleucylalanylaspartylglycylprolylthreonylisoleucylglutaminylas
paraginylalanylthreonylleucylarginylalanylphenylalanylalanylalanylgly
cylvalylthreonylprolylalanylglutaminylcysteinylphenylalanylglutamylm
ethionylleucylalanylleucylisoleucylarginylglutaminyllysylhistidylprolylt
hreonylisoleucylprolylisoleucylglycylleucylleucylmethionyltyrosylalan
ylasparaginylleucylvalylphenylalanylasparaginyllysylglycylisoleucylas
partylglutamylphenylalanyltyrosylalanylglutaminylcysteinylglutamylly
sylvalylglycylvalylaspartylserylvalylleucylvalylalanylaspartylvalylprol
ylvalylglutaminylglutamylserylalanylprolylphenylalanylarginylglutami
nylalanylalanylleucylarginylhistidylasparaginylvalylalanylprolylisoleuc
ylphenylalanylisoleucylcysteinylprolylprolylaspartylalanylaspartylaspa
rtylaspartylleucylleucylarginylglutaminylisoleucylalanylseryltyrosylgly
cylarginylglycyltyrosylthreonyltyrosylleucylleucylserylarginylalanylgly
cylvalylthreonylglycylalanylglutamylasparaginylarginylalanylalanylleu
cylprolylleucylasparaginylhistidylleucylvalylalanyllysylleucyllysylgluta
myltyrosylasparaginylalanylalanylprolylprolylleucylglutaminylglycylph
enylalanylglycylisoleucylserylalanylprolylaspartylglutaminylvalyllysyl
alanylalanylisoleucylaspartylalanylglycylalanylalanylglycylalanylisole
ucylserylglycylserylalanylisoleucylvalyllysylisoleucylisoleucylglutamyl
glutaminylhistidylasparaginylisoleucylglutamylprolylglutamyllysylmet
hionylleucylalanylalanylleucyllysylvalylphenylalanylvalylglutaminylpr
olylmethionyllysylalanylalanylthreonylarginylacetylseryltyrosylserylis
oleucylthreonylserylprolylserylglutaminylphenylalanylvalylphenylalan
ylleucylserylserylvalyltryptophylalanylaspartylprolylisoleucylglutamyl
leucylleucylasparaginylvalylcysteinylthreonylserylserylleucylglycylasp
araginylglutaminylphenylalanylglutaminylthreonylglutaminylglutamin
ylalanylarginylthreonylthreonylglutaminylvalylglutaminylglutaminylph
enylalanylserylglutaminylvalyltryptophyllysylprolylphenylalanylprolyl
glutaminylserylthreonylvalylarginylphenylalanylprolylglycylaspartylva
lyltyrosyllysylvalyltyrosylarginyltyrosylasparaginylalanylvalylleucylas
partylprolylleucylisoleucylthreonylalanylleucylleucylglycylthreonylphe
nylalanylaspartylthreonylarginylasparaginylarginylisoleucylisoleucylgl
utamylvalylglutamylasparaginylglutaminylglutaminylserylprolylthreon

ylthreonylalanylglutamylthreonylleucylaspartylalanylthreonylarginylar
ginylvalylaspartylaspartylalanylthreonylvalylalanylisoleucylarginylser
ylalanylasparaginylisoleucylasparaginylleucylvalylasparaginylglutamy
lleucylvalylarginylglycylthreonylglycylleucyltyrosylasparaginylglutami
nylasparaginylthreonylphenylalanylglutamylserylmethionylserylglycyl
leucylvalyltryptophylthreonylserylalanylprolylalanyltitinmethionylglut
aminylarginyltyrosylglutamylserylleucylphenylalanylalanylisoleucylcy
steinylprolylprolylaspartylalanylaspartylaspartylaspartylleucylleucylar
ginylglutaminylisoleucylalanylseryltyrosylglycylarginylglycyltyrosylthr
eonyltyrosylleucylleucylserylarginylalanylglycylvalylthreonylglycylala
nylglutamylasparaginylarginylalanylalanylleucylprolylleucylasparagin
ylhistidylleucylvalylalanyllysylleucyllysylglutamyltyrosylasparaginylal
anylalanylprolylprolylleucylglutaminylglycylphenylalanylglycylisoleuc
ylserylalanylprolylaspartylglutaminylvalyllysylalanylalanylisoleucylas
partylalanylglycylalanylalanylglycylalanylisoleucylserylglycylserylalan
ylisoleucylvalyllysylisoleucylisoleucylglutamylglutaminylhistidylaspar
aginylisoleucylglutamylprolylglutamyllysylmethionylleucylalanylalanyl
leucyllysylvalylphenylalanylvalylglutaminylprolylmethionyllysylalanyl
alanylthreonylarginylacetylseryltyrosylserylisoleucylthreonylserylprol
ylserylglutaminylphenylalanylvalylphenylalanylleucylserylserylvalyltr
yptophylalanylaspartylprolylisoleucylglutamylleucylleucylasparaginylv
alylcysteinylthreonylserylserylleucylglycylasparaginylglutaminylphen
ylalanylglutaminylthreonylglutaminylglutaminylalanylarginylthreonylt
hreonylglutaminylvalylglutaminylglutaminylphenylalanylserylglutamin
ylvalyltryptophyllysylprolylphenylalanylprolylglutaminylserylthreonyl
valylarginylphenylalanylprolylglycylaspartylvalyltyrosyllysylvalyltyros
ylarginyltyrosylasparaginylalanylvalylleucylaspartylprolylleucylisoleu
cylthreonylalanylleucylleucylglycylthreonylphenylalanylaspartylthreon
ylarginylasparaginylarginylisoleucylisoleucylglutamylvalylglutamylasp
araginylglutaminylglutaminylserylprolylthreonylthreonylalanylglutam
ylthreonylleucylaspartylalanylthreonylarginylarginylvalylaspartylaspa
rtylalanylthreonylvalylalanylisoleucylarginylserylalanylasparaginylisol
eucylasparaginylleucylvalylasparaginylglutamylleucylvalylarginylglyc
ylthreonylglycylleucyltyrosylasparaginylglutaminylasparaginylthreony
lphenylalanylglutamylserylmethionylserylglycylleucylvalyltryptophylt
hreonylserylalanylprolylalanyltitinmethionylglutaminylarginyltyrosylgl
utamylserylleucylphenylalanylalanylisoleucylcysteinylprolylprolylaspa
rtylalanylaspartylaspartylaspartylleucylleucylarginylglutaminylisoleuc
ylalanylseryltyrosylglycylarginylglycyltyrosylthreonyltyrosylleucylleuc
ylserylarginylalanylglycylvalylthreonylglycylalanylglutamylasparaginy

larginylalanylalanylleucylprolylleucylasparaginylhistidylleucylvalylala
nyllysylleucyllysylglutamyltyrosylasparaginylalanylalanylprolylprolyll
eucylglutaminylglycylphenylalanylglycylisoleucylserylalanylprolylaspa
rtylglutaminylvalyllysylalanylalanylisoleucylaspartylalanylglycylalanyl
alanylglycylalanylisoleucylserylglycylserylalanylisoleucylvalyllysylisol
eucylisoleucylglutamylglutaminylhistidylasparaginylisoleucylglutamyl
prolylglutamyllysylmethionylleucylalanylalanylleucyllysylvalylphenyla
lanylvalylglutaminylprolylmethionyllysylalanylalanylthreonylarginylac
etylseryltyrosylserylisoleucylthreonylserylprolylserylglutaminylphenyl
alanylvalylphenylalanylleucylserylserylvalyltryptophylalanylaspartylp
rolylisoleucylglutamylleucylleucylasparaginylvalylcysteinylthreonylser
ylserylleucylglycylasparaginylglutaminylphenylalanylglutaminylthreon
ylglutaminylglutaminylalanylarginylthreonylthreonylglutaminylvalylgl
utaminylglutaminylphenylalanylserylglutaminylvalyltryptophyllysylpro
lylphenylalanylprolylglutaminylserylthreonylvalylarginylphenylalanylp
rolylglycylaspartylvalyltyrosyllysylvalyltyrosylarginyltyrosylasparagin
ylalanylvalylleucylaspartylprolylleucylisoleucylthreonylalanylleucylleu
cylglycylthreonylphenylalanylaspartylthreonylarginylasparaginylargin
ylisoleucylisoleucylglutamylvalylglutamylasparaginylglutaminylgluta
minylserylprolylthreonylthreonylalanylglutamylthreonylleucylaspartyl
alanylthreonylarginylarginylvalylaspartylaspartylalanylthreonylvalylal
anylisoleucylarginylserylalanylasparaginylisoleucylasparaginylleucylv
alylasparaginylglutamylleucylvalylarginylglycylthreonylglycylleucyltyr
osylasparaginylglutaminylasparaginylthreonylphenylalanylglutamylse
rylmethionylserylglycylleucylvalyltryptophylthreonylserylalanylprolyl
alanyltitinmethionylglutaminylarginyltyrosylglutamylserylleucylphenyl
alanylalanylisoleucylcysteinylprolylprolylaspartylalanylaspartylaspart
ylaspartylleucylleucylarginylglutaminylisoleucylalanylseryltyrosylglyc
ylarginylglycyltyrosylthreonyltyrosylleucylleucylserylarginylalanylglyc
ylvalylthreonylglycylalanylglutamylasparaginylarginylalanylalanylleuc
ylprolylleucylasparaginylhistidylleucylvalylalanyllysylleucyllysylgluta
myltyrosylasparaginylalanylalanylprolylprolylleucylglutaminylglycylph
enylalanylglycylisoleucylserylalanylprolylaspartylglutaminylvalyllysyl
alanylalanylisoleucylaspartylalanylglycylalanylalanylglycylalanylisole
ucylserylglycylserylalanylisoleucylvalyllysylisoleucylisoleucylglutamyl
glutaminylhistidylasparaginylisoleucylglutamylprolylglutamyllysylmet
hionylleucylalanylalanylleucyllysylvalylphenylalanylvalylglutaminylpr
olylmethionyllysylalanylalanylthreonylarginylacetylseryltyrosylserylis
oleucylthreonylserylprolylserylglutaminylphenylalanylvalylphenylalan
ylleucylserylserylvalyltryptophylalanylaspartylprolylisoleucylglutamyl

leucylleucylasparaginylvalylcysteinylthreonylserylserylleucylglycylasp
araginylglutaminylphenylalanylglutaminylthreonylglutaminylglutamin
ylalanylarginylthreonylthreonylglutaminylvalylglutaminylglutaminylph
enylalanylserylglutaminylvalyltryptophyllysylprolylphenylalanylprolyl
glutaminylserylthreonylvalylarginylphenylalanylprolylglycylaspartylva
lyltyrosyllysylvalyltyrosylarginyltyrosylasparaginylalanylvalylleucylas
partylprolylleucylisoleucylthreonylalanylleucylleucylglycylthreonylphe
nylalanylaspartylthreonylarginylasparaginylarginylisoleucylisoleucylgl
utamylvalylglutamylasparaginylglutaminylglutaminylserylprolylthreon
ylthreonylalanylglutamylthreonylleucylaspartylalanylthreonylarginylar
ginylvalylaspartylaspartylalanylthreonylvalylalanylisoleucylarginylser
ylalanylasparaginylisoleucylasparaginylleucylvalylasparaginylglutamy
lleucylvalylarginylglycylthreonylglycylleucyltyrosylasparaginylglutami
nylasparaginylthreonylphenylalanylglutamylserylmethionylserylglycyl
leucylvalyltryptophylthreonylserylalanylprolylalanyltitinmethionylglut
aminylarginyltyrosylglutamylserylleucylphenylalanylalanylmethionylt
hreonylthreonylglutaminylarginyltyrosylglutamylserylleucylphenylala
nylalanylglutaminylleucyllysylglutamylarginyllysylglutamylglycylalany
lphenylalanylvalylprolylphenylalanylvalylthreonylleucylglycylaspartyl
prolylglycylisoleucylglutamylglutaminylserylleucyllysylisoleucylaspart
ylthreonylleucylisoleucylglutamylalanylglycylalanylaspartylalanylleuc
ylglutamylleucylglycylisoleucylprolylphenylalanylserylaspartylprolylle
ucylalanylaspartylglycylprolylthreonylisoleucylglutaminylasparaginyla
lanylthreonylleucylarginylalanylphenylalanylalanylalanylglycylvalylthr
eonylprolylalanylglutaminylcysteinylphenylalanylglutamylmethionylle
ucylalanylleucylisoleucylarginylglutaminyllysylhistidylprolylthreonylis
oleucylprolylisoleucylglycylleucylleucylmethionyltyrosylalanylasparag
inylleucylvalylphenylalanylasparaginyllysylglycylisoleucylaspartylglut
amylphenylalanyltyrosylalanylglutaminylcysteinylglutamyllysylvalylgl
ycylvalylaspartylserylvalylleucylvalylalanylaspartylvalylprolylvalylglu
taminylglutamylserylalanylprolylphenylalanylarginylglutaminylalanyla
lanylleucylarginylhistidylasparaginylvalylalanylprolylisoleucylphenylal
anylisoleucylcysteinylprolylprolylaspartylalanylaspartylaspartylaspart
ylleucylleucylarginylglutaminylisoleucylalanylseryltyrosylglycylarginyl
glycyltyrosylthreonyltyrosylleucylleucylserylarginylalanylglycylvalylth
reonylglycylalanylglutamylasparaginylarginylalanylalanylleucylprolyll
eucylasparaginylhistidylleucylvalylalanyllysylleucyllysylglutamyltyros
ylasparaginylalanylalanylprolylprolylleucylglutaminylglycylphenylalan
ylglycylisoleucylserylalanylprolylaspartylglutaminylvalyllysylalanylala
nylisoleucylaspartylalanylglycylalanylalanylglycylalanylisoleucylseryl

glycylserylalanylisoleucylvalyllysylisoleucylisoleucylglutamylglutamin
ylhistidylasparaginylisoleucylglutamylprolylglutamyllysylmethionylleu
cylalanylalanylleucyllysylvalylphenylalanylvalylglutaminylprolylmethi
onyllysylalanylalanylthreonylarginylacetylseryltyrosylserylisoleucylth
reonylserylprolylserylglutaminylphenylalanylvalylphenylalanylleucyls
erylserylvalyltryptophylalanylaspartylprolylisoleucylglutamylleucylleu
cylasparaginylvalylcysteinylthreonylserylserylleucylglycylasparaginyl
glutaminylphenylalanylglutaminylthreonylglutaminylglutaminylalanyla
rginylthreonylthreonylglutaminylvalylglutaminylglutaminylphenylalan
ylserylglutaminylvalyltryptophyllysylprolylphenylalanylprolylglutamin
ylserylthreonylvalylarginylphenylalanylprolylglycylaspartylvalyltyrosy
llysylvalyltyrosylarginyltyrosylasparaginylalanylvalylleucylaspartylpr
olylleucylisoleucylthreonylalanylleucylleucylglycylthreonylphenylalany
laspartylthreonylarginylasparaginylarginylisoleucylisoleucylglutamylv
alylglutamylasparaginylglutaminylglutaminylserylprolylthreonylthreon
ylalanylglutamylthreonylleucylaspartylalanylthreonylarginylarginylval
ylaspartylaspartylalanylthreonylvalylalanylisoleucylarginylserylalanyl
asparaginylisoleucylasparaginylleucylvalylasparaginylglutamylleucylv
alylarginylglycylthreonylglycylleucyltyrosylasparaginylglutaminylaspa
raginylthreonylphenylalanylglutamylserylmethionylserylglycylleucylv
alyltryptophylthreonylserylalanylprolylalanyltitinmethionylglutaminyla
rginyltyrosylglutamylserylleucylphenylalanylalanylisoleucylcysteinylp
rolylprolylaspartylalanylaspartylaspartylaspartylleucylleucylarginylglu
taminylisoleucylalanylseryltyrosylglycylarginylglycyltyrosylthreonylty
rosylleucylleucylserylarginylalanylglycylvalylthreonylglycylalanylgluta
mylasparaginylarginylalanylalanylleucylprolylleucylasparaginylhistidy
lleucylvalylalanyllysylleucyllysylglutamyltyrosylasparaginylalanylalan
ylprolylprolylleucylglutaminylglycylphenylalanylglycylisoleucylserylal
anylprolylaspartylglutaminylvalyllysylalanylalanylisoleucylaspartylala
nylglycylalanylalanylglycylalanylisoleucylserylglycylserylalanylisoleuc
ylvalyllysylisoleucylisoleucylglutamylglutaminylhistidylasparaginylisol
eucylglutamylprolylglutamyllysylmethionylleucylalanylalanylleucyllys
ylvalylphenylalanylvalylglutaminylprolylmethionyllysylalanylalanylthr
eonylarginylacetylseryltyrosylserylisoleucylthreonylserylprolylserylgl
utaminylphenylalanylvalylphenylalanylleucylserylserylvalyltryptophyl
alanylaspartylprolylisoleucylglutamylleucylleucylasparaginylvalylcyst
einylthreonylserylserylleucylglycylasparaginylglutaminylphenylalanyl
glutaminylthreonylglutaminylglutaminylalanylarginylthreonylthreonyl
glutaminylvalylglutaminylglutaminylphenylalanylserylglutaminylvalylt
ryptophyllysylprolylphenylalanylprolylglutaminylserylthreonylvalylarg

inylphenylalanylprolylglycylaspartylvalyltyrosyllysylvalyltyrosylarginy
ltyrosylasparaginylalanylvalylleucylaspartylprolylleucylisoleucylthreo
nylalanylleucylleucylglycylthreonylphenylalanylaspartylthreonylarginy
lasparaginylarginylisoleucylisoleucylglutamylvalylglutamylasparaginyl
glutaminylglutaminylserylprolylthreonylthreonylalanylglutamylthreon
ylleucylaspartylalanylthreonylarginylarginylvalylaspartylaspartylalany
lthreonylvalylalanylisoleucylarginylserylalanylasparaginylisoleucylasp
araginylleucylvalylasparaginylglutamylleucylvalylarginylglycylthreony
lglycylleucyltyrosylasparaginylglutaminylasparaginylthreonylphenylal
anylglutamylserylmethionylserylglycylleucylvalyltryptophylthreonylse
rylalanylprolylalanyltitinmethionylglutaminylarginyltyrosylglutamylse
rylleucylphenylalanylalanylisoleucylcysteinylprolylprolylaspartylalanyl
aspartylaspartylaspartylleucylleucylarginylglutaminylisoleucylalanyls
eryltyrosylglycylarginylglycyltyrosylthreonyltyrosylleucylleucylserylar
ginylalanylglycylvalylthreonylglycylalanylglutamylasparaginylarginyla
lanylalanylleucylprolylleucylasparaginylhistidylleucylvalylalanyllysylle
ucyllysylglutamyltyrosylasparaginylalanylalanylprolylprolylleucylgluta
minylglycylphenylalanylglycylisoleucylserylalanylprolylaspartylglutam
inylvalyllysylalanylalanylisoleucylaspartylalanylglycylalanylalanylglyc
ylalanylisoleucylserylglycylserylalanylisoleucylvalyllysylisoleucylisole
ucylglutamylglutaminylhistidylasparaginylisoleucylglutamylprolylgluta
myllysylmethionylleucylalanylalanylleucyllysylvalylphenylalanylvalylg
lutaminylprolylmethionyllysylalanylalanylthreonylarginylacetylserylty
rosylserylisoleucylthreonylserylprolylserylglutaminylphenylalanylvaly
lphenylalanylleucylserylserylvalyltryptophylalanylaspartylprolylisoleu
cylglutamylleucylleucylasparaginylvalylcysteinylthreonylserylserylleu
cylglycylasparaginylglutaminylphenylalanylglutaminylthreonylglutami
nylglutaminylalanylarginylthreonylthreonylglutaminylvalylglutaminylg
lutaminylphenylalanylserylglutaminylvalyltryptophyllysylprolylphenyl
alanylprolylglutaminylserylthreonylvalylarginylphenylalanylprolylglyc
ylaspartylvalyltyrosyllysylvalyltyrosylarginyltyrosylasparaginylalanyl
valylleucylaspartylprolylleucylisoleucylthreonylalanylleucylleucylglycy
lthreonylphenylalanylaspartylthreonylarginylasparaginylarginylisoleuc
ylisoleucylglutamylvalylglutamylasparaginylglutaminylglutaminylseryl
prolylthreonylthreonylalanylglutamylthreonylleucylaspartylalanylthre
onylarginylarginylvalylaspartylaspartylalanylthreonylvalylalanylisoleu
cylarginylserylalanylasparaginylisoleucylasparaginylleucylvalylaspara
ginylglutamylleucylvalylarginylglycylthreonylglycylleucyltyrosylaspar
aginylglutaminylasparaginylthreonylphenylalanylglutamylserylmethio
nylserylglycylleucylvalyltryptophylthreonylserylalanylprolylalanyltitin

methionylglutaminylarginyltyrosylglutamylserylleucylphenylalanylala
nylisoleucylcysteinylprolylprolylaspartylalanylaspartylaspartylasparty
lleucylleucylarginylglutaminylisoleucylalanylseryltyrosylglycylarginylg
lycyltyrosylthreonyltyrosylleucylleucylserylarginylalanylglycylvalylthr
eonylglycylalanylglutamylasparaginylarginylalanylalanylleucylprolylle
ucylasparaginylhistidylleucylvalylalanyllysylleucyllysylglutamyltyrosyl
asparaginylalanylalanylprolylprolylleucylglutaminylglycylphenylalanyl
glycylisoleucylserylalanylprolylaspartylglutaminylvalyllysylalanylalan
ylisoleucylaspartylalanylglycylalanylalanylglycylalanylisoleucylserylgl
ycylserylalanylisoleucylvalyllysylisoleucylisoleucylglutamylglutaminyl
histidylasparaginylisoleucylglutamylprolylglutamyllysylmethionylleuc
ylalanylalanylleucyllysylvalylphenylalanylvalylglutaminylprolylmethio
nyllysylalanylalanylthreonylarginylacetylseryltyrosylserylisoleucylthr
eonylserylprolylserylglutaminylphenylalanylvalylphenylalanylleucylse
rylserylvalyltryptophylalanylaspartylprolylisoleucylglutamylleucylleuc
ylasparaginylvalylcysteinylthreonylserylserylleucylglycylasparaginylgl
utaminylphenylalanylglutaminylthreonylglutaminylglutaminylalanylar
ginylthreonylthreonylglutaminylvalylglutaminylglutaminylphenylalanyl
serylglutaminylvalyltryptophyllysylprolylphenylalanylprolylglutaminyl
serylthreonylvalylarginylphenylalanylprolylglycylaspartylvalyltyrosyll
ysylvalyltyrosylarginyltyrosylasparaginylalanylvalylleucylaspartylprol
ylleucylisoleucylthreonylalanylleucylleucylglycylthreonylphenylalanyla
spartylthreonylarginylasparaginylarginylisoleucylisoleucylglutamylval
ylglutamylasparaginylglutaminylglutaminylserylprolylthreonylthreonyl
alanylglutamylthreonylleucylaspartylalanylthreonylarginylarginylvalyl
aspartylaspartylalanylthreonylvalylalanylisoleucylarginylserylalanylas
paraginylisoleucylasparaginylleucylvalylasparaginylglutamylleucylval
ylarginylglycylthreonylglycylleucyltyrosylasparaginylglutaminylaspara
ginylthreonylphenylalanylglutamylserylmethionylserylglycylleucylvaly
ltryptophylthreonylserylalanylprolylalanyltitinmethionylglutaminylargi
nyltyrosylglutamylserylleucylphenylalanylalanylmethionylthreonylthre
onylglutaminylarginyltyrosylglutamylserylleucylphenylalanylalanylglu
taminylleucyllysylglutamylarginyllysylglutamylglycylalanylphenylalan
ylvalylprolylphenylalanylvalylthreonylleucylglycylaspartylprolylglycyli
soleucylglutamylglutaminylserylleucyllysylisoleucylaspartylthreonylle
ucylisoleucylglutamylalanylglycylalanylaspartylalanylleucylglutamylle
ucylglycylisoleucylprolylphenylalanylserylaspartylprolylleucylalanylas
partylglycylprolylthreonylisoleucylglutaminylasparaginylalanylthreony
lleucylarginylalanylphenylalanylalanylalanylglycylvalylthreonylprolyla
lanylglutaminylcysteinylphenylalanylglutamylmethionylleucylalanylleu

cylisoleucylarginylglutaminyllysylhistidylprolylthreonylisoleucylprolyli
soleucylglycyllleucyllleucylmethionyltyrosylalanylasparaginyllleucylvalyl
lphenylalanylasparaginyllysylglycylisoleucylaspartylglutamylphenylal
anyltyrosylalanylglutaminylcysteinylglutamyllysylvalylglycylvalylaspa
rtylserylvalylleucylvalylalanylaspartylvalylprolylvalylglutaminylgluta
mylserylalanylprolylphenylalanylarginylglutaminylalanylalanylleucyla
rginylhistidylasparaginylvalylalanylprolylisoleucylphenylalanylisoleuc
ylcysteinylprolylprolylaspartylalanylaspartylaspartylaspartylleucylleu
cylarginylglutaminylisoleucylalanylseryltyrosylglycylarginylglycyltyro
sylthreonyltyrosylleucylleucylserylarginylalanylglycylvalylthreonylgly
cylalanylglutamylasparaginylarginylalanylalanylleucylprolylleucylaspa
raginylhistidylleucylvalylalanyllysylleucyllysylglutamyltyrosylasparagi
nylalanylalanylprolylprolylleucylglutaminylglycylphenylalanylglycyliso
leucylserylalanylprolylaspartylglutaminylvalyllysylalanylalanylisoleuc
ylaspartylalanylglycylalanylalanylglycylalanylisoleucylserylglycylseryl
alanylisoleucylvalyllysylisoleucylisoleucylglutamylglutaminylhistidylas
paraginylisoleucylglutamylprolylglutamyllysylmethionylleucylalanylal
anylleucyllysylvalylphenylalanylvalylglutaminylprolylmethionyllysylal
anylalanylthreonylarginylacetylseryltyrosylserylisoleucylthreonylseryl
prolylserylglutaminylphenylalanylvalylphenylalanylleucylserylserylval
yltryptophylalanylaspartylprolylisoleucylglutamylleucylleucylasparagi
nylvalylcysteinylthreonylserylserylleucylglycylasparaginylglutaminylp
henylalanylglutaminylthreonylglutaminylglutaminylalanylarginylthreo
nylthreonylglutaminylvalylglutaminylglutaminylphenylalanylserylgluta
minylvalyltryptophyllysylprolylphenylalanylprolylglutaminylserylthreo
nylvalylarginylphenylalanylprolylglycylaspartylvalyltyrosyllysylvalylty
rosylarginyltyrosylasparaginylalanylvalylleucylaspartylprolylleucylisol
eucylthreonylalanylleucylleucylglycylthreonylphenylalanylaspartylthre
onylarginylasparaginylarginylisoleucylisoleucylglutamylvalylglutamyl
asparaginylglutaminylglutaminylserylprolylthreonylthreonylalanylglut
amylthreonylleucylaspartylalanylthreonylarginylarginylvalylaspartyla
spartylalanylthreonylvalylalanylisoleucylarginylserylalanylasparaginyl
isoleucylasparaginylleucylvalylasparaginylglutamylleucylvalylarginylg
lycylthreonylglycylleucyltyrosylasparaginylglutaminylasparaginylthre
onylphenylalanylglutamylserylmethionylserylglycylleucylvalyltryptoph
ylthreonylserylalanylprolylalanyltitinmethionylglutaminylarginyltyrosy
lglutamylserylleucylphenylalanylalanylisoleucylcysteinylprolylprolylas
partylalanylaspartylaspartylaspartylleucylleucylarginylglutaminylisole
ucylalanylseryltyrosylglycylarginylglycyltyrosylthreonyltyrosylleucylle
ucylserylarginylalanylglycylvalylthreonylglycylalanylglutamylasparagi

nylarginylalanylalanylleucylprolylleucylasparaginylhistidylleucylvalyla
lanyllysylleucyllysylglutamyltyrosylasparaginylalanylalanylprolylproly
lleucylglutaminylglycylphenylalanylglycylisoleucylserylalanylprolylasp
artylglutaminylvalyllysylalanylalanylisoleucylaspartylalanylglycylalan
ylalanylglycylalanylisoleucylserylglycylserylalanylisoleucylvalyllysylis
oleucylisoleucylglutamylglutaminylhistidylasparaginylisoleucylglutam
ylprolylglutamyllysylmethionylleucylalanylalanylleucyllysylvalylpheny
lalanylvalylglutaminylprolylmethionyllysylalanylalanylthreonylarginyl
acetylseryltyrosylserylisoleucylthreonylserylprolylserylglutaminylphe
nylalanylvalylphenylalanylleucylserylserylvalyltryptophylalanylaspart
ylprolylisoleucylglutamylleucylleucylasparaginylvalylcysteinylthreonyl
serylserylleucylglycylasparaginylglutaminylphenylalanylglutaminylthr
eonylglutaminylglutaminylalanylarginylthreonylthreonylglutaminylval
ylglutaminylglutaminylphenylalanylserylglutaminylvalyltryptophyllysy
lprolylphenylalanylprolylglutaminylserylthreonylvalylarginylphenylala
nylprolylglycylaspartylvalyltyrosyllysylvalyltyrosylarginyltyrosylaspar
aginylalanylvalylleucylaspartylprolylleucylisoleucylthreonylalanylleuc
ylleucylglycylthreonylphenylalanylaspartylthreonylarginylasparaginyl
arginylisoleucylisoleucylglutamylvalylglutamylasparaginylglutaminylg
lutaminylserylprolylthreonylthreonylalanylglutamylthreonylleucylaspa
rtylalanylthreonylarginylarginylvalylaspartylaspartylalanylthreonylval
ylalanylisoleucylarginylserylalanylasparaginylisoleucylasparaginylleuc
ylvalylasparaginylglutamylleucylvalylarginylglycylthreonylglycylleucyl
tyrosylasparaginylglutaminylasparaginylthreonylphenylalanylglutamyl
serylmethionylserylglycylleucylvalyltryptophylthreonylserylalanylprol
ylalanyltitinmethionylglutaminylarginyltyrosylglutamylserylleucylphen
ylalanylalanylisoleucylcysteinylprolylprolylaspartylalanylaspartylaspa
rtylaspartylleucylleucylarginylglutaminylisoleucylalanylseryltyrosylgly
cylarginylglycyltyrosylthreonyltyrosylleucylleucylserylarginylalanylgly
cylvalylthreonylglycylalanylglutamylasparaginylarginylalanylalanylleu
cylprolylleucylasparaginylhistidylleucylvalylalanyllysylleucyllysylgluta
myltyrosylasparaginylalanylalanylprolylprolylleucylglutaminylglycylph
enylalanylglycylisoleucylserylalanylprolylaspartylglutaminylvalyllysyl
alanylalanylisoleucylaspartylalanylglycylalanylalanylglycylalanylisole
ucylserylglycylserylalanylisoleucylvalyllysylisoleucylisoleucylglutamyl
glutaminylhistidylasparaginylisoleucylglutamylprolylglutamyllysylmet
hionylleucylalanylalanylleucyllysylvalylphenylalanylvalylglutaminylpr
olylmethionyllysylalanylalanylthreonylarginylacetylseryltyrosylserylis
oleucylthreonylserylprolylserylglutaminylphenylalanylvalylphenylalan
ylleucylserylserylvalyltryptophylalanylaspartylprolylisoleucylglutamyl

leucylleucylasparaginylvalylcysteinylthreonylserylserylleucylglycylasp
araginylglutaminylphenylalanylglutaminylthreonylglutaminylglutamin
ylalanylarginylthreonylthreonylglutaminylvalylglutaminylglutaminylph
enylalanylserylglutaminylvalyltryptophyllysylprolylphenylalanylprolyl
glutaminylserylthreonylvalylarginylphenylalanylprolylglycylaspartylva
lyltyrosyllysylvalyltyrosylarginyltyrosylasparaginylalanylvalylleucylas
partylprolylleucylisoleucylthreonylalanylleucylleucylglycylthreonylphe
nylalanylaspartylthreonylarginylasparaginylarginylisoleucylisoleucylgl
utamylvalylglutamylasparaginylglutaminylglutaminylserylprolylthreon
ylthreonylalanylglutamylthreonylleucylaspartylalanylthreonylarginylar
ginylvalylaspartylaspartylalanylthreonylvalylalanylisoleucylarginylser
ylalanylasparaginylisoleucylasparaginylleucylvalylasparaginylglutamy
lleucylvalylarginylglycylthreonylglycylleucyltyrosylasparaginylglutami
nylasparaginylthreonylphenylalanylglutamylserylmethionylserylglycyl
leucylvalyltryptophylthreonylserylalanylprolylalanyltitinmethionylglut
aminylarginyltyrosylglutamylserylleucylphenylalanylalanylisoleucylcy
steinylprolylprolylaspartylalanylaspartylaspartylaspartylleucylleucylar
ginylglutaminylisoleucylalanylseryltyrosylglycylarginylglycyltyrosylthr
eonyltyrosylleucylleucylserylarginylalanylglycylvalylthreonylglycylala
nylglutamylasparaginylarginylalanylalanylleucylprolylleucylasparagin
ylhistidylleucylvalylalanyllysylleucyllysylglutamyltyrosylasparaginylal
anylalanylprolylprolylleucylglutaminylglycylphenylalanylglycylisoleuc
ylserylalanylprolylaspartylglutaminylvalyllysylalanylalanylisoleucylas
partylalanylglycylalanylalanylglycylalanylisoleucylserylglycylserylalan
ylisoleucylvalyllysylisoleucylisoleucylglutamylglutaminylhistidylaspar
aginylisoleucylglutamylprolylglutamyllysylmethionylleucylalanylalanyl
leucyllysylvalylphenylalanylvalylglutaminylprolylmethionyllysylalanyl
alanylthreonylarginylacetylseryltyrosylserylisoleucylthreonylserylprol
ylserylglutaminylphenylalanylvalylphenylalanylleucylserylserylvalyltr
yptophylalanylaspartylprolylisoleucylglutamylleucylleucylasparaginylv
alylcysteinylthreonylserylserylleucylglycylasparaginylglutaminylphen
ylalanylglutaminylthreonylglutaminylglutaminylalanylarginylthreonylt
hreonylglutaminylvalylglutaminylglutaminylphenylalanylserylglutamin
ylvalyltryptophyllysylprolylphenylalanylprolylglutaminylserylthreonyl
valylarginylphenylalanylprolylglycylaspartylvalyltyrosyllysylvalyltyros
ylarginyltyrosylasparaginylalanylvalylleucylaspartylprolylleucylisoleu
cylthreonylalanylleucylleucylglycylthreonylphenylalanylaspartylthreon
ylarginylasparaginylarginylisoleucylisoleucylglutamylvalylglutamylasp
araginylglutaminylglutaminylserylprolylthreonylthreonylalanylglutam
ylthreonylleucylaspartylalanylthreonylarginylarginylvalylaspartylaspa

rtylalanylthreonylvalylalanylisoleucylarginylserylalanylasparaginylisol
eucylasparaginylleucylvalylasparaginylglutamylleucylvalylarginylglyc
ylthreonylglycylleucyltyrosylasparaginylglutaminylasparaginylthreony
lphenylalanylglutamylserylmethionylserylglycylleucylvalyltryptophylt
hreonylserylalanylprolylalanyltitinmethionylglutaminylarginyltyrosylgl
utamylserylleucylphenylalanylalanylmethionylthreonylthreonylglutami
nylarginyltyrosylglutamylserylleucylphenylalanylalanylglutaminylleuc
yllysylglutamylarginyllysylglutamylglycylalanylphenylalanylvalylproly
lphenylalanylvalylthreonylleucylglycylaspartylprolylglycylisoleucylglut
amylglutaminylserylleucyllysylisoleucylaspartylthreonylleucylisoleucy
lglutamylalanylglycylalanylaspartylalanylleucylglutamylleucylglycylis
oleucylprolylphenylalanylserylaspartylprolylleucylalanylaspartylglycyl
prolylthreonylisoleucylglutaminylasparaginylalanylthreonylleucylargin
ylalanylphenylalanylalanylalanylglycylvalylthreonylprolylalanylglutam
inylcysteinylphenylalanylglutamylmethionylleucylalanylleucylisoleucyl
arginylglutaminyllysylhistidylprolylthreonylisoleucylprolylisoleucylgly
cylleucylleucylmethionyltyrosylalanylasparaginylleucylvalylphenylala
nylasparaginyllysylglycylisoleucylaspartylglutamylphenylalanyltyrosyl
alanylglutaminylcysteinylglutamyllysylvalylglycylvalylaspartylserylval
ylleucylvalylalanylaspartylvalylprolylvalylglutaminylglutamylserylalan
ylprolylphenylalanylarginylglutaminylalanylalanylleucylarginylhistidyl
asparaginylvalylalanylprolylisoleucylphenylalanylisoleucylcysteinylpro
lylprolylaspartylalanylaspartylaspartylaspartylleucylleucylarginylgluta
minylisoleucylalanylseryltyrosylglycylarginylglycyltyrosylthreonyltyro
sylleucylleucylserylarginylalanylglycylvalylthreonylglycylalanylglutam
ylasparaginylarginylalanylalanylleucylprolylleucylasparaginylhistidylle
ucylvalylalanyllysylleucyllysylglutamyltyrosylasparaginylalanylalanyl
prolylprolylleucylglutaminylglycylphenylalanylglycylisoleucylserylalan
ylprolylaspartylglutaminylvalyllysylalanylalanylisoleucylaspartylalany
lglycylalanylalanylglycylalanylisoleucylserylglycylserylalanylisoleucyl
valyllysylisoleucylisoleucylglutamylglutaminylhistidylasparaginylisole
ucylglutamylprolylglutamyllysylmethionylleucylalanylalanylleucyllysyl
valylphenylalanylvalylglutaminylprolylmethionyllysylalanylalanylthreo
nylarginylacetylseryltyrosylserylisoleucylthreonylserylprolylserylgluta
minylphenylalanylvalylphenylalanylleucylserylserylvalyltryptophylala
nylaspartylprolylisoleucylglutamylleucylleucylasparaginylvalylcystein
ylthreonylserylserylleucylglycylasparaginylglutaminylphenylalanylglut
aminylthreonylglutaminylglutaminylalanylarginylthreonylthreonylglut
aminylvalylglutaminylglutaminylphenylalanylserylglutaminylvalyltrypt
ophyllysylprolylphenylalanylprolylglutaminylserylthreonylvalylarginyl

phenylalanylprolylglycylaspartylvalyltyrosyllysylvalyltyrosylarginyltyr
osylasparaginylalanylvalylleucylaspartylprolylleucylisoleucylthreonyla
lanylleucylleucylglycylthreonylphenylalanylaspartylthreonylarginylasp
araginylarginylisoleucylisoleucylglutamylvalylglutamylasparaginylglut
aminylglutaminylserylprolylthreonylthreonylalanylglutamylthreonylle
ucylaspartylalanylthreonylarginylarginylvalylaspartylaspartylalanylthr
eonylvalylalanylisoleucylarginylserylalanylasparaginylisoleucylaspara
ginylleucylvalylasparaginylglutamylleucylvalylarginylglycylthreonylgl
ycylleucyltyrosylasparaginylglutaminylasparaginylthreonylphenylalan
ylglutamylserylmethionylserylglycylleucylvalyltryptophylthreonylseryl
alanylprolylalanyltitinmethionylglutaminylarginyltyrosylglutamylseryll
eucylphenylalanylalanylisoleucylcysteinylprolylprolylaspartylalanylas
partylaspartylaspartylleucylleucylarginylglutaminylisoleucylalanylsery
ltyrosylglycylarginylglycyltyrosylthreonyltyrosylleucylleucylserylargin
ylalanylglycylvalylthreonylglycylalanylglutamylasparaginylarginylalan
ylalanylleucylprolylleucylasparaginylhistidylleucylvalylalanyllysylleuc
yllysylglutamyltyrosylasparaginylalanylalanylprolylprolylleucylglutam
inylglycylphenylalanylglycylisoleucylserylalanylprolylaspartylglutamin
ylvalyllysylalanylalanylisoleucylaspartylalanylglycylalanylalanylglycyl
alanylisoleucylserylglycylserylalanylisoleucylvalyllysylisoleucylisoleuc
ylglutamylglutaminylhistidylasparaginylisoleucylglutamylprolylglutam
yllysylmethionylleucylalanylalanylleucyllysylvalylphenylalanylvalylglu
taminylprolylmethionyllysylalanylalanylthreonylarginylacetylseryltyro
sylserylisoleucylthreonylserylprolylserylglutaminylphenylalanylvalylp
henylalanylleucylserylserylvalyltryptophylalanylaspartylprolylisoleucy
lglutamylleucylleucylasparaginylvalylcysteinylthreonylserylserylleucyl
glycylasparaginylglutaminylphenylalanylglutaminylthreonylglutaminyl
glutaminylalanylarginylthreonylthreonylglutaminylvalylglutaminylglut
aminylphenylalanylserylglutaminylvalyltryptophyllysylprolylphenylala
nylprolylglutaminylserylthreonylvalylarginylphenylalanylprolylglycyla
spartylvalyltyrosyllysylvalyltyrosylarginyltyrosylasparaginylalanylval
ylleucylaspartylprolylleucylisoleucylthreonylalanylleucylleucylglycylth
reonylphenylalanylaspartylthreonylarginylasparaginylarginylisoleucyli
soleucylglutamylvalylglutamylasparaginylglutaminylglutaminylserylpr
olylthreonylthreonylalanylglutamylthreonylleucylaspartylalanylthreon
ylarginylarginylvalylaspartylaspartylalanylthreonylvalylalanylisoleucy
larginylserylalanylasparaginylisoleucylasparaginylleucylvalylasparagi
nylglutamylleucylvalylarginylglycylthreonylglycylleucyltyrosylasparag
inylglutaminylasparaginylthreonylphenylalanylglutamylserylmethionyl
serylglycylleucylvalyltryptophylthreonylserylalanylprolylalanyltitinme

thionylglutaminylarginyltyrosylglutamylserylleucylphenylalanylalanyli
soleucylcysteinylprolylprolylaspartylalanylaspartylaspartylaspartylleu
cylleucylarginylglutaminylisoleucylalanylseryltyrosylglycylarginylglyc
yltyrosylthreonyltyrosylleucylleucylserylarginylalanylglycylvalylthreo
nylglycylalanylglutamylasparaginylarginylalanylalanylleucylprolylleuc
ylasparaginylhistidylleucylvalylalanyllysylleucyllysylglutamyltyrosylas
paraginylalanylalanylprolylprolylleucylglutaminylglycylphenylalanylgl
ycylisoleucylserylalanylprolylaspartylglutaminylvalyllysylalanylalanyli
soleucylaspartylalanylglycylalanylalanylglycylalanylisoleucylserylglyc
ylserylalanylisoleucylvalyllysylisoleucylisoleucylglutamylglutaminylhi
stidylasparaginylisoleucylglutamylprolylglutamyllysylmethionylleucyl
alanylalanylleucyllysylvalylphenylalanylvalylglutaminylprolylmethiony
llysylalanylalanylthreonylarginylacetylseryltyrosylserylisoleucylthreo
nylserylprolylserylglutaminylphenylalanylvalylphenylalanylleucylseryl
serylvalyltryptophylalanylaspartylprolylisoleucylglutamylleucylleucyla
sparaginylvalylcysteinylthreonylserylserylleucylglycylasparaginylglut
aminylphenylalanylglutaminylthreonylglutaminylglutaminylalanylargin
ylthreonylthreonylglutaminylvalylglutaminylglutaminylphenylalanylse
rylglutaminylvalyltryptophyllysylprolylphenylalanylprolylglutaminylse
rylthreonylvalylarginylphenylalanylprolylglycylaspartylvalyltyrosyllys
ylvalyltyrosylarginyltyrosylasparaginylalanylvalylleucylaspartylprolyll
eucylisoleucylthreonylalanylleucylleucylglycylthreonylphenylalanylasp
artylthreonylarginylasparaginylarginylisoleucylisoleucylglutamylvalyl
glutamylasparaginylglutaminylglutaminylserylprolylthreonylthreonylal
anylglutamylthreonylleucylaspartylalanylthreonylarginylarginylvalylas
partylaspartylalanylthreonylvalylalanylisoleucylarginylserylalanylaspa
raginylisoleucylasparaginylleucylvalylasparaginylglutamylleucylvalyla
rginylglycylthreonylglycylleucyltyrosylasparaginylglutaminylasparagin
ylthreonylphenylalanylglutamylserylmethionylserylglycylleucylvalyltr
yptophylthreonylserylalanylprolylalanyltitinmethionylglutaminylarginy
ltyrosylglutamylserylleucylphenylalanylalanylisoleucylcysteinylprolylp
rolylaspartylalanylaspartylaspartylaspartylleucylleucylarginylglutamin
ylisoleucylalanylseryltyrosylglycylarginylglycyltyrosylthreonyltyrosyll
eucylleucylserylarginylalanylglycylvalylthreonylglycylalanylglutamyla
sparaginylarginylalanylalanylleucylprolylleucylasparaginylhistidylleuc
ylvalylalanyllysylleucyllysylglutamyltyrosylasparaginylalanylalanylpro
lylprolylleucylglutaminylglycylphenylalanylglycylisoleucylserylalanylp
rolylaspartylglutaminylvalyllysylalanylalanylisoleucylaspartylalanylgl
ycylalanylalanylglycylalanylisoleucylserylglycylserylalanylisoleucylval
yllysylisoleucylisoleucylglutamylglutaminylhistidylasparaginylisoleucy

lglutamylprolylglutamyllysylmethionylleucylalanylalanylleucyllysylval
ylphenylalanylvalylglutaminylprolylmethionyllysylalanylalanylthreonyl
arginylacetylseryltyrosylserylisoleucylthreonylserylprolylserylglutami
nylphenylalanylvalylphenylalanylleucylserylserylvalyltryptophylalanyl
aspartylprolylisoleucylglutamylleucylleucylasparaginylvalylcysteinylth
reonylserylserylleucylglycylasparaginylglutaminylphenylalanylglutami
nylthreonylglutaminylglutaminylalanylarginylthreonylthreonylglutami
nylvalylglutaminylglutaminylphenylalanylserylglutaminylvalyltryptoph
yllysylprolylphenylalanylprolylglutaminylserylthreonylvalylarginylphe
nylalanylprolylglycylaspartylvalyltyrosyllysylvalyltyrosylarginyltyrosy
laspataginylalanylvalylleucylaspartylprolylleucylisoleucylthreonylalan
ylleucylleucylglycylthreonylphenylalanylaspartylthreonylarginylaspara
ginylarginylisoleucylisoleucylglutamylvalylglutamylasparaginylglutam
inylglutaminylserylprolylthreonylthreonylalanylglutamylthreonylleucyl
aspartylalanylthreonylarginylarginylvalylaspartylaspartylalanylthreon
ylvalylalanylisoleucylarginylserylalanylasparaginylisoleucylasparagin
ylleucylvalylasparaginylglutamylleucylvalylarginylglycylthreonylglycyl
leucyltyrosylasparaginylglutaminylasparaginylthreonylphenylalanylglu
tamylserylmethionylserylglycylleucylvalyltryptophylthreonylserylalan
ylprolylalanyltitinmethionylglutaminylarginyltyrosylglutamylserylleuc
ylphenylalanylalanylmethionylthreonylthreonylglutaminylarginyltyros
ylglutamylserylleucylphenylalanylalanylglutaminylleucyllysylglutamyl
arginyllysylglutamylglycylalanylphenylalanylvalylprolylphenylalanylva
lylthreonylleucylglycylaspartylprolylglycylisoleucylglutamylglutaminyl
serylleucyllysylisoleucylaspartylthreonylleucylisoleucylglutamylalanyl
glycylalanylaspartylalanylleucylglutamylleucylglycylisoleucylprolylphe
nylalanylserylaspartylprolylleucylalanylaspartylglycylprolylthreonylis
oleucylglutaminylasparaginylalanylthreonylleucylarginylalanylphenyla
lanylalanylalanylglycylvalylthreonylprolylalanylglutaminylcysteinylph
enylalanylglutamylmethionylleucylalanylleucylisoleucylarginylglutami
nyllysylhistidylprolylthreonylisoleucylprolylisoleucylglycylleucylleucyl
methionyltyrosylalanylasparaginylleucylvalylphenylalanylasparaginyll
ysylglycylisoleucylaspartylglutamylphenylalanyltyrosylalanylglutamin
ylcysteinylglutamyllysylvalylglycylvalylaspartylserylvalylleucylvalylal
anylaspartylvalylprolylvalylglutaminylglutamylserylalanylprolylphenyl
alanylarginylglutaminylalanylalanylleucylarginylhistidylasparaginylval
ylalanylprolylisoleucylphenylalanylisoleucylcysteinylprolylprolylaspart
ylalanylaspartylaspartylaspartylleucylleucylarginylglutaminylisoleucyl
alanylseryltyrosylglycylarginylglycyltyrosylthreonyltyrosylleucylleucyl
serylarginylalanylglycylvalylthreonylglycylalanylglutamylasparaginyla

rginylalanylalanylleucylprolylleucylasparaginylhistidylleucylvalylalany
llysylleucyllysylglutamyltyrosylasparaginylalanylalanylprolylprolylleu
cylglutaminylglycylphenylalanylglycylisoleucylserylalanylprolylaspart
ylglutaminylvalyllysylalanylalanylisoleucylaspartylalanylglycylalanylal
anylglycylalanylisoleucylserylglycylserylalanylisoleucylvalyllysylisole
ucylisoleucylglutamylglutaminylhistidylasparaginylisoleucylglutamylpr
olylglutamyllysylmethionylleucylalanylalanylleucyllysylvalylphenylala
nylvalylglutaminylprolylmethionyllysylalanylalanylthreonylarginylacet
ylseryltyrosylserylisoleucylthreonylserylprolylserylglutaminylphenylal
anylvalylphenylalanylleucylserylserylvalyltryptophylalanylaspartylpro
lylisoleucylglutamylleucylleucylasparaginylvalylcysteinylthreonylseryl
serylleucylglycylasparaginylglutaminylphenylalanylglutaminylthreonyl
glutaminylglutaminylalanylarginylthreonylthreonylglutaminylvalylglut
aminylglutaminylphenylalanylserylglutaminylvalyltryptophyllysylproly
lphenylalanylprolylglutaminylserylthreonylvalylarginylphenylalanylpro
lylglycylaspartylvalyltyrosyllysylvalyltyrosylarginyltyrosylasparaginyl
alanylvalylleucylaspartylprolylleucylisoleucylthreonylalanylleucylleuc
ylglycylthreonylphenylalanylaspartylthreonylarginylasparaginylarginyl
isoleucylisoleucylglutamylvalylglutamylasparaginylglutaminylglutami
nylserylprolylthreonylthreonylalanylglutamylthreonylleucylaspartylala
nylthreonylarginylarginylvalylaspartylaspartylalanylthreonylvalylalan
ylisoleucylarginylserylalanylasparaginylisoleucylasparaginylleucylvaly
lasparaginylglutamylleucylvalylarginylglycylthreonylglycylleucyltyros
ylasparaginylglutaminylasparaginylthreonylphenylalanylglutamylseryl
methionylserylglycylleucylvalyltryptophylthreonylserylalanylprolylala
nyltitinmethionylglutaminylarginyltyrosylglutamylserylleucylphenylala
nylalanylisoleucylcysteinylprolylprolylaspartylalanylaspartylaspartyla
spartylleucylleucylarginylglutaminylisoleucylalanylseryltyrosylglycyla
rginylglycyltyrosylthreonyltyrosylleucylleucylserylarginylalanylglycylv
alylthreonylglycylalanylglutamylasparaginylarginylalanylalanylleucylp
rolylleucylasparaginylhistidylleucylvalylalanyllysylleucyllysylglutamyl
tyrosylasparaginylalanylalanylprolylprolylleucylglutaminylglycylpheny
lalanylglycylisoleucylserylalanylprolylaspartylglutaminylvalyllysylalan
ylalanylisoleucylaspartylalanylglycylalanylalanylglycylalanylisoleucyls
erylglycylserylalanylisoleucylvalyllysylisoleucylisoleucylglutamylgluta
minylhistidylasparaginylisoleucylglutamylprolylglutamyllysylmethiony
lleucylalanylalanylleucyllysylvalylphenylalanylvalylglutaminylprolylm
ethionyllysylalanylalanylthreonylarginylacetylseryltyrosylserylisoleuc
ylthreonylserylprolylserylglutaminylphenylalanylvalylphenylalanylleuc
ylserylserylvalyltryptophylalanylaspartylprolylisoleucylglutamylleucyl

leucylasparaginylvalylcysteinylthreonylserylserylleucylglycylasparagi
nylglutaminylphenylalanylglutaminylthreonylglutaminylglutaminylalan
ylarginylthreonylthreonylglutaminylvalylglutaminylglutaminylphenylal
anylserylglutaminylvalyltryptophyllysylprolylphenylalanylprolylglutam
inylserylthreonylvalylarginylphenylalanylprolylglycylaspartylvalyltyro
syllysylvalyltyrosylarginyltyrosylasparaginylalanylvalylleucylaspartyl
prolylleucylisoleucylthreonylalanylleucylleucylglycylthreonylphenylala
nylaspartylthreonylarginylasparaginylarginylisoleucylisoleucylglutamy
lvalylglutamylasparaginylglutaminylglutaminylserylprolylthreonylthre
onylalanylglutamylthreonylleucylaspartylalanylthreonylarginylarginyl
valylaspartylaspartylalanylthreonylvalylalanylisoleucylarginylserylala
nylasparaginylisoleucylasparaginylleucylvalylasparaginylglutamylleuc
ylvalylarginylglycylthreonylglycylleucyltyrosylasparaginylglutaminyla
sparaginylthreonylphenylalanylglutamylserylmethionylserylglycylleuc
ylvalyltryptophylthreonylserylalanylprolylalanyltitinmethionylglutamin
ylarginyltyrosylglutamylserylleucylphenylalanylalanylisoleucylcystein
ylprolylprolylaspartylalanylaspartylaspartylaspartylleucylleucylarginyl
glutaminylisoleucylalanylseryltyrosylglycylarginylglycyltyrosylthreony
ltyrosylleucylleucylserylarginylalanylglycylvalylthreonylglycylalanylgl
utamylasparaginylarginylalanylalanylleucylprolylleucylasparaginylhist
idylleucylvalylalanyllysylleucyllysylglutamyltyrosylasparaginylalanyla
lanylprolylprolylleucylglutaminylglycylphenylalanylglycylisoleucylsery
lalanylprolylaspartylglutaminylvalyllysylalanylalanylisoleucylaspartyl
alanylglycylalanylalanylglycylalanylisoleucylserylglycylserylalanylisol
eucylvalyllysylisoleucylisoleucylglutamylglutaminylhistidylasparaginyl
isoleucylglutamylprolylglutamyllysylmethionylleucylalanylalanylleucyl
lysylvalylphenylalanylvalylglutaminylprolylmethionyllysylalanylalanyl
threonylarginylacetylseryltyrosylserylisoleucylthreonylserylprolylsery
lglutaminylphenylalanylvalylphenylalanylleucylserylserylvalyltryptoph
ylalanylaspartylprolylisoleucylglutamylleucylleucylasparaginylvalylcy
steinylthreonylserylserylleucylglycylasparaginylglutaminylphenylalan
ylglutaminylthreonylglutaminylglutaminylalanylarginylthreonylthreon
ylglutaminylvalylglutaminylglutaminylphenylalanylserylglutaminylval
yltryptophyllysylprolylphenylalanylprolylglutaminylserylthreonylvalyl
arginylphenylalanylprolylglycylaspartylvalyltyrosyllysylvalyltyrosylar
ginyltyrosylasparaginylalanylvalylleucylaspartylprolylleucylisoleucylth
reonylalanylleucylleucylglycylthreonylphenylalanylaspartylthreonylar
ginylasparaginylarginylisoleucylisoleucylglutamylvalylglutamylaspara
ginylglutaminylglutaminylserylprolylthreonylthreonylalanylglutamylth
reonylleucylaspartylalanylthreonylarginylarginylvalylaspartylaspartyl

alanylthreonylvalylalanylisoleucylarginylserylalanylasparaginylisoleuc
ylasparaginylleucylvalylasparaginylglutamylleucylvalylarginylglycylth
reonylglycylleucyltyrosylasparaginylglutaminylasparaginylthreonylph
enylalanylglutamylserylmethionylserylglycylleucylvalyltryptophylthre
onylserylalanylprolylalanyltitinmethionylglutaminylarginyltyrosylgluta
mylserylleucylphenylalanylalanylisoleucylcysteinylprolylprolylaspartyl
alanylaspartylaspartylaspartylleucylleucylarginylglutaminylisoleucylal
anylseryltyrosylglycylarginylglycyltyrosylthreonyltyrosylleucylleucyls
erylarginylalanylglycylvalylthreonylglycylalanylglutamylasparaginylar
ginylalanylalanylleucylprolylleucylasparaginylhistidylleucylvalylalanyll
ysylleucyllysylglutamyltyrosylasparaginylalanylalanylprolylprolylleuc
ylglutaminylglycylphenylalanylglycylisoleucylserylalanylprolylaspartyl
glutaminylvalyllysylalanylalanylisoleucylaspartylalanylglycylalanylala
nylglycylalanylisoleucylserylglycylserylalanylisoleucylvalyllysylisoleu
cylisoleucylglutamylglutaminylhistidylasparaginylisoleucylglutamylpro
lylglutamyllysylmethionylleucylalanylalanylleucyllysylvalylphenylalan
ylvalylglutaminylprolylmethionyllysylalanylalanylthreonylarginylacety
lseryltyrosylserylisoleucylthreonylserylprolylserylglutaminylphenylala
nylvalylphenylalanylleucylserylserylvalyltryptophylalanylaspartylprol
ylisoleucylglutamylleucylleucylasparaginylvalylcysteinylthreonylseryl
serylleucylglycylasparaginylglutaminylphenylalanylglutaminylthreonyl
glutaminylglutaminylalanylarginylthreonylthreonylglutaminylvalylglut
aminylglutaminylphenylalanylserylglutaminylvalyltryptophyllysylproly
lphenylalanylprolylglutaminylserylthreonylvalylarginylphenylalanylpro
lylglycylaspartylvalyltyrosyllysylvalyltyrosylarginyltyrosylasparaginyl
alanylvalylleucylaspartylprolylleucylisoleucylthreonylalanylleucylleuc
ylglycylthreonylphenylalanylaspartylthreonylarginylasparaginylarginyl
isoleucylisoleucylglutamylvalylglutamylasparaginylglutaminylglutami
nylserylprolylthreonylthreonylalanylglutamylthreonylleucylaspartylala
nylthreonylarginylarginylvalylaspartylaspartylalanylthreonylvalylalan
ylisoleucylarginylserylalanylasparaginylisoleucylasparaginylleucylvaly
lasparaginylglutamylleucylvalylarginylglycylthreonylglycylleucyltyros
ylasparaginylglutaminylasparaginylthreonylphenylalanylglutamylseryl
methionylserylglycylleucylvalyltryptophylthreonylserylalanylprolylala
nyltitinmethionylglutaminylarginyltyrosylglutamylserylleucylphenylala
nylalanylmethionylthreonylthreonylglutaminylarginyltyrosylglutamyls
erylleucylphenylalanylalanylglutaminylleucyllysylglutamylarginyllysyl
glutamylglycylalanylphenylalanylvalylprolylphenylalanylvalylthreonyll
eucylglycylaspartylprolylglycylisoleucylglutamylglutaminylserylleucyll
ysylisoleucylaspartylthreonylleucylisoleucylglutamylalanylglycylalanyl

aspartylalanylleucylglutamylleucylglycylisoleucylprolylphenylalanylse
rylaspartylprolylleucylalanylaspartylglycylprolylthreonylisoleucylgluta
minylasparaginylalanylthreonylleucylarginylalanylphenylalanylalanyla
lanylglycylvalylthreonylprolylalanylglutaminylcysteinylphenylalanylgl
utamylmethionylleucylalanylleucylisoleucylarginylglutaminyllysylhisti
dylprolylthreonylisoleucylprolylisoleucylglycylleucylleucylmethionylty
rosylalanylasparaginylleucylvalylphenylalanylasparaginyllysylglycylis
oleucylaspartylglutamylphenylalanyltyrosylalanylglutaminylcysteinylg
lutamyllysylvalylglycylvalylaspartylserylvalylleucylvalylalanylaspartyl
valylprolylvalylglutaminylglutamylserylalanylprolylphenylalanylarginy
lglutaminylalanylalanylleucylarginylhistidylasparaginylvalylalanylprol
ylisoleucylphenylalanylisoleucylcysteinylprolylprolylaspartylalanylasp
artylaspartylaspartylleucylleucylarginylglutaminylisoleucylalanylseryl
tyrosylglycylarginylglycyltyrosylthreonyltyrosylleucylleucylserylargin
ylalanylglycylvalylthreonylglycylalanylglutamylasparaginylarginylalan
ylalanylleucylprolylleucylasparaginylhistidylleucylvalylalanyllysylleuc
yllysylglutamyltyrosylasparaginylalanylalanylprolylprolylleucylglutam
inylglycylphenylalanylglycylisoleucylserylalanylprolylaspartylglutamin
ylvalyllysylalanylalanylisoleucylaspartylalanylglycylalanylalanylglycyl
alanylisoleucylserylglycylserylalanylisoleucylvalyllysylisoleucylisoleuc
ylglutamylglutaminylhistidylasparaginylisoleucylglutamylprolylglutam
yllysylmethionylleucylalanylalanylleucyllysylvalylphenylalanylvalylglu
taminylprolylmethionyllysylalanylalanylthreonylarginylacetylseryltyro
sylserylisoleucylthreonylserylprolylserylglutaminylphenylalanylvalylp
henylalanylleucylserylserylvalyltryptophylalanylaspartylprolylisoleucy
lglutamylleucylleucylasparaginylvalylcysteinylthreonylserylserylleucyl
glycylasparaginylglutaminylphenylalanylglutaminylthreonylglutaminyl
glutaminylalanylarginylthreonylthreonylglutaminylvalylglutaminylglut
aminylphenylalanylserylglutaminylvalyltryptophyllysylprolylphenylala
nylprolylglutaminylserylthreonylvalylarginylphenylalanylprolylglycyla
spartylvalyltyrosyllysylvalyltyrosylarginyltyrosylasparaginylalanylval
ylleucylaspartylprolylleucylisoleucylthreonylalanylleucylleucylglycylth
reonylphenylalanylaspartylthreonylarginylasparaginylarginylisoleucyli
soleucylglutamylvalylglutamylasparaginylglutaminylglutaminylserylpr
olylthreonylthreonylalanylglutamylthreonylleucylaspartylalanylthreon
ylarginylarginylvalylaspartylaspartylalanylthreonylvalylalanylisoleucy
larginylserylalanylasparaginylisoleucylasparaginylleucylvalylasparagi
nylglutamylleucylvalylarginylglycylthreonylglycylleucyltyrosylasparag
inylglutaminylasparaginylthreonylphenylalanylglutamylserylmethionyl
serylglycylleucylvalyltryptophylthreonylserylalanylprolylalanyltitinme

thionylglutaminylarginyltyrosylglutamylserylleucylphenylalanylalanyli
soleucylcysteinylprolylprolylaspartylalanylaspartylaspartylaspartylleu
cylleucylarginylglutaminylisoleucylalanylseryltyrosylglycylarginylglyc
yltyrosylthreonyltyrosylleucylleucylserylarginylalanylglycylvalylthreo
nylglycylalanylglutamylasparaginylarginylalanylalanylleucylprolylleuc
ylasparaginylhistidylleucylvalylalanyllysylleucyllysylglutamyltyrosylas
paraginylalanylalanylprolylprolylleucylglutaminylglycylphenylalanylgl
ycylisoleucylserylalanylprolylaspartylglutaminylvalyllysylalanylalanyli
soleucylaspartylalanylglycylalanylalanylglycylalanylisoleucylserylglyc
ylserylalanylisoleucylvalyllysylisoleucylisoleucylglutamylglutaminylhi
stidylasparaginylisoleucylglutamylprolylglutamyllysylmethionylleucyl
alanylalanylleucyllysylvalylphenylalanylvalylglutaminylprolylmethiony
llysylalanylalanylthreonylarginylacetylseryltyrosylserylisoleucylthreo
nylserylprolylserylglutaminylphenylalanylvalylphenylalanylleucylseryl
serylvalyltryptophylalanylaspartylprolylisoleucylglutamylleucylleucyla
sparaginylvalylcysteinylthreonylserylserylleucylglycylasparaginylglut
aminylphenylalanylglutaminylthreonylglutaminylglutaminylalanylargin
ylthreonylthreonylglutaminylvalylglutaminylglutaminylphenylalanylse
rylglutaminylvalyltryptophyllysylprolylphenylalanylprolylglutaminylse
rylthreonylvalylarginylphenylalanylprolylglycylaspartylvalyltyrosyllys
ylvalyltyrosylarginyltyrosylasparaginylalanylvalylleucylaspartylprolyll
eucylisoleucylthreonylalanylleucylleucylglycylthreonylphenylalanylasp
artylthreonylarginylasparaginylarginylisoleucylisoleucylglutamylvalyl
glutamylasparaginylglutaminylglutaminylserylprolylthreonylthreonylal
anylglutamylthreonylleucylaspartylalanylthreonylarginylarginylvalylas
partylaspartylalanylthreonylvalylalanylisoleucylarginylserylalanylaspa
raginylisoleucylasparaginylleucylvalylasparaginylglutamylleucylvalyla
rginylglycylthreonylglycylleucyltyrosylasparaginylglutaminylasparagin
ylthreonylphenylalanylglutamylserylmethionylserylglycylleucylvalyltr
yptophylthreonylserylalanylprolylalanyltitinmethionylglutaminylarginy
ltyrosylglutamylserylleucylphenylalanylalanylisoleucylcysteinylprolylp
rolylaspartylalanylaspartylaspartylaspartylleucylleucylarginylglutamin
ylisoleucylalanylseryltyrosylglycylarginylglycyltyrosylthreonyltyrosyll
eucylleucylserylarginylalanylglycylvalylthreonylglycylalanylglutamyla
sparaginylarginylalanylalanylleucylprolylleucylasparaginylhistidylleuc
ylvalylalanyllysylleucyllysylglutamyltyrosylasparaginylalanylalanylpro
lylprolylleucylglutaminylglycylphenylalanylglycylisoleucylserylalanylp
rolylaspartylglutaminylvalyllysylalanylalanylisoleucylaspartylalanylgl
ycylalanylalanylglycylalanylisoleucylserylglycylserylalanylisoleucylval
yllysylisoleucylisoleucylglutamylglutaminylhistidylasparaginylisoleucy

lglutamylprolylglutamyllysylmethionylleucylalanylalanylleucyllysylval
ylphenylalanylvalylglutaminylprolylmethionyllysylalanylalanylthreonyl
arginylacetylseryltyrosylserylisoleucylthreonylserylprolylserylglutami
nylphenylalanylvalylphenylalanylleucylserylserylvalyltryptophylalanyl
aspartylprolylisoleucylglutamylleucylleucylasparaginylvalylcysteinylth
reonylserylserylleucylglycylasparaginylglutaminylphenylalanylglutami
nylthreonylglutaminylglutaminylalanylarginylthreonylthreonylglutami
nylvalylglutaminylglutaminylphenylalanylserylglutaminylvalyltryptoph
yllysylprolylphenylalanylprolylglutaminylserylthreonylvalylarginylphe
nylalanylprolylglycylaspartylvalyltyrosyllysylvalyltyrosylarginyltyrosy
lasparaginylalanylvalylleucylaspartylprolylleucylisoleucylthreonylalan
ylleucylleucylglycylthreonylphenylalanylaspartylthreonylarginylaspara
ginylarginylisoleucylisoleucylglutamylvalylglutamylasparaginylglutam
inylglutaminylserylprolylthreonylthreonylalanylglutamylthreonylleucyl
aspartylalanylthreonylarginylarginylvalylaspartylaspartylalanylthreon
ylvalylalanylisoleucylarginylserylalanylasparaginylisoleucylasparagin
ylleucylvalylasparaginylglutamylleucylvalylarginylglycylthreonylglycyl
leucyltyrosylasparaginylglutaminylasparaginylthreonylphenylalanylglu
tamylserylmethionylserylglycylleucylvalyltryptophylthreonylserylalan
ylprolylalanyltitinmethionylglutaminylarginyltyrosylglutamylserylleuc
ylphenylalanylalanylisoleucylcysteinylprolylprolylaspartylalanylaspart
ylaspartylaspartylleucylleucylarginylglutaminylisoleucylalanylseryltyr
osylglycylarginylglycyltyrosylthreonyltyrosylleucylleucylserylarginylal
anylglycylvalylthreonylglycylalanylglutamylasparaginylarginylalanylal
anylleucylprolylleucylasparaginylhistidylleucylvalylalanyllysylleucylly
sylglutamyltyrosylasparaginylalanylalanylprolylprolylleucylglutaminyl
glycylphenylalanylglycylisoleucylserylalanylprolylaspartylglutaminylv
alyllysylalanylalanylisoleucylaspartylalanylglycylalanylalanylglycylala
nylisoleucylserylglycylserylalanylisoleucylvalyllysylisoleucylisoleucylg
lutamylglutaminylhistidylasparaginylisoleucylglutamylprolylglutamyll
ysylmethionylleucylalanylalanylleucyllysylvalylphenylalanylvalylgluta
minylprolylmethionyllysylalanylalanylthreonylarginylacetylseryltyrosy
lserylisoleucylthreonylserylprolylserylglutaminylphenylalanylvalylphe
nylalanylleucylserylserylvalyltryptophylalanylaspartylprolylisoleucylgl
utamylleucylleucylasparaginylvalylcysteinylthreonylserylserylleucylgl
ycylasparaginylglutaminylphenylalanylglutaminylthreonylglutaminylgl
utaminylalanylarginylthreonylthreonylglutaminylvalylglutaminylgluta
minylphenylalanylserylglutaminylvalyltryptophyllysylprolylphenylalan
ylprolylglutaminylserylthreonylvalylarginylphenylalanylprolylglycylas
partylvalyltyrosyllysylvalyltyrosylarginyltyrosylasparaginylalanylvalyl

leucylaspartylprolylleucylisoleucylthreonylalanylleucylleucylglycylthre
onylphenylalanylaspartylthreonylarginylasparaginylarginylisoleucyliso
leucylglutamylvalylglutamylasparaginylglutaminylglutaminylserylprol
ylthreonylthreonylalanylglutamylthreonylleucylaspartylalanylthreonyl
arginylarginylvalylaspartylaspartylalanylthreonylvalylalanylisoleucyla
rginylserylalanylasparaginylisoleucylasparaginylleucylvalylasparaginy
lglutamylleucylvalylarginylglycylthreonylglycylleucyltyrosylasparagin
ylglutaminylasparaginylthreonylphenylalanylglutamylserylmethionyls
erylglycylleucylvalyltryptophylthreonylserylalanylprolylalanyltitinmet
hionylglutaminylarginyltyrosylglutamylserylleucylphenylalanylalanyl
methionylthreonylthreonylglutaminylarginyltyrosylglutamylserylleucyl
phenylalanylalanylglutaminylleucyllysylglutamylarginyllysylglutamylg
lycylalanylphenylalanylvalylprolylphenylalanylvalylthreonylleucylglyc
ylaspartylprolylglycylisoleucylglutamylglutaminylserylleucyllysylisole
ucylaspartylthreonylleucylisoleucylglutamylalanylglycylalanylaspartyl
alanylleucylglutamylleucylglycylisoleucylprolylphenylalanylserylaspar
tylprolylleucylalanylaspartylglycylprolylthreonylisoleucylglutaminylas
paraginylalanylthreonylleucylarginylalanylphenylalanylalanylalanylgly
cylvalylthreonylprolylalanylglutaminylcysteinylphenylalanylglutamylm
ethionylleucylalanylleucylisoleucylarginylglutaminyllysylhistidylprolylt
hreonylisoleucylprolylisoleucylglycylleucylleucylmethionyltyrosylalan
ylasparaginylleucylvalylphenylalanylasparaginyllysylglycylisoleucylas
partylglutamylphenylalanyltyrosylalanylglutaminylcysteinylglutamylly
sylvalylglycylvalylaspartylserylvalylleucylvalylalanylaspartylvalylprol
ylvalylglutaminylglutamylserylalanylprolylphenylalanylarginylglutami
nylalanylalanylleucylarginylhistidylasparaginylvalylalanylprolylisoleuc
ylphenylalanylisoleucylcysteinylprolylprolylaspartylalanylaspartylaspa
rtylaspartylleucylleucylarginylglutaminylisoleucylalanylseryltyrosylgly
cylarginylglycyltyrosylthreonyltyrosylleucylleucylserylarginylalanylgly
cylvalylthreonylglycylalanylglutamylasparaginylarginylalanylalanylleu
cylprolylleucylasparaginylhistidylleucylvalylalanyllysylleucyllysylgluta
myltyrosylasparaginylalanylalanylprolylprolylleucylglutaminylglycylph
enylalanylglycylisoleucylserylalanylprolylaspartylglutaminylvalyllysyl
alanylalanylisoleucylaspartylalanylglycylalanylalanylglycylalanylisole
ucylserylglycylserylalanylisoleucylvalyllysylisoleucylisoleucylglutamyl
glutaminylhistidylasparaginylisoleucylglutamylprolylglutamyllysylmet
hionylleucylalanylalanylleucyllysylvalylphenylalanylvalylglutaminylpr
olylmethionyllysylalanylalanylthreonylarginylacetylseryltyrosylserylis
oleucylthreonylserylprolylserylglutaminylphenylalanylvalylphenylalan
ylleucylserylserylvalyltryptophylalanylaspartylprolylisoleucylglutamyl

leucylleucylasparaginylvalylcysteinylthreonylserylserylleucylglycylasp
araginylglutaminylphenylalanylglutaminylthreonylglutaminylglutamin
ylalanylarginylthreonylthreonylglutaminylvalylglutaminylglutaminylph
enylalanylserylglutaminylvalyltryptophyllysylprolylphenylalanylprolyl
glutaminylserylthreonylvalylarginylphenylalanylprolylglycylaspartylva
lyltyrosyllysylvalyltyrosylarginyltyrosylasparaginylalanylvalylleucylas
partylprolylleucylisoleucylthreonylalanylleucylleucylglycylthreonylphe
nylalanylaspartylthreonylarginylasparaginylarginylisoleucylisoleucylgl
utamylvalylglutamylasparaginylglutaminylglutaminylserylprolylthreon
ylthreonylalanylglutamylthreonylleucylaspartylalanylthreonylarginylar
ginylvalylaspartylaspartylalanylthreonylvalylalanylisoleucylarginylser
ylalanylasparaginylisoleucylasparaginylleucylvalylasparaginylglutamy
lleucylvalylarginylglycylthreonylglycylleucyltyrosylasparaginylglutami
nylasparaginylthreonylphenylalanylglutamylserylmethionylserylglycyl
leucylvalyltryptophylthreonylserylalanylprolylalanyltitinmethionylglut
aminylarginyltyrosylglutamylserylleucylphenylalanylalanylisoleucylcy
steinylprolylprolylaspartylalanylaspartylaspartylaspartylleucylleucylar
ginylglutaminylisoleucylalanylseryltyrosylglycylarginylglycyltyrosylthr
eonyltyrosylleucylleucylserylarginylalanylglycylvalylthreonylglycylala
nylglutamylasparaginylarginylalanylalanylleucylprolylleucylasparagin
ylhistidylleucylvalylalanyllysylleucyllysylglutamyltyrosylasparaginylal
anylalanylprolylprolylleucylglutaminylglycylphenylalanylglycylisoleuc
ylserylalanylprolylaspartylglutaminylvalyllysylalanylalanylisoleucylas
partylalanylglycylalanylalanylglycylalanylisoleucylserylglycylserylalan
ylisoleucylvalyllysylisoleucylisoleucylglutamylglutaminylhistidylaspar
aginylisoleucylglutamylproylglutamyllysylmethionylleucylalanylalanyll
eucyllysylvalylphenylalanylvalylglutaminylprolylmethionyllysylalanyla
lanylthreonylarginylacetylseryltyrosylserylisoleucylthreonylserylproly
lserylglutaminylphenylalanylvalylphenylalanylleucylserylserylvalyltry
ptophylalanylaspartylprolylisoleucylglutamylleucylleucylasparaginylva
lylcysteinylthreonylserylserylleucylglycylasparaginylglutaminylphenyl
alanylglutaminylthreonylglutaminylglutaminylalanylarginylthreonylthr
eonylglutaminylvalylglutaminylglutaminylphenylalanylserylglutaminyl
valyltryptophyllysylprolylphenylalanylprolylglutaminylserylthreonylva
lylarginylphenylalanylprolylglycylaspartylvalyltyrosyllysylvalyltyrosyl
arginyltyrosylasparaginylalanylvalylleucylaspartylprolylleucylisoleucy
lthreonylalanylleucylleucylglycylthreonylphenylalanylaspartylthreonyl
arginylasparaginylarginylisoleucylisoleucylglutamylvalylglutamylaspa
raginylglutaminylglutaminylserylprolylthreonylthreonylalanylglutamyl
threonylleucylaspartylalanylthreonylarginylarginylvalylaspartylaspart

ylalanylthreonylvalylalanylisoleucylarginylserylalanylasparaginylisole
ucylasparaginylleucylvalylasparaginylglutamylleucylvalylarginylglycyl
threonylglycylleucyltyrosylasparaginylglutaminylasparaginylthreonylp
henylalanylglutamylserylmethionylserylglycylleucylvalyltryptophylthr
eonylserylalanylprolylalanyltitinmethionylglutaminylarginyltyrosylglut
amylserylleucylphenylalanylalanylisoleucylcysteinylprolylprolylaspart
ylalanylaspartylaspartylaspartylleucylleucylarginylglutaminylisoleucyl
alanylseryltyrosylglycylarginylglycyltyrosylthreonyltyrosylleucylleucyl
serylarginylalanylglycylvalylthreonylglycylalanylglutamylasparaginyla
rginylalanylalanylleucylprolylleucylasparaginylhistidylleucylvalylalany
llysylleucyllysylglutamyltyrosylasparaginylalanylalanylprolylprolylleu
cylglutaminylglycylphenylalanylglycylisoleucylserylalanylprolylaspart
ylglutaminylvalyllysylalanylalanylisoleucylaspartylalanylglycylalanylal
anylglycylalanylisoleucylserylglycylserylalanylisoleucylvalyllysylisole
ucylisoleucylglutamylglutaminylhistidylasparaginylisoleucylglutamylpr
olylglutamyllysylmethionylleucylalanylalanylleucyllysylvalylphenylala
nylvalylglutaminylprolylmethionyllysylalanylalanylthreonylarginylacet
ylseryltyrosylserylisoleucylthreonylserylprolylserylglutaminylphenylal
anylvalylphenylalanylleucylserylserylvalyltryptophylalanylaspartylpro
lylisoleucylglutamylleucylleucylasparaginylvalylcysteinylthreonylseryl
serylleucylglycylasparaginylglutaminylphenylalanylglutaminylthreonyl
glutaminylglutaminylalanylarginylthreonylthreonylglutaminylvalylglut
aminylglutaminylphenylalanylserylglutaminylvalyltryptophyllysylproly
lphenylalanylprolylglutaminylserylthreonylvalylarginylphenylalanylpro
lylglycylaspartylvalyltyrosyllysylvalyltyrosylarginyltyrosylasparaginyl
alanylvalylleucylaspartylprolylleucylisoleucylthreonylalanylleucylleuc
ylglycylthreonylphenylalanylaspartylthreonylarginylasparaginylarginyl
isoleucylisoleucylglutamylvalylglutamylasparaginylglutaminylglutami
nylserylprolylthreonylthreonylalanylglutamylthreonylleucylaspartylala
nylthreonylarginylarginylvalylaspartylaspartylalanylthreonylvalylalan
ylisoleucylarginylserylalanylasparaginylisoleucylasparaginylleucylvaly
lasparaginylglutamylleucylvalylarginylglycylthreonylglycylleucyltyros
ylasparaginylglutaminylasparaginylthreonylphenylalanylglutamylseryl
methionylserylglycylleucylvalyltryptophylthreonylserylalanylprolylala
nyltitinmethionylglutaminylarginyltyrosylglutamylserylleucylphenylala
nylalanylisoleucylcysteinylprolylprolylaspartylalanylaspartylaspartyla
spartylleucylleucylarginylglutaminylisoleucylalanylseryltyrosylglycyla
rginylglycyltyrosylthreonyltyrosylleucylleucylserylarginylalanylglycylv
alylthreonylglycylalanylglutamylasparaginylarginylalanylalanylleucylp
rolylleucylasparaginylhistidylleucylvalylalanyllysylleucyllysylglutamyl

tyrosylasparaginylalanylalanylprolylprolylleucylglutaminylglycylpheny
lalanylglycylisoleucylserylalanylprolylaspartylglutaminylvalyllysylalan
ylalanylisoleucylaspartylalanylglycylalanylalanylglycylalanylisoleucyls
erylglycylserylalanylisoleucylvalyllysylisoleucylisoleucylglutamylgluta
minylhistidylasparaginylisoleucylglutamylprolylglutamyllysylmethiony
lleucylalanylalanylleucyllysylvalylphenylalanylvalylglutaminylprolylm
ethionyllysylalanylalanylthreonylarginylacetylseryltyrosylserylisoleuc
ylthreonylserylprolylserylglutaminylphenylalanylvalylphenylalanylleuc
ylserylserylvalyltryptophylalanylaspartylprolylisoleucylglutamylleucyl
leucylasparaginylvalylcysteinylthreonylserylserylleucylglycylasparagi
nylglutaminylphenylalanylglutaminylthreonylglutaminylglutaminylalan
ylarginylthreonylthreonylglutaminylvalylglutaminylglutaminylphenylal
anylserylglutaminylvalyltryptophyllysylprolylphenylalanylprolylglutam
inylserylthreonylvalylarginylphenylalanylprolylglycylaspartylvalyltyro
syllysylvalyltyrosylarginyltyrosylasparaginylalanylvalylleucylaspartyl
prolylleucylisoleucylthreonylalanylleucylleucylglycylthreonylphenylala
nylaspartylthreonylarginylasparaginylarginylisoleucylisoleucylglutamy
lvalylglutamylasparaginylglutaminylglutaminylserylprolylthreonylthre
onylalanylglutamylthreonylleucylaspartylalanylthreonylarginylarginyl
valylaspartylaspartylalanylthreonylvalylalanylisoleucylarginylserylala
nylasparaginylisoleucylasparaginylleucylvalylasparaginylglutamylleuc
ylvalylarginylglycylthreonylglycylleucyltyrosylasparaginylglutaminyla
sparaginylthreonylphenylalanylglutamylserylmethionylserylglycylleuc
ylvalyltryptophylthreonylserylalanylprolylalanyltitinmethionylglutamin
ylarginyltyrosylglutamylserylleucylphenylalanylalanylmethionylthreon
ylthreonylglutaminylarginyltyrosylglutamylserylleucylphenylalanylala
nylglutaminylleucyllysylglutamylarginyllysylglutamylglycylalanylphen
ylalanylvalylprolylphenylalanylvalylthreonylleucylglycylaspartylprolyl
glycylisoleucylglutamylglutaminylserylleucyllysylisoleucylaspartylthre
onylleucylisoleucylglutamylalanylglycylalanylaspartylalanylleucylgluta
mylleucylglycylisoleucylprolylphenylalanylserylaspartylprolylleucylala
nylaspartylglycylprolylthreonylisoleucylglutaminylasparaginylalanylth
reonylleucylarginylalanylphenylalanylalanylalanylglycylvalylthreonylp
rolylalanylglutaminylcysteinylphenylalanylglutamylmethionylleucylala
nylleucylisoleucylarginylglutaminyllysylhistidylprolylthreonylisoleucyl
prolylisoleucylglycylleucylleucylmethionyltyrosylalanylasparaginylleu
cylvalylphenylalanylasparaginyllysylglycylisoleucylaspartylglutamylph
enylalanyltyrosylalanylglutaminylcysteinylglutamyllysylvalylglycylval
ylaspartylserylvalylleucylvalylalanylaspartylvalylprolylvalylglutaminyl
glutamylserylalanylprolylphenylalanylarginylglutaminylalanylalanylle

ucylarginylhistidylasparaginylvalylalanylprolylisoleucylphenylalanylis
oleucylcysteinylprolylprolylaspartylalanylaspartylaspartylaspartylleuc
ylleucylarginylglutaminylisoleucylalanylseryltyrosylglycylarginylglycyl
tyrosylthreonyltyrosylleucylleucylserylarginylalanylglycylvalylthreony
lglycylalanylglutamylasparaginylarginylalanylalanylleucylprolylleucyla
sparaginylhistidylleucylvalylalanylllysylleucylllysylglutamyltyrosylaspa
raginylalanylalanylprolylprolylleucylglutaminylglycylphenylalanylglyc
ylisoleucylserylalanylprolylaspartylglutaminylvalylllysylalanylalanyliso
leucylaspartylalanylglycylalanylalanylglycylalanylisoleucylserylglycyls
erylalanylisoleucylvalylllysylisoleucylisoleucylglutamylglutaminylhistid
ylasparaginylisoleucylglutamylprolylglutamylllysylmethionylleucylalan
ylalanylleucylllysylvalylphenylalanylvalylglutaminylprolylmethionylllys
ylalanylalanylthreonylarginylacetylseryltyrosylserylisoleucylthreonyls
erylprolylserylglutaminylphenylalanylvalylphenylalanylleucylserylsery
lvalyltryptophylalanylaspartylprolylisoleucylglutamylleucylleucylaspar
aginylvalylcysteinylthreonylserylserylleucylglycylasparaginylglutamin
ylphenylalanylglutaminylthreonylglutaminylglutaminylalanylarginylthr
eonylthreonylglutaminylvalylglutaminylglutaminylphenylalanylserylgl
utaminylvalyltryptophylllysylprolylphenylalanylprolylglutaminylserylth
reonylvalylarginylphenylalanylprolylglycylaspartylvalyltyrosylllysylval
yltyrosylarginyltyrosylasparaginylalanylvalylleucylaspartylprolylleucy
lisoleucylthreonylalanylleucylleucylglycylthreonylphenylalanylaspartyl
threonylarginylasparaginylarginylisoleucylisoleucylglutamylvalylgluta
mylasparaginylglutaminylglutaminylserylprolylthreonylthreonylalanyl
glutamylthreonylleucylaspartylalanylthreonylarginylarginylvalylaspart
ylaspartylalanylthreonylvalylalanylisoleucylarginylserylalanylasparagi
nylisoleucylasparaginylleucylvalylasparaginylglutamylleucylvalylargin
ylglycylthreonylglycylleucyltyrosylasparaginylglutaminylasparaginylth
reonylphenylalanylglutamylserylmethionylserylglycylleucylvalyltrypto
phylthreonylserylalanylprolylalanyltitinmethionylglutaminylarginyltyr
osylglutamylserylleucylphenylalanylalanylisoleucylcysteinylprolylprol
ylaspartylalanylaspartylaspartylaspartylleucylleucylarginylglutaminyli
soleucylalanylseryltyrosylglycylarginylglycyltyrosylthreonyltyrosylleu
cylleucylserylarginylalanylglycylvalylthreonylglycylalanylglutamylasp
araginylarginylalanylalanylleucylprolylleucylasparaginylhistidylleucylv
alylalanylllysylleucylllysylglutamyltyrosylasparaginylalanylalanylprolyl
prolylleucylglutaminylglycylphenylalanylglycylisoleucylserylalanylprol
ylaspartylglutaminylvalylllysylalanylalanylisoleucylaspartylalanylglycy
lalanylalanylglycylalanylisoleucylserylglycylserylalanylisoleucylvalylly
sylisoleucylisoleucylglutamylglutaminylhistidylasparaginylisoleucylglu

tamylprolylglutamyllysylmethionylleucylalanylalanylleucyllysylvalylph
enylalanylvalylglutaminylprolylmethionyllysylalanylalanylthreonylargi
nylacetylseryltyrosylserylisoleucylthreonylserylprolylserylglutaminylp
henylalanylvalylphenylalanylleucylserylserylvalyltryptophylalanylaspa
rtylprolylisoleucylglutamylleucylleucylasparaginylvalylcysteinylthreon
ylserylserylleucylglycylasparaginylglutaminylphenylalanylglutaminylt
hreonylglutaminylglutaminylalanylarginylthreonylthreonylglutaminylv
alylglutaminylglutaminylphenylalanylserylglutaminylvalyltryptophylly
sylprolylphenylalanylprolylglutaminylserylthreonylvalylarginylphenyla
lanylprolylglycylaspartylvalyltyrosyllysylvalyltyrosylarginyltyrosylasp
araginylalanylvalylleucylaspartylprolylleucylisoleucylthreonylalanylle
ucylleucylglycylthreonylphenylalanylaspartylthreonylarginylasparagin
ylarginylisoleucylisoleucylglutamylvalylglutamylasparaginylglutaminy
lglutaminylserylprolylthreonylthreonylalanylglutamylthreonylleucylas
partylalanylthreonylarginylarginylvalylaspartylaspartylalanylthreonyl
valylalanylisoleucylarginylserylalanylasparaginylisoleucylasparaginyll
eucylvalylasparaginylglutamylleucylvalylarginylglycylthreonylglycylle
ucyltyrosylasparaginylglutaminylasparaginylthreonylphenylalanylglut
amylserylmethionylserylglycylleucylvalyltryptophylthreonylserylalany
lprolylalanyltitinmethionylglutaminylarginyltyrosylglutamylserylleucyl
phenylalanylalanylisoleucylcysteinylprolylprolylaspartylalanylaspartyl
aspartylaspartylleucylleucylarginylglutaminylisoleucylalanylseryltyros
ylglycylarginylglycyltyrosylthreonyltyrosylleucylleucylserylarginylalan
ylglycylvalylthreonylglycylalanylglutamylasparaginylarginylalanylalan
ylleucylprolylleucylasparaginylhistidylleucylvalylalanyllysylleucyllysyl
glutamyltyrosylasparaginylalanylalanylprolylprolylleucylglutaminylgly
cylphenylalanylglycylisoleucylserylalanylprolylaspartylglutaminylvalyl
lysylalanylalanylisoleucylaspartylalanylglycylalanylalanylglycylalanyli
soleucylserylglycylserylalanylisoleucylvalyllysylisoleucylisoleucylglut
amylglutaminylhistidylasparaginylisoleucylglutamylprolylglutamyllysy
lmethionylleucylalanylalanylleucyllysylvalylphenylalanylvalylglutamin
ylprolylmethionyllysylalanylalanylthreonylarginylacetylseryltyrosylser
ylisoleucylthreonylserylprolylserylglutaminylphenylalanylvalylphenyla
lanylleucylserylserylvalyltryptophylalanylaspartylprolylisoleucylgluta
mylleucylleucylasparaginylvalylcysteinylthreonylserylserylleucylglycy
lasparaginylglutaminylphenylalanylglutaminylthreonylglutaminylgluta
minylalanylarginylthreonylthreonylglutaminylvalylglutaminylglutamin
ylphenylalanylserylglutaminylvalyltryptophyllysylprolylphenylalanylpr
olylglutaminylserylthreonylvalylarginylphenylalanylprolylglycylaspart
ylvalyltyrosyllysylvalyltyrosylarginyltyrosylasparaginylalanylvalylleuc

ylaspartylprolylleucylisoleucylthreonylalanylleucylleucylglycylthreonyl
phenylalanylaspartylthreonylarginylasparaginylarginylisoleucylisoleuc
ylglutamylvalylglutamylasparaginylglutaminylglutaminylserylprolylthr
eonylthreonylalanylglutamylthreonylleucylaspartylalanylthreonylargin
ylarginylvalylaspartylaspartylalanylthreonylvalylalanylisoleucylarginy
lserylalanylasparaginylisoleucylasparaginylleucylvalylasparaginylglut
amylleucylvalylarginylglycylthreonylglycylleucyltyrosylasparaginylglu
taminylasparaginylthreonylphenylalanylglutamylserylmethionylserylgl
ycylleucylvalyltryptophylthreonylserylalanylprolylalanyltitinmethionyl
glutaminylarginyltyrosylglutamylserylleucylphenylalanylalanylisoleuc
ylcysteinylprolylprolylaspartylalanylaspartylaspartylaspartylleucylleu
cylarginylglutaminylisoleucylalanylseryltyrosylglycylarginylglycyltyro
sylthreonyltyrosylleucylleucylserylarginylalanylglycylvalylthreonylgly
cylalanylglutamylasparaginylarginylalanylalanylleucylprolylleucylaspa
raginylhistidylleucylvalylalanyllysylleucyllysylglutamyltyrosylasparagi
nylalanylalanylprolylprolylleucylglutaminylglycylphenylalanylglycyliso
leucylserylalanylprolylaspartylglutaminylvalyllysylalanylalanylisoleuc
ylaspartylalanylglycylalanylalanylglycylalanylisoleucylserylglycylseryl
alanylisoleucylvalyllysylisoleucylisoleucylglutamylglutaminylhistidylas
paraginylisoleucylglutamylprolylglutamyllysylmethionylleucylalanylal
anylleucyllysylvalylphenylalanylvalylglutaminylprolylmethionyllysylal
anylalanylthreonylarginylacetylseryltyrosylserylisoleucylthreonylseryl
prolylserylglutaminylphenylalanylvalylphenylalanylleucylserylserylval
yltryptophylalanylaspartylprolylisoleucylglutamylleucylleucylasparagi
nylvalylcysteinylthreonylserylserylleucylglycylasparaginylglutaminylp
henylalanylglutaminylthreonylglutaminylglutaminylalanylarginylthreo
nylthreonylglutaminylvalylglutaminylglutaminylphenylalanylserylgluta
minylvalyltryptophyllysylprolylphenylalanylprolylglutaminylserylthreo
nylvalylarginylphenylalanylprolylglycylaspartylvalyltyrosyllysylvalylty
rosylarginyltyrosylasparaginylalanylvalylleucylaspartylprolylleucylisol
eucylthreonylalanylleucylleucylglycylthreonylphenylalanylaspartylthre
onylarginylasparaginylarginylisoleucylisoleucylglutamylvalylglutamyl
asparaginylglutaminylglutaminylserylprolylthreonylthreonylalanylglut
amylthreonylleucylaspartylalanylthreonylarginylarginylvalylaspartyla
spartylalanylthreonylvalylalanylisoleucylarginylserylalanylasparaginyl
isoleucylasparaginylleucylvalylasparaginylglutamylleucylvalylarginylg
lycylthreonylglycylleucyltyrosylasparaginylglutaminylasparaginylthre
onylphenylalanylglutamylserylmethionylserylglycylleucylvalyltryptoph
ylthreonylserylalanylprolylalanyltitinmethionylglutaminylarginyltyrosy
lglutamylserylleucylphenylalanylalanylmethionylthreonylthreonylgluta

minylarginyltyrosylglutamylserylleucylphenylalanylalanylglutaminylle
ucyllysylglutamylarginyllysylglutamylglycylalanylphenylalanylvalylpro
lylphenylalanylvalylthreonylleucylglycylaspartylprolylglycylisoleucylgl
utamylglutaminylserylleucyllysylisoleucylaspartylthreonylleucylisoleu
cylglutamylalanylglycylalanylaspartylalanylleucylglutamylleucylglycyl
isoleucylprolylphenylalanylserylaspartylprolylleucylalanylaspartylglyc
ylprolylthreonylisoleucylglutaminylasparaginylalanylthreonylleucylarg
inylalanylphenylalanylalanylalanylglycylvalylthreonylprolylalanylgluta
minylcysteinylphenylalanylglutamylmethionylleucylalanylleucylisoleuc
ylarginylglutaminyllysylhistidylprolylthreonylisoleucylprolylisoleucylgl
ycylleucylleucylmethionyltyrosylalanylasparaginylleucylvalylphenylal
anylasparaginyllysylglycylisoleucylaspartylglutamylphenylalanyltyros
ylalanylglutaminylcysteinylglutamyllysylvalylglycylvalylaspartylserylv
alylleucylvalylalanylaspartylvalylprolylvalylglutaminylglutamylserylal
anylprolylphenylalanylarginylglutaminylalanylalanylleucylarginylhistid
ylasparaginylvalylalanylprolylisoleucylphenylalanylisoleucylcysteinylp
rolylprolylaspartylalanylaspartylaspartylaspartylleucylleucylarginylglu
taminylisoleucylalanylseryltyrosylglycylarginylglycyltyrosylthreonylty
rosylleucylleucylserylarginylalanylglycylvalylthreonylglycylalanylgluta
mylasparaginylarginylalanylalanylleucylprolylleucylasparaginylhistidy
lleucylvalylalanyllysylleucyllysylglutamyltyrosylasparaginylalanylalan
ylprolylprolylleucylglutaminylglycylphenylalanylglycylisoleucylserylal
anylprolylaspartylglutaminylvalyllysylalanylalanylisoleucylaspartylala
nylglycylalanylalanylglycylalanylisoleucylserylglycylserylalanylisoleuc
ylvalyllysylisoleucylisoleucylglutamylglutaminylhistidylasparaginylisol
eucylglutamylprolylglutamyllysylmethionylleucylalanylalanylleucyllys
ylvalylphenylalanylvalylglutaminylprolylmethionyllysylalanylalanylthr
eonylarginylacetylseryltyrosylserylisoleucylthreonylserylprolylserylgl
utaminylphenylalanylvalylphenylalanylleucylserylserylvalyltryptophyl
alanylaspartylprolylisoleucylglutamylleucylleucylasparaginylvalylcyst
einylthreonylserylserylleucylglycylasparaginylglutaminylphenylalanyl
glutaminylthreonylglutaminylglutaminylalanylarginylthreonylthreonyl
glutaminylvalylglutaminylglutaminylphenylalanylserylglutaminylvalylt
ryptophyllysylprolylphenylalanylprolylglutaminylserylthreonylvalylarg
inylphenylalanylprolylglycylaspartylvalyltyrosyllysylvalyltyrosylarginy
ltyrosylasparaginylalanylvalylleucylaspartylprolylleucylisoleucylthreo
nylalanylleucylleucylglycylthreonylphenylalanylaspartylthreonylarginy
lasparaginylarginylisoleucylisoleucylglutamylvalylglutamylasparaginyl
glutaminylglutaminylserylprolylthreonylthreonylalanylglutamylthreon
ylleucylaspartylalanylthreonylarginylarginylvalylaspartylaspartylalany

lthreonylvalylalanylisoleucylarginylserylalanylasparaginylisoleucylasp
araginylleucylvalylasparaginylglutamylleucylvalylarginylglycylthreony
lglycylleucyltyrosylasparaginylglutaminylasparaginylthreonylphenylal
anylglutamylserylmethionylserylglycylleucylvalyltryptophylthreonylse
rylalanylprolylalanyltitinmethionylglutaminylarginyltyrosylglutamylse
rylleucylphenylalanylalanylisoleucylcysteinylprolylprolylaspartylalanyl
aspartylaspartylaspartylleucylleucylarginylglutaminylisoleucylalanyls
eryltyrosylglycylarginylglycyltyrosylthreonyltyrosylleucylleucylserylar
ginylalanylglycylvalylthreonylglycylalanylglutamylasparaginylarginyla
lanylalanylleucylprolylleucylasparaginylhistidylleucylvalylalanyllysylle
ucyllysylglutamyltyrosylasparaginylalanylalanylprolylprolylleucylgluta
minylglycylphenylalanylglycylisoleucylserylalanylprolylaspartylglutam
inylvalyllysylalanylalanylisoleucylaspartylalanylglycylalanylalanylglyc
ylalanylisoleucylserylglycylserylalanylisoleucylvalyllysylisoleucylisole
ucylglutamylglutaminylhistidylasparaginylisoleucylglutamylprolylgluta
myllysylmethionylleucylalanylalanylleucyllysylvalylphenylalanylvalylg
lutaminylprolylmethionyllysylalanylalanylthreonylarginylacetylserylty
rosylserylisoleucylthreonylserylprolylserylglutaminylphenylalanylvaly
lphenylalanylleucylserylserylvalyltryptophylalanylaspartylprolylisoleu
cylglutamylleucylleucylasparaginylvalylcysteinylthreonylserylserylleu
cylglycylasparaginylglutaminylphenylalanylglutaminylthreonylglutami
nylglutaminylalanylarginylthreonylthreonylglutaminylvalylglutaminylg
lutaminylphenylalanylserylglutaminylvalyltryptophyllysylprolylphenyl
alanylprolylglutaminylserylthreonylvalylarginylphenylalanylprolylglyc
ylaspartylvalyltyrosyllysylvalyltyrosylarginyltyrosylasparaginylalanyl
valylleucylaspartylprolylleucylisoleucylthreonylalanylleucylleucylglycy
lthreonylphenylalanylaspartylthreonylarginylasparaginylarginylisoleuc
ylisoleucylglutamylvalylglutamylasparaginylglutaminylglutaminylseryl
prolylthreonylthreonylalanylglutamylthreonylleucylaspartylalanylthre
onylarginylarginylvalylaspartylaspartylalanylthreonylvalylalanylisoleu
cylarginylserylalanylasparaginylisoleucylasparaginylleucylvalylaspara
ginylglutamylleucylvalylarginylglycylthreonylglycylleucyltyrosylaspar
aginylglutaminylasparaginylthreonylphenylalanylglutamylserylmethio
nylserylglycylleucylvalyltryptophylthreonylserylalanylprolylalanyltitin
methionylglutaminylarginyltyrosylglutamylserylleucylphenylalanylala
nylisoleucylcysteinylprolylprolylaspartylalanylaspartylaspartylasparty
lleucylleucylarginylglutaminylisoleucylalanylseryltyrosylglycylarginylg
lycyltyrosylthreonyltyrosylleucylleucylserylarginylalanylglycylvalylthr
eonylglycylalanylglutamylasparaginylarginylalanylalanylleucylprolylle
ucylasparaginylhistidylleucylvalylalanyllysylleucyllysylglutamyltyrosyl

asparaginylalanylalanylprolylprolylleucylglutaminylglycylphenylalanyl
glycylisoleucylserylalanylprolylaspartylglutaminylvalyllysylalanylalan
ylisoleucylaspartylalanylglycylalanylalanylglycylalanylisoleucylserylgl
ycylserylalanylisoleucylvalyllysylisoleucylisoleucylglutamylglutaminyl
histidylasparaginylisoleucylglutamylprolylglutamyllysylmethionylleuc
ylalanylalanylleucyllysylvalylphenylalanylvalylglutaminylprolylmethio
nyllysylalanylalanylthreonylarginylacetylseryltyrosylserylisoleucylthr
eonylserylprolylserylglutaminylphenylalanylvalylphenylalanylleucylse
rylserylvalyltryptophylalanylaspartylprolylisoleucylglutamylleucylleuc
ylasparaginylvalylcysteinylthreonylserylserylleucylglycylasparaginylgl
utaminylphenylalanylglutaminylthreonylglutaminylglutaminylalanylar
ginylthreonylthreonylglutaminylvalylglutaminylglutaminylphenylalanyl
serylglutaminylvalyltryptophyllysylprolylphenylalanylprolylglutaminyl
serylthreonylvalylarginylphenylalanylprolylglycylaspartylvalyltyrosyll
ysylvalyltyrosylarginyltyrosylasparaginylalanylvalylleucylaspartylprol
ylleucylisoleucylthreonylalanylleucylleucylglycylthreonylphenylalanyla
spartylthreonylarginylasparaginylarginylisoleucylisoleucylglutamylval
ylglutamylasparaginylglutaminylglutaminylserylprolylthreonylthreonyl
alanylglutamylthreonylleucylaspartylalanylthreonylarginylarginylvalyl
aspartylaspartylalanylthreonylvalylalanylisoleucylarginylserylalanylas
paraginylisoleucylasparaginylleucylvalylasparaginylglutamylleucylval
ylarginylglycylthreonylglycylleucyltyrosylasparaginylglutaminylaspara
ginylthreonylphenylalanylglutamylserylmethionylserylglycylleucylvaly
ltryptophylthreonylserylalanylprolylalanyltitinmethionylglutaminylargi
nyltyrosylglutamylserylleucylphenylalanylalanylisoleucylcysteinylprol
ylprolylaspartylalanylaspartylaspartylaspartylleucylleucylarginylgluta
minylisoleucylalanylseryltyrosylglycylarginylglycyltyrosylthreonyltyro
sylleucylleucylserylarginylalanylglycylvalylthreonylglycylalanylglutam
ylasparaginylarginylalanylalanylleucylprolylleucylasparaginylhistidylle
ucylvalylalanyllysylleucyllysylglutamyltyrosylasparaginylalanylalanyl
prolylprolylleucylglutaminylglycylphenylalanylglycylisoleucylserylalan
ylprolylaspartylglutaminylvalyllysylalanylalanylisoleucylaspartylalany
lglycylalanylalanylglycylalanylisoleucylserylglycylserylalanylisoleucyl
valyllysylisoleucylisoleucylglutamylglutaminylhistidylasparaginylisole
ucylglutamylprolylglutamyllysylmethionylleucylalanylalanylleucyllysyl
valylphenylalanylvalylglutaminylprolylmethionyllysylalanylalanylthreo
nylarginylacetylseryltyrosylserylisoleucylthreonylserylprolylserylgluta
minylphenylalanylvalylphenylalanylleucylserylserylvalyltryptophylala
nylaspartylprolylisoleucylglutamylleucylleucylasparaginylvalylcystein
ylthreonylserylserylleucylglycylasparaginylglutaminylphenylalanylglut

aminylthreonylglutaminylglutaminylalanylarginylthreonylthreonylglut
aminylvalylglutaminylglutaminylphenylalanylserylglutaminylvalyltrypt
ophyllysylprolylphenylalanylprolylglutaminylserylthreonylvalylarginyl
phenylalanylprolylglycylaspartylvalyltyrosyllysylvalyltyrosylarginyltyr
osylasparaginylalanylvalylleucylaspartylprolylleucylisoleucylthreonyla
lanylleucylleucylglycylthreonylphenylalanylaspartylthreonylarginylasp
araginylarginylisoleucylisoleucylglutamylvalylglutamylasparaginylglut
aminylglutaminylserylprolylthreonylthreonylalanylglutamylthreonylle
ucylaspartylalanylthreonylarginylarginylvalylaspartylaspartylalanylthr
eonylvalylalanylisoleucylarginylserylalanylasparaginylisoleucylaspara
ginylleucylvalylasparaginylglutamylleucylvalylarginylglycylthreonylgl
ycylleucyltyrosylasparaginylglutaminylasparaginylthreonylphenylalan
ylglutamylserylmethionylserylglycylleucylvalyltryptophylthreonylseryl
alanylprolylalanyltitinmethionylglutaminylarginyltyrosylglutamylseryll
eucylphenylalanylalanylprolylprolylleucylglutaminylglycylphenylalanyl
glycylisoleucylserylalanylprolylaspartylglutaminylvalyllysylalanylalan
ylisoleucylaspartylalanylglycylalanylalanylglycylalanylisoleucylserylgl
ycylserylalanylisoleucylvalyllysylisoleucylisoleucylglutamylglutaminyl
histidylasparaginylisoleucylglutamylprolylglutamyllysylmethionylleuc
ylalanylalanylleucyllysylvalylphenylalanylvalylglutaminylprolylmethio
nyllysylalanylalanylthreonylarginylacetylseryltyrosylserylisoleucylthr
eonylserylprolylserylglutaminylphenylalanylvalylphenylalanylleucylse
rylserylvalyltryptophylalanylaspartylprolylisoleucylglutamylleucylleuc
ylasparaginylvalylcysteinylthreonylserylserylleucylglycylasparaginylgl
utaminylphenylalanylglutaminylthreonylglutaminylglutaminylalanylar
ginylthreonylthreonylglutaminylvalylglutaminylglutaminylphenylalanyl
serylglutaminylvalyltryptophyllysylprolylphenylalanylprolylglutaminyl
serylthreonylvalylarginylphenylalanylprolylglycylaspartylvalyltyrosyll
ysylvalyltyrosylarginyltyrosylasparaginylalanylvalylleucylaspartylprol
ylleucylisoleucylthreonylalanylleucylleucylglycylthreonylphenylalanyla
spartylthreonylarginylasparaginylarginylisoleucylisoleucylglutamylval
ylglutamylasparaginylglutaminylglutaminylserylprolylthreonylthreonyl
alanylglutamylthreonylleucylaspartylalanylthreonylarginylarginylvalyl
aspartylaspartylalanylthreonylvalylalanylisoleucylarginylserylalanylas
paraginylisoleucylasparaginylleucylvalylasparaginylglutamylleucylval
ylarginylglycylthreonylglycylleucyltyrosylasparaginylglutaminylaspara
ginylthreonylphenylalanylglutamylserylmethionylserylglycylleucylvaly
ltryptophylthreonylserylalanylprolylalanyltitinmethionylglutaminylargi
nyltyrosylglutamylserylleucylphenylalanylalanylprolylprolylleucylgluta
minylglycylphenylalanylglycylisoleucylserylalanylprolylaspartylglutam

inylvalyllysylalanylalanylisoleucylaspartylalanylglycylalanylalanylglyc
ylalanylisoleucylserylglycylserylalanylisoleucylvalyllysylisoleucylisole
ucylglutamylglutaminylhistidylasparaginylisoleucylglutamylprolylgluta
myllysylmethionylleucylalanylalanylleucyllysylvalylphenylalanylvalylg
lutaminylprolylmethionyllysylalanylalanylthreonylarginylacetylserylty
rosylserylisoleucylthreonylserylprolylserylglutaminylphenylalanylvaly
lphenylalanylleucylserylserylvalyltryptophylalanylaspartylprolylisoleu
cylglutamylleucylleucylasparaginylvalylcysteinylthreonylserylserylleu
cylglycylasparaginylglutaminylphenylalanylglutaminylthreonylglutami
nylglutaminylalanylarginylthreonylthreonylglutaminylvalylglutaminylg
lutaminylphenylalanylserylglutaminylvalyltryptophyllysylprolylphenyl
alanylprolylglutaminylserylthreonylvalylarginylphenylalanylprolylglyc
ylaspartylvalyltyrosyllysylvalyltyrosylarginyltyrosylasparaginylalanyl
valylleucylaspartylprolylleucylisoleucylthreonylalanylleucylleucylglycy
lthreonylphenylalanylaspartylthreonylarginylasparaginylarginylisoleuc
ylisoleucylglutamylvalylglutamylasparaginylglutaminylglutaminylseryl
glutamylasparaginylglutaminylglutaminylserylglutamylasparaginylglut
aminylglutaminylserxisoleucine.

Obviously, I've picked this as my last word b/c it's the
longest word I 'know' of. But, how do I 'know' of it?
When I 1st ran across 'the longest word in English' it was
in Mrs. Byrne's Dictionary of Unusual, Obscure, and
Preposterous Words (1974) & it was the chemical name for
tryptophan synthetase A protein that was not nearly as
long as this one (a mere 1,913 letters - according to the
dictionary). I copied that letter-for-letter for
something I wrote for a publication called Edge Wise
(1998) edited by etta cetera. Now, online, a "Sarah
McCulloch" claims that this 189,819 letter word (her
count) is the "full chemical name of the protein Titin".
Now it's unclear to me what her source for this is or
whether the source is reliable or whether the spelling is
correct or whether she's bullshitting (I give her the
benefit of the doubt that she's not). I'm not even sure
whether a highly educated chemist wd 'know', whether a
specialist re Titin wd 'know'. Who's going to proofread
this word? Not me. (Not today at least) It wd be a
shame to mispronounce my last word or to pronounce the

wrong chemical name. How wd I ever live it down?
[naturally, I also think that that ONE WORD's being longer
than the rest of this interview is fucking hilarious]

Imagine that I *cd* pronounce this word in its entirety as
my last word! That wd be quite an accomplishment - esp
for someone in the highly reduced state of functioning
that precedes death. Think of how *long* it wd take just to
pronounce the thing! People have been reported to've
continued talking briefly after being decapitated by a
guillotine. Wd I be able to say this word as my head fell
into the basket below the blade?

If I were writing a story about a person trying to trick
the grim reaper into a reprieve, it might incorporate
this. The person might ask for death to be postponed long
enuf for them to correctly say a last word of their own
choosing. Then they cd try to read the above. Given that
they'd be unlikely to succeed at this, their death cd be
indefinitely postponed. Then again, trying to pronounce
this word over & over might be such a bore that they'd
welcome death in the long run.

Titin

- tENTATIVELY, a cONVENIENCE & Ivan Panchenko - May 30 & 31, 2015

In an interview conducted with me by Alan Davies ("tENTATIVELY, aN iNTERVIEW")
& published online I state [slightly altered here]:

"I've picked this [the full version of "Titin"] as my last word b/c it's the longest word
I 'know' of. [August 23, 2014 note: [..] From June, 2013, to February, 2014 I made a
7:35:41 movie called "Titin" which features the word + footage made with my friend
Elisa that includes skydiving & a visit to the Bayernhof Museum. I'd like to screen the
movie somewhere, preferably as an installation. [..]] But, how do I 'know' of it?
When I 1st ran across 'the longest word in English' it was in Mrs. Byrne's Dictionary
of Unusual, Obscure, and Preposterous Words (1974) & it was the chemical name for
tryptophan synthetase A protein that was not nearly as long as this one (a mere 1,913
letters - according to the dictionary). I copied that letter-for-letter for something I
wrote for a publication called Edge Wise (1998) edited by etta cetera. Now, online, a
"Sarah McCulloch" claims that this 189,819 letter word (her count) is the "full
chemical name of the protein Titin". Now it's unclear to me what her source for this is
or whether the source is reliable or whether the spelling is correct or whether she's
bullshitting (I give her the benefit of the doubt that she's not). I'm not even sure
whether a highly educated chemist wd 'know', whether a specialist re Titin wd 'know'.
Who's going to proofread this word? Not me. (Not today at least) It wd be a shame to
mispronounce my last word or to pronounce the wrong chemical name. How wd I ever
live it down? [naturally, I also think that that ONE WORD's being longer than the rest
of this interview is fucking hilarious]"

"Imagine that I cd pronounce this word in its entirety as my last word! That wd be
quite an accomplishment - esp for someone in the highly reduced state of functioning
that precedes death. Think of how long it wd take just to pronounce the thing! People
have been reported to've continued talking briefly after being decapitated by a
guillotine. Wd I be able to say this word as my head fell into the basket below the
blade?"

I did eventually proof-read the word, decided that there were 5 errors in McCulloch's
posting of it, that it's actually 189,824 letters long, & posted my corrections to her
blog - as well as making various versions of the word to be used in my "Titin" movie.
For me, that was the end of that. Lo & Behold! I was then surprised, on May 25 & 26,
2015, to receive an email from "Ivan Panchenko", someone that, as far as I recall, I
wasn't previously in correspondence with, in which he corrected McCulloch's version at
 a much deeper level. He claimed that 3 of my corrections were mistakes (I'll
provisionally take his apparently meticulous word for it - I'm not about to scrutinize
my process any further at this late date). An edited version of his correspondence
follows:

May 25, 2015 2:16:57 PM EDT

I saw that you proofread the 189,819-letter name of titin and wanted to point out that the flaw in it is actually much bigger. As you may know, the name states a peptide sequence (I supply the number of occurences):

Alanine   A alanyl   3060
Arginine   R arginyl   1337
Asparagine   N asparaginyl 1219
Aspartic acid D aspartyl   1215
Cysteine   C cysteinyl   202
Glutamine   Q glutaminyl   1738
Glutamic acid E glutamyl   1178
Glycine   G glycyl   1419
Histidine   H histidyl   202
Isoleucine   I isoleucyl   1507
Leucine   L leucyl   2348
Lysine   K lysyl   854
Methionine   M methionyl   385
Phenylalanine F phenylalanyl 1100
Proline   P prolyl   1524
Serine   S seryl   1814
Threonine   T threonyl   1788
Tryptophane   W tryptophyl   245
Tyrosine   Y tyrosyl   870
Valine   V valyl   1933

The names for the acyl groups are derived by replacing the suffix "-ine" or "-ane" by "-yl" with the exception of "asparaginyl-" for asparagine (because of the aspartic acid "aspartyl-"), "glutaminyl-" for glutamine (because of the glutamic acid "glutamyl-") and "cysteinyl-" for cysteine (because of the cysteic acid). This is according to 3AA-9.3. (IUPAC): http://www.chem.qmul.ac.uk/iupac/AminoAcid/AA610.html#AA93

However, Sarah's name contains some parts that should not be there. I will abbreviate them with:

Xac acetyl 82
Xet ethionyl 1
Xse serx   1
Xti titin   81

You correctly identified "ethionyl" and "serx", while I could not find "asparty" without an "l" at the end, "alyl" without a "v" at the beginning and "hreonyl" without a "t" at the beginning. Ethionine is a nonproteinogenic amino acid, so one can assume that it is a typo and should be "methionyl". But there are two more flaws: Acetic acid is not an amino acid at all, and "titin" is a self-reference, referring to the whole protein supposedly named by this word. Is it just an accidental error (if it is, how did it come about?) or deliberate nonsense? Correcting the typos and letting

p = PPLQGFGISAPDQVKAAIDAGAAGAISGSAIVKIIEQHNIEPEKMLAALKVFVQPMKAATRX acSYSITSPSQFVFLSSVWADPIELLNVCTSSLGNQFQTQQARTTQVQQFSQVWKPFPQSTVRFP GDVYKVYRYNAVLDPLITALLGTFDTRNRIIEVENQQSPTTAETLDATRRVDDATVAIRSANINLV NELVRGTGLYNQNTFESMSGLVWTSAPAXtiMQRYESLFA i = ICPPDADDDLLRQIASYGRGYTYLLSRAGVTGAENRAALPLNHLVAKLKEYNAA

m = MTTQRYESLFAQLKERKEGAFVPFVTLGDPGIEQSLKIDTLIEAGADALELGIPFSDPLADGP
TIQNATLRAFAAGVTPAQCFEMLALIRQKHPTIPIGLLMYANLVFNKGIDEFYAQCEKVGVDSVLV
ADVPVQESAPFRQAALRHNVAPIF(ip)^4

the whole sequence can be compressed by: m^20, p, p.substr(0, 165), p.substr(160, 165)^2, I. One can impress their friends by memorizing just this. Some were already skeptical about "serx" and "titin": http://en.wiktionary.org/wiki/Appendix_talk:List_of_protologisms/Long_words/Titin It seems that no one has noticed the repetitive pattern, and I doubt this is real. I asked Sarah about "serx", but she did not answer, neither me nor RunasSudo who commented:

"How did you come up with this?

Given that this appears to be the only definitive version of this on the Internet, and people like tENTATIVELY, a cONVENIENCE have found errors in it, your methodology and sources would be good to know." (April 25, 2014 at 3:07 am)

Erik Leppen analyzed the letter frequency and found out there is only one x:

"So, I think this is the best "find x" type of question ever possible :D"

Sarah would recognize the mistake if it was her word and not supposed to be a myth, but only answered: "Hah, good stuff, Eric. Love your LEGO models. :)"

There actually is an accurate 189,819-letter name of titin, the name of TTN.AA in kinbase.com (just get the FASTA file and compile the name by the table above, with "-ine" instead of "-yl" at the end): http://kinase.com/web/current/kinbase/gene/5994

It seems to have appeared in Wikisource for the first time: https://wikisource.org/wiki/Methionylthreonylthreonyl...isoleucine

Because of the same letter number, I suppose that Sarah's name is based upon it; but it does not make any sense, as we have seen. The accurate name cannot be said to be the longest IUPAC name either, because there are isoforms of titin that surpass this length, and you can make up chemical names as large as you want (for instance, "ennennennennenn...ium" refers to element 99999...).

Best regards
Ivan Panchenko

May 26, 2015 4:20:26 AM EDT

My claim is that correcting the typos does not lead to a genuine name either and that it is deliberate nonsense because 1) "acetyl" and "titin" do not make sense as part of a peptide sequence, 2) there is a repetitive pattern that seems very unrealistic (with "m^20", I mean twenty times m, so the name seems to have emerged out of copy & paste), 3) the name seems to be an obfuscation of an accurate (!) 189,819-letter name that can still be found, for instance, here: https://www.englishforums.com/English/LongestWordEverDictionary/6/crrl/post.htm#310857

If you download the sequence in kinase.com and replace every "A" with "alanyl", every "R" with "arginyl" etc., and the last "yl" with "ine", you get exactly this name, so it is typo-free and does contain exactly 189,819 letters, but note that this is /not/ the name you analyzed (at sarahmcculloch.com).

[..]

I review[ed] this video: https://www.youtube.com/watch?v=NFR-ADakI-c

My result is that 1) the name in the pastebin link (in the description) is that of nesprin-1 (not identical to what the guy read), 2) the video was cut at ~ 21:35, 29:50, 43:10, 53:20, 1:05:00, 1:15:45, 1:26:25, 1:34:35, 1:46:50, 1:58:55, 2:09:20, 2:20:00, 2:30:35, 2:40:55, 2:51:25, 3:01:55, and 3:17:45, 3) he dropped "serx" and "titin", and always said "cysteyl" instead of "cysteinyl". The other deviations are "isoisoleucyl" and a skipped "iso" at 19 places. This has an impact to the number of letters (188,949, not 189,819). He recited the word in Russian, where it has 185,429 letters, but it can also be seen as English with a Russian accent.

So the whole thing is quite confused!!

There is also this statement by Guinness World Records: "The systematic name for the deoxyribonucleic acid (DNA) of the human mitochondria contains 16,569 nucleotide residues and is thus c. 207,000 letters long. It was published in key form in Nature on 9 Apr 1981."

The sequence (original as well as revised) can be found here: http://www.mitomap.org/bin/view.pl/MITOMAP/MitoSeqs

I counted it has 5,123 times adenine, 5,175 times cytosine, 2,177 times guanine and 4,094 times thymine, and was puzzled for a long time on how to transform it to a name of this length. Bonnie Taylor from message.snopes.com guessed "that would be something like "deoxyriboadenyl, deoxyriboguanyl, deoxyribocytosyl, lather, rinse, repeat … acid."", but rounded to the nearest thousand, the name would be too long, even if you use "deoxyadenosyl", "deoxycytidyl", "deoxyguanosyl" and "deoxythymidyl". If "adenyl", "cystosyl" etc. are used, the name is too short.

She later wrote: "I just realized that the sequence presented in the paper shows 16-thousand-some individual bases of single-stranded DNA. The complete genome reported for double-stranded DNA, then, would contain twice the number of bases (or 16-thousand-some base pairs), so a "name" of 207,000 "letters" could refer to the names of the individual bases themselves and not nucleosides"

http://message.snopes.com/showthread.php?t=30025

I think this is the case, while 207,000 is not the actual rounded length, but rather an estimation obtained by assuming that every of the four bases occurs with the same frequency. After all, they used the word "[is] thus [c. 207,000 letters long]".

Best regards (and sorry for bad grammar)
Ivan Panchenko

I'm probably not going to follow-up on Panchenko's analysis, thusly making myself a bad scientist, because my purpose isn't to be a scientist but to revel in the absurdity & wonderfully detailed obsessive possibilities of human cognition. Ivan Panchenko, who, for all I know, is a Relativistic Astrophysicist working sometimes out of the STERNBERG ASTRONOMICAL INSTITUTE at Moscow State University or a fictional identity ambiguously evocative of a lawyer or an athlete or, to quote Panchenko out-of-context, "somehow a pink unicorn in my fridge", really made my day.

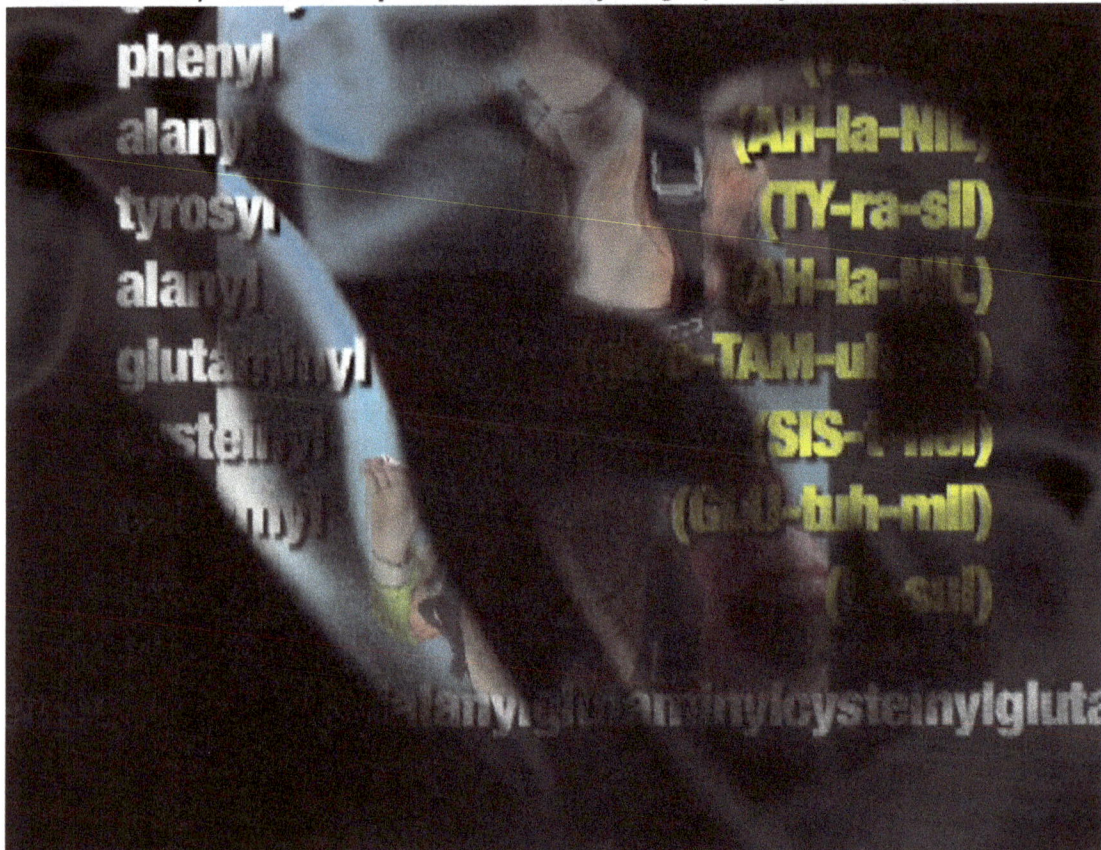

It also really made my day to find that a Google search for "Relativistic Astrophysics" did NOT yield a Wikipedia entry but instead directed me to more primary scientific sources. I was interested to learn that Alessandro Patruno provides a list of "Seven Android Apps for Relativistic Astrophysics Lovers" wch he rates & describes (descriptions not included here):

1. Black Hole Calculator (5 stars)
2. BOINC (2 stars)
3. Accretion Disk (2 star)
4. ArXiv Mobile (4 stars)
5. Space Scoop (1 star)
6. Verbosus (3 stars)
7. MERLOT OER (3 stars)

- https://apatruno.wordpress.com/2014/04/28/
seven-android-apps-for-relativistic-astrophysics-lovers/

But, then, what we're really addressing here is what wd "an-ending" to this inter

```
* * * * * * * * * * * * * * * * * * * * * * * * * * * * * * * * * * * *
```

[*footnote 1*]

review of
<u>Bombay Gin 1998</u>
by tENTATIVELY, a cONVENIENCE - August 9, 2010
http://www.goodreads.com/book/show/8817213-bombay-gin-1998

Aw, shucks! I gave this a 5 star rating mainly b/c there's something by Kenneth Patchen in it that I hadn't previously read. Strangely, there's no art, no photography, no images other than what's on the cover - the front of wch reproduces a Patchen picture poem.

There's a Terri Smith poem "Somewhere Over St. Louis *i.m. William Burroughs*" - Burroughs died the yr before. Here's the 2nd stanza:

"unmitigated muckraker, you shovel
bowel born instinct piecemeal
to page. You, cynical saint, dangle
crook'd words of cold steel"

I'm touched. There're Shijo translations from Gary Allen & his students in Korea. There's Ferlinghetti's "The Breeding Blues". There're even "Three Tourette Rhapsodies" from Jonathan Lethem! *THAT* I didn't expect. This wd've been a yr before Lethem's novel w/ a protaganist w/ Tourettes, "Motherless Brooklyn", was published. As such, these "Rhapsodies" are a sneak preview of sorts.

I found Michael Martone's "from: The Blue Guide to Indiana" esp inspired. In it he describes a theme park created by the Pharmaceuticals industry:

"THE GELATIN CAPSULE HOUSE OF HORRORS

The Gelatin Capsule you ride in proceeds to dissolve as you travel along a highly detailed and thoroughly accurate recreation of the alimentary canal. Thrills await as you cascade through the simulated mucus covered rooms, sluiced from the pharynx to the esophagus to the stomach and on to the intestines, both large and small. You race against time and the prospect of untimely elimination, hoping that you will be, through the marvels of virtual reality and computer generated animation, absorbed into *The Body's Bloodstream*, an entirely separate ride, and on your way to where you can do the most organic good."

Christopher & Jack Collom's "Driving South to Calgary" was a hoot too:

"On my way back from the Devonian,
Plate tectonic traffic made me late
So I grew winches, to pull myself up the eigenetic ridge,
It was a Carboniferous shame you didn't swallow me whole;"

Then there's Jennifer Asteris's "96 Dinosaurs in Motion *Poem based on cut up contents from Discover Magazine*:

"1800-year-old Pompeiian, frozen
to the same tune?
Pitcairn Island relics
end a region's sense
of vanished society. Today
found civilizations significantly
improve picture."

After having complained in a recent review of other Bombay Gins that they're entirely too lacking in humor, I read this issue wch's CHOCK-FULL OF IT! Susan Moon's "Woman Weds Rental Car":

"A woman poet was married to a Toyota Camry in a Catholic ceremony in New Hampshire this week. She had rented the car in an Avis agency in Boston after the unhappy end of a love affair, and planned to cheer herself up by driving to New Hampshire for the weekend to admire the fall foliage. However, she fell in love with the Toyota on the "Mass Pike.""

Have you ever sd "I love this thing!" to be then told by a friend "Well, then, why don't you marry it?!"

After substantially disliking something by Bobbie Louise Hawkins in another BG I found myself liking her "Various Voices" in wch she writes from a man's perspective w/ skill & humor. & I liked John Moulder's "Brainstorm":

"The mind must be agile and the wit sharp to write clever poems.
The intellect must be changed and the control sensitive to write published poems.
The absence of intellect must be stable and the wit tenderhearted to write public poems."

ETC! But the clincher was Patchen's "Excerpt from *In Quest of Candlelighters*. Patchen always has such an interesting flow flickering over odd turns of phrase ("We had hearts the field white white.") & borderline vernacular musings such as:

"I'd like to be God for about five minutes O wouldn't I just throw my weight around.

I guess I'd just about fix it so nobody'd ever have to be hungry again or cold

or lonely

or sitting waiting for the dirty bastards to start another war

O wouldn't I give the beautiful a workout"]

[*footnote 2*]

review of
Franklin W. Dixon's <u>The Clue in the Embers</u>
by tENTATIVELY, a cONVENIENCE - April 7, 2012
http://www.goodreads.com/book/show/13583071-the-clue-in-the-embers

In the past yr, my friend, the poet & essayist Alan Davies, conducted an email interview w/ me in wch he wrote: "I would be interested in knowing which books first struck you / as a boy / which authors — and the reading of what things might have pointed (pushed?) you in the direction of writing and the other arts." This unleashed a flood of memories about childhood reading wch led to my thinking of The Hardy Boys.

The Hardy Boys bks, a series of mysteries starring teenage brothers Frank & Joe & a supporting cast of friends, were probably staple reading for most white boys like myself from the time of their inception in 1927 'til when? I'm not sure what the answer to that is. At any rate, I probably read every one I cd get my hands on from ages 7 to 9 if not beyond. Then, of course, my tastes got more sophisticated, & I moved on w/ no desire to revisit childish things. Now, tho, I find it moderately fascinating to reread something that I wd've last read 50 yrs ago to reappraise the culture that they represented at the time.

As I replied to Alan regarding a list of bks that I'd read as a child:

"It's not too hard to find things that these bks had in common that're still meaningful to me today. The White bks anthropomorphized a mouse & a spider, etc - wch fed into my natural inclination to identify w/ non-human life. Of course, Carroll & Tolkien did much the same thing. There's science, there's myth, there's fantasy; nonsense,

struggle, freedom, hero's journeys. Twain's sense of
justice.

"Kids bks seem to be generally written by people w/ a sense
of ethics, people who want to inspire children to aspire
to leading a life of integrity pushing for just societies."

SO, it was of interest to me to read in Wikipedia's Hardy Boys entry:

"The Hardy Boys have evolved in various ways since their first appearance in 1927.
Beginning in 1959, the books were extensively revised, largely to eliminate racial
stereotypes. The books were also written in a simpler style in an attempt to compete
with television. Some critics argue that in the process the Hardy Boys changed,
becoming more respectful of the law and simultaneously more affluent, "agents of the
adult ruling class" rather than characters who aided the poor."

- http://en.wikipedia.org/wiki/The_Hardy_Boys

I think that I wd've read both the original, pre-revision versions, & the post-1959 ones.
The cover I uploaded for the edition I read wd've been from the earlier versions. This
bk read like a serial. Most, if not all, chapters end w/ a 'cliff-hanger'. I'm reminded of
the more recent Raiders of the Lost Ark movies insofar as this bk, & probably all of the
series, immediately starts off w/ something over-the-top & keeps going. This one, in
particular, is 'exotic', from the perspective of a middle-class American boy.

On the 1st page, the Hardys learn that their friend has inherited some shrunken heads.
Now this, for me, was esp vivid b/c when I was a kid rubber novelty shrunken heads
were common & I had one. When I was about 18, in 1971 or 72, I started trying to write
a somewhat Captain Beefheart inspired poem that probably had some formal
restriction on it that eventually defeated me. The subject? Shrunken heads. I
sometimes wonder what happened to that failed attempt. Most likely I destroyed it. I'm
sure I've wondered since then where I got the info about shrunken heads that I used in
it. Then I reread The Clue in the Embers where shrunken heads are explained as
follows & realized that I'd probably gotten it from there!:

"The savage Andean Indians used to take the heads of their enemies in local warfare.
After the removal of the skull from the severed head, the rest was reduced by boiling to
the size of a man's fist. The eyes and lips were pinned and laced, and the interior
treated with hot stones and sand. With the use of a local herb, the hair remained long
and kept its original luster."

Assuming such details to be at least somewhat accurate rather than purely fictional, I
like such touches in The Clue in the Embers. There're a few others. Mostly what
amuses me about them is the way the Hardy family is presented as 'normal' while the
sons are plunged into life-threatening, world-traveling adventures on a rapid-fire basis

at the same time that they go on dates & do other 'normal' kid things. Take this paragraph from page 3:

""I'll sure need some nourishment if I'm going to hassle with a lot of shrunken heads," Frank declared. "Joe, let's finish that clam chowder Mother made yesterday. It always tastes better the second day.""

Ha ha! Nothing like a little of mom's clam chowder before an inspection of a shrunken head collection! Now the character who inherits this stuff immediately gets a threatening phone call from a man named "Valez". I then wondered whether there'd be racial stereotyping of Latino guys as sinister. On page 7 it's written:

"Glancing around the platform, the boys saw no one who resembled what they thought Valez might look like. Most of the faces were familiar and the others were those of teen-agers."

Ok, what did they think Valez might look like? They didn't have much to go on since they'd only heard his voice over the phone & didn't even know if his name was a pseudonym or not. When reading, before I read the Wikipedia entry quoted above, I thought that the author avoided racial stereotypes by eliminating the people at the train stn b/c they were either familiar or were too young. 'Dixon' *didn't* write something like 'They didn't see any swarthy skulking sinister South Americans.' As such, I found the story throughout to walk a thin line between stereotypes & attempts to be sensitive & anti-racist.

The 'exotica' plunges on when the Hardys are attacked by a blowgun. I'm sure this was the type of detail that was meant to be particularly thrilling. How common was blowgun imagery in 1955? I don't know. I reckon it was plentiful. Then, by page 36, a man w/ tattoos is introduced. Tattoos definitely weren't common in my neck of the woods in 1955 so this wd've been 'exotica' from my childish perspective too. Putting him in context, he's a seaman. In the narrow-minded world I was raised in, a tattooed man wd've probably been pretty frightening to my mom. Here, he's described as having a "voice no less friendly than his handshake."

I don't know what it's like for boys growing up in the 21st century, but in my youth becoming a boy scout & learning to "be prepared" was the 'norm'. I hated the cub scouts & the boy scouts. In The Clue in the Embers, the Hardys always have a flashlight handy & have no problem repairing a broken window. What wd most kids use for lite these days? Their cellphones? & wd they be able to repair a broken window?

By page 101, Valez is suspected of being an illegal immigrant. An illegal immigrant from south of the US border? Is there a racist generalization at work here? Again, a thin line.

&, then, in the midst of action like Joe's being waylaid & trussed-up, curses, shrunken heads, blowdart arrowheads, etc, the boys go out on a date w/ the girls for a picnic & some fun at the Amusement Park. I mean, they're not under any stress or anything, right? They just take it all in stride. &, of course, the reader is being set up for something *almost* serious to happen in this idyllic picnic setting. I think of things like Leopold & Loeb, rich kids who kidnapped a boy, possibly sexually molested him, & killed him, trying to get ransom - all in an attempt to commit a 'perfect crime' - not b/c they needed the money. If James Ellroy were to rewrite a Hardy Boys story I reckon it might go somewhat more along such lines.

The previously mentioned 'curse' involved the making of a cone of ashes from mahogany - &. perhaps such a practice exists or existed. It's one of the details in the bk that I suspect came from some sort of anthropological source.

Back to the stereotyping tightrope:

"Aunt Gertrude spoke up for the first time and snapped. "Why those Indians might kill you if they found you looking for their treasure!"

"Mr. Putnam smiled tolerantly. "The Indians in Guatemala respect the white man. The boys wouldn't have any trouble with them, but I also doubt that they would receive any clues about the treasure. No, you're more likely to have trouble with an occasional band of hostile, renegade Ladinos who have fled to the mountain regions.

""Ladinos," the explorer explained, "are Spanish-speaking, mixed-breed people. They are very proud and do no manual work like laboring in the fields or carrying loads. Mainly, they own stores and cantinas in the towns and villages and hold political offices.""

Now, I sortof *cringe* when I read of people described in terms of "breeding". It makes me think of 'good breeding' (rich people) & 'ill bred' (poor people) or of mating a poodle w/ a pit-bull or something. It reeks of nazi *genetics*.

2/3rds of the way thru the bk, one of the villains, a man, is in disguise as a woman. Oh! The 1950s! Nowadays that wd *scream* of *drag queen* but, here, it's just a "disguise". Later, Tony's luggage goes missing & he moans about what he's going to do w/o his clothes.

""You'll have to dress like an Injun!" Joe laughed and folded his arms across his chest Indian style. "You heap big chief of our tribe.""

This is where it gets even more ridiculous. Maybe we have Mark Twain to thank for the use of "Injun" as an acceptable "Americanism'. After all, "Injun Joe" was a famous character of his, a *villain* - &, as much as I love Twain, his depiction of Native Americans in Roughing It (if I remember correctly) is completely racist, demeaning, insensitive, & hateful. It's not quite so bad here. Nonetheless, Tony's imitation of a indigenous person in Guatemala is immediately convincing to the natives. Not fucking likely.

""Suppose we all wander into the village," Frank proposed. "By the time we get there they'll probably have elected Tony chief of the tribe!""

In the meantime, NO, the locals aren't that stupid, thank goodness:

"Tony sobered. "This shaman business was a fake," he said. "They knew right away I wasn't an Indian."

In the meantime, they barely survive a volcano (might as well throw one of those in, right?) & a native ritual where they're trussed. Perhaps the most annoying scene for me, & the one most reflective of an uncritical attitude towards the 'white man's' imperialist 'right' to go anywhere he wants, is when the Hardys & friend Chet decided to just go into a bldg that has 2 people blocking the entrance. When they're stopped from entering they get outraged & immediately attack the guards - How dare anyone stop them from going anywhere they want to!

&, of course, they find the treasure, big surprise, & hand it over to the government w/ the blessing of the wise old 'Indian' chief whose people accumulated the treasure in the 1st place. Right, like the government's going to then distribute the wealth for the good of the people! I wonder what the rewritten version's like? Does the government come in & slaughter all the 'Indians' to take their land? That wd be more realistic.

But, of course, this is a kid's adventure tale meant to instill a sense of sensible daring in boys & not to delve into the complex miseries of human rottenness &.. yeah, I enjoyed it as such.

****

review of
'Victor Appleton II"s Tom Swift and His Flying Lab
by tENTATIVELY, a cONVENIENCE - July 16, 2012
http://www.goodreads.com/book/show/264792.Tom_Swift_and_His_Flying_Lab

This is the 3rd serialized bk targeted to boys that I've (re)read in the recent past in my project of revisiting bks I originally read probably between ages 7 & 9. This revisitation project started as a side-effect of answering an interview question posited to me by my friend the poet/essayist Alan Davies regarding what I read as a child. In answer, I mentioned the Tom Swift Jr series. Given that I read them 50 yrs or so ago, I didn't necessarily remember them vividly.

The 1st Tom Swift series (Sr, as it were), starting in 1910, was ghostwritten under the pseudonym "Victor Appleton", & this 2nd series, starting in 1954, under "Victor Appleton II". Since I was born in 1953, I think of this series as being somewhat directed at my generation of post-'WWII' baby-boomers.

I've already reviewed the Hardy Boys bk <u>The Clue in the Embers</u> (http://www.goodreads.com/book/show/13583071-the-clue-in-the-embers) & the "Rick Brant Electronic Adventure" <u>The Lost City</u> (http://www.goodreads.com/book/show/4547891-the-lost-city). In both of these reviews, I try to both explain what was inspiring & likable to me about these bks & try to analyze their subtext of popular American attitudes at the time - esp racist & imperialist ones.

Hardy Boys:

"""Ladinos," the explorer explained, "are Spanish-speaking, mixed-breed people. They are very proud and do no manual work like laboring in the fields or carrying loads. Mainly, they own stores and cantinas in the towns and villages and hold political offices.""

"Now, I sortof *cringe* when I read of people described in terms of "breeding". It makes me think of 'good breeding' (rich people) & 'ill bred' (poor people) or of mating a poodle w/ a pit-bull or something. It reeks of nazi *genetics*."

Rick Brant:

"In other words, this is formulaic writing meant to encourage 'white' boys to be resourceful in 'conquering' the world - wch is, of course, their oyster.

"This isn't really as 'bad' as my use of the word 'conquering' implies. The use of far-flung locales (in relation to the New Jersey origins of the young men) is a way of introducing parts of the world to the readers to get their imaginations 'out of the box' & into a wider world. In this story, the main villain is an impeccably dressed 'white' man from the Netherlands wearing a clean white suit - & 'our heros' fall for him as someone to be trusted b/c of this appearance. On the other hand, the most helpful character is an impoverished young Indian lad who's dirty & ragged & who speaks pigeon-English & who the protagonists make the mistake of not taking seriously. SO, there's a bit of parody of American stereotyping."

I vaguely remember liking the Hardy Boys the most & Tom Swift Jr not so much. I might've read every HB I cd get my hands on & just a few TSs from time-to-time. As I was about to (re)read this 1 I had a slight expectation that I'd like it more now b/c it's more SF than the HB bks. Instead, I disliked it considerably more than the Hardy Boys or the Rick Brant b/c the negative (for me) political subtext was even more exaggerated.

Basically, tho, the formulaicness commented on in my Brant review extends across all 3 of these serials. Some young 'white' men, probably based in the North East United States, have an extraordinary father from whom they learn extraordinary skills. They become embroiled in some activity that involves an 'exotic' locale (South America in this bk & in <u>The Clue in the Embers</u>, the Himalayas in <u>The Lost City</u>) & whatever scientific activity they're involved w/ becomes immediately sabotaged by mysterious people. Chances are they're 'rebels' or some other sort of threatening military possibility not 'validated' by a government recognized by the US.

The protagonists, like cartoon characters, spring back from their frequent injuries & death-defying predicaments w/ only minor consequences. Hence, no matter how many times they're hit on the head, they never suffer permanent brain-damage that creates personality change. No matter how many times they run from landslides or volcanos they never even sprain an ankle. If only! In the end, of course, their superhuman courage, technical know-how, & red-blooded Americanism triumphs over all those sniveling evil inferior peoples & some sort of 'advance' is made in the world at large. In other words, this is pure fantasy disguised as some sort of 'realistic' daydream for 'white' boys growing up into Future Leaders. I wonder: how many CIA agents grew up on this stuff & bought it hook, line, & sinker?

I don't mind being stimulated to fantastic daydreams, having an imagination is important. I DO mind the imperialistic dehumanizing that demonizes people in such a casual way. Ultimately, it paves the ideological road to plunder.

An organization called "Hemispak" is introduced as a key player early on:

""Hemispak! The scientific society of the Americas!" Mr. Swift cried. "The group formed to pool information and resources for the protection of the Western Hemisphere!"

Wow! Right away I'm reminded of the S.O.A. (School of the Americas) now known as WHINSEC:

"**The Western Hemisphere Institute for Security Cooperation (WHINSEC)** (formerly named **School of the Americas**) is a United States Department of Defense Institute located at Fort Benning near Columbus, Georgia in the United States. Authorized by US Congress through 10 USC 2166 in 2001, WHINSEC "Provides professional education and training to eligible personnel of nations of the Western Hemisphere within the context of the democratic principles set forth in the Charter of the Organization of American States (such charter being a treaty to which the United States is a party), while fostering mutual knowledge, transparency, confidence, and cooperation among the participating nations and promoting democratic values, respect for human rights, and knowledge and understanding of United States customs and traditions. Throughout the decade since its establishment, WHINSEC has provided training for more than 13,000 US and International students. Its educational format incorporates guest lecturers and subject matter experts from sectors of US and International government, non-government, human rights, law enforcement, academic institutions and interagency departments to share best practices in pursuit of improved security cooperation between all nations of the Western Hemisphere." - http://en.wikipedia.org/wiki/Western_Hemisphere_Institute_for_Security_Cooperation

"World War II was the "good war". After that conflict, most Americans believed that US intentions in the world were noble -- the US was the punisher of aggression and a warrior for freedom. This image was for generations of Americans the measure by which they judged their country in world affairs. The war in Vietnam ended the illusion that America was always on the "right side". Today, America's image as a defender of democracy and justice has been further eroded by the School of the Americas (SOA), which trains Latin American and Caribbean military officers and soldiers to subvert democracy and kill hope in their own countries.

"Founded by the United States in 1946, the SOA was initially located in Panama, but in 1984 it was kicked out under the terms of the Panama Canal Treaty and moved to the army base at Fort Benning, Georgia. Then-President of Panama Jorge Illueca called it "the biggest base for de-stabilization in Latin America," and a major Panamanian newspaper dubbed it " The School of Assassins."" - http://www.thirdworldtraveler.com/ Terrorism/SOA.html

Perhaps it seems far-fetched of me to bring up Tom Swift and His Flying Lab's Hemispak & the S.O.A.. Consider this, by the next page (p 21) after Hemispak's introduction, the threat of torture is given by a still-unknown enemy. Torture? In a kid's bk? As it turns out, the torture is being threatened by some 'rebels':

""my country is having trouble with a certain group of its people - the Veranos. Verano is really a splinter state, run by rebels who broke away from the mother country. They carry on continual guerrilla warfare against us." - p 32

On no more info than the word of a newly met man, the Swifts immediately accept this word w/o further explanation & accept the Veranos as their enemy. No questions are asked as to WHY the 'rebels' might rebel - such niceties don't fit into this world of simpletons.

""Will you and your father help us thwart these dangerous rebels?"

"TOM'S EYES gleamed with eagerness as he waited a moment for his father's reply to the South American's question. This could be a high adventure!

""We need the help of you Swifts and your wonderful inventions," continued Señor Ricardo as he pressed his case, "both to locate our missing scientists and to investigate the presence of uranium deposits."

""I'd like to do it!" Tom cried. "What do you think, Dad?"

"Mr. Swift, more cautious, asked whether Ricardo's government had tried to find the scientists.

""Yes, but we have not succeeded," the South American replied. "We believe if someone from a North American country came there the rebels would not - what you say - catch on."" - pp 34-35

This is so ridiculous at so many levels that it irks me to even feel compelled to explain it to any degree. ONE "North American" (read: US) family (who happen to be fabulously wealthy & powerful - but, of course, they 'deserve' it?!) will succeed where a government has failed despite being unfamiliar w/ the country they're about to intercede in. Furthermore, the rebels will be taken off-guard even tho that's already been demonstrated to be not true by the rebels having already started to try to prevent the Swift's interference. Go figger.

Another subtext of all this crap is that the Swifts & their allies are just nice ordinary folks who happen to be scientific geniuses. B/c they're American scientists anything that they do is for the good of mankind. Sure, the enemy scientists are clever too (even, perhaps, diabolically clever - as the 'bad guys' are in Michael Crichton's propagandistic State of Fear: http://www.goodreads.com/book/show/ 15860.State_of_Fear) but, you know, they're **the bad guys** & we don't even need to question their motives, do we? I mean, they're just greedy or sumpin'. Science is good, American science is even better, the world's resources belong in the hands of American scientists & their allies (read: puppets). In this case, the resource that's the crux of the matter is uranium.

""Are we going to dig tonight for that stuff what's goin' to make us all rich?" Chow asked. "I sure could use any extry wad of bills."

""That'll be Tom's next neat trick," Bud spoke up. "How to turn uranium into a bank roll in one easy lesson."" - p 146

Now, THAT, of course, isn't GREED. It's just good old American boy common sense & good humor. Really, tho, the fantasy of this bk is filled w/ get-rich-quick schemes. Tom Swift Sr & Jr can both invent the most miraculous things in very short time *and* get them built at their (not-very) well-protected HQ by their employees in record time. Atomic thrusters? Coming right up! All b/c of their natural genius combined w/ good old American know-how.

"It took the combined efforts of all four of the party to maneuver the tremendous nylon netting over the body and wings of the plane. For half an hour they sweated and strained, but at last the job was done." - p 146

"At this very moment the two men were hard at work in good-sized pits which they had laboriously hewed out of the rocky tableland between the two peaks." - p 158

Are these guys on speed?! B/c, even if they were, the above wd be impossible. To hand-wrangle a giant camouflage netting over a huge jet in a half hr by hand is pretty unrealistic. To dig "good-sized pits" w/ picks & shovel in a matter less than 2 hrs out of ROCK is utterly ridiculous. Have these ghost writers ever done any manual labor?!

Ok, ok, it's a kid's bk, a fantasy, it's not supposed to be realistic. But my argument here is that this is propaganda aimed at boys to inculcate them w/ a feeling of being supermen. As they grow into adults they can always get Free Trade slave labor to do the actual work.

Despite the Swifts being taken in by imposters (&, of course, gassed or clunked on the head or what-not w/o serious after-effect), they're still quick to jump to conclusions that're so lacking in deductive substance one's amazed by their otherwise 'brilliant' careers as scientists:

""From South America!" Tom cried. "If that man dropped this, then I'd say he's one of the rebels."" - p 47

"Then Tom questioned, "Who is their leader? Apparently they're only stooges for a higher-up - someone of a different nationality, perhaps." - p 188

Eureka! The rebels in South America are just stooges (unlike Tom & his friends) for a foreign power. I wonder who that cd be? At the formulaic usual moment when our heros are held captive & when their captor needn't worry any longer about their knowing everything b/c they're about to die or whatever:

""First, I will tell you a little about myself. I am a Eurasian by birth."

[His dad must've been Fu Manchu!]

"*Eurasian!* Hanson and Chow instantly thought of Leeskol, the Eurasian who Rip Hulse had captured. Had the two been in league?"

"The man continued, "By choice I serve Europe or Asia, whichever suits my purposes best."

""You mean you ain't got a country you stick to?" Chow burst out.

""Is that so necessary?" the man asked suavely, a sardonic smile playing over his face.

""It sure is!" Chow cried. "Why, you low-down-"" - p 193

Chow reminds me of the captured Texan soldiers interviewed in the 2004 documentary Control Room: 'I just follow orders.' Patriotism vs free thinking. This Swift bk pretends to support the latter while firmly supporting the former - just like all the other American propaganda I grew up w/.

""I said you were smart," he remarked. "Now you are becoming sensible too. You will call me Vladimir."" - p 195

Yep, we weren't fooled! This Eurasian's one of those commie Russkies! &, yep, Tom's a quick thinker alright (as will be most of his readers):

""Ordep?" Tom repeated to himself. Then he realized what it was - Pedro spelled backward!" - p 94

All of these boys bks have comic supporting characters. In the Hardy Boys it's Chet Morton, who loves to eat alot. In Tom Swift Jr it's Chow, the cook, who loves to eat alot. Overeaters are comic relief. At bottom, of course, these characters are another variety of good ole boy:

"Chow waved a stout rope he was carrying.

""I'll tie that Leeskol up myself! Nobody can double-cross Uncle Sam when I'm around an' get away with it!"" - p 122

Yee-haw! Ride 'em cowboy! Yep, the myth of the Cowboys & the Injuns lives on:

"the Indians suddenly appeared again.

""They're going to shoot!" Hanson cried. "Run!"

""Wait!" Chow cried.

"To everyone's amazement, he stepped forward and haltingly spoke a jargon of guttural sounds. Slowly, smiles of understanding broke out on the faces of the Indians.

""What are you telling them?" Tom asked.

""That I fetched 'em some presents from the Lone Star State."

""Presents?"

""Sure thing. I'd never get caught in Injun country without some little ole knickknacks."

"From a pocket he pulled several cheap bracelets, rings, brooches, and four pearl necklaces, and distributed them." - pp 122-123

Well.. not only do these good ole boys have their own security force at the family plant, they also have the power to call upon the local police force every day or so as their various family members get shot at or kidnapped or whatever (how DO they survive?!). But, NO, *that's not all*:

"Tom put in a long-distance call to the capital of Bapcho [the code-name for the South American country] asking for the president's office. After a seemingly interminable wait, he was finally connected." - p 132

Yep, Tom can just go to one of them thar Banana Republics & call up the president. But he *had to wait*! We'll have to do something about that!

& what's the motive for all this? ""And what ore! The richest deposit in the world - and all for Verano and her ally. It will make her the richest nation in this part of the globe. And wealth means power!"" - p 201

Right. That last quote's from a rebel leader & it's obviously meant to be 'bad guy' logic but, of course, it's no different from the 'good guy' logic. It's just that it's ok for the rich American industrialists to go into a South American country & plunder its natural resources that can be used for making nuclear weapons & it's NOT ok for those evil commies to do it. I shd qualify here that communism is never mentioned directly, it's only implied.

Online, the Swift bks are credited w/ foreseeing inventions. In the light of my political criticism above, I found this particularly interesting:
"Several inventions, including the taser, have been directly inspired by the fictional inventions. "TASER" is an acronym for "Thomas A. Swift's Electric Rifle."" - http://en.wikipedia.org/wiki/Tom_Swift

Alan Davies bio:

Alan Davies was spawned on the Canadian prairies / and lived in various spots across that country through high school. Then / college in Massachusetts / a year in Boulder / and final removal to New York City. He is the author of a bunch of books / including – Name / Candor / Signage / Rave / Active 24 Hours. Two books have just been released – Raw War / and Odes & fragments. In addition to poetry / Alan writes essays and book reviews as well as philosophy and critical theory and the like.

idonot@mail.com

The dead soldier's silence sings our national anthem.

tENTATIVELY, a cONVENIENCE self-describes as a:

Mad Scientist / d composer / Sound Thinker / Thought Collector / As Been /
PIN-UP (Postal Interaction Network Underground Participant) /
Headless Deadbeat of the Pup tENT Cult /
booed usician / Low Classicist / H.D.J. (Hard Disc Jockey) /
Psychopathfinder / Jack-Off-Of-All-Trades / criminally sane /
Homonymphonemiac / Practicing PromoTextual /
Air Dresser /
Sprocket Scientist / headitor & earchivist / Explicator /
Sexorcist /
Professional Resister of Character Defamation /
Proponent of Classification-Resistant What-Have-Yous /
tOGGLE nUT cASE /

Princess of Dorkness's Right Hand Man /
Human Attention-ExSpanDex Speculum /
Imp Activist /
SPLEENIUS / Cognitive Dissident

He's written 13 bks (ALL published) [including tENTATIVELY, aN iNTERVIEW], made
560 movies [as of September, 2018], has over 215 audio publications, is an early &
very active member of the neoist movement & a SAINT in the Church of the
SubGenius. More info than anyone is ever likely to read is available here:

http://idioideo.pleintekst.nl

- a website many people report as something they're unable to connect to.
In such a case it's recommended that one try:

http://www.youtube.com/user/onesownthoughts

or:

http://www.goodreads.com/author/show/1054095.tENTATIVELY_a_cONVENIENCE

www.ingramcontent.com/pod-product-compliance
Lightning Source LLC
Chambersburg PA
CBHW080925050426
42334CB00056B/2939